FOULA

Island West of the Sun

D1609759

FOULA
ISLAND WEST OF THE SUN

by

Sheila Gear

Photographs by Jim Gear

ROBERT HALE · LONDON

© *Sheila Gear 1983*
First published in Great Britain 1983
Reprinted 1988

ISBN 0 7091 9673 3

Robert Hale Limited
Clerkenwell House
Clerkenwell Green
London EC1R 0HT

Photoset in Great Britain by
Rowland Phototypesetting Limited, Bury St Edmunds, Suffolk
and printed by St Edmundsbury Press Limited,
Bury St Edmunds, Suffolk. Bound by
Hunter & Foulis Limited

Contents

1 Half an Island   11
2 A Summer Day   20
3 The Crü   32
4 The Sea Around Us   42
5 Time for Reflection   55
6 Hairst Days   65
7 First Catch Your Lamb   76
8 Ponies for Sale   85
9 Shortening Days   94
10 Midwinter Foys   102
11 Snowfall   115
12 A Promise of Spring   124
13 Lambing   136
14 Voar   149
15 Foals and Fowls   159
16 June   175
17 Goodbye to the Cows   186
18 High Summer   195
19 What of the Future   205
Glossary   215
Index   221

List of illustrations

Between pages 80 and 81
Foula croft house
The author's children
Foula from the north
Unloading the mailboat
The view from Summons Head
Fulmars taking fish offal
Hauling up a lobster creel
The Voe in a storm
Rossies Loch and hills
Hamnafield, the Sneug and the Kame
Bloburn and Harrier
Ham Voe from the top of the hill
Looking along the Nort Bank to the mainland

Between pages 160 and 161
Flossie and Marcie with the author's husband
Meeting the sheep . . .
. . . and feeding the foals
A plane-load of ponies
Loading a pony onto the mailboat
A peat bank
The islanders learn to cut peat at an early age
The hay harvest
A hay rack
The beach under snow
Digging out a sheep
Snow has its pleasures too
A bonxie displaying
Nories (puffins)

To Ross, Kevin and Penny

O a simmer's night whin I look oot ta da wastird
    An see Foula standin oot fornenst da sky
I feel happy, an yit sad, and hae a langin
    Ats aafil hard for me ta pit ta wirds.

I feel dir somethin I sood keen at A'm forgotten
    I try ta tink, bit canna mind ava.
I wiss at I could stop da clock forever
    An at da sam time canna wait ta win awa.

Bit noo an den I canna help bit winder
    Whaat it is at comes ower me an why;
O a simmer's night whin I look oot ta da wastird
    An see Foula standin oot fornenst da sky.

Rhoda Bulter

FOULA

1

Half an Island

Qua'll come oot ta Foula wi me?
Qua'll come oot ta Foula wi me?
Qua'll come oot ta Foula wi me?
Oot wi a windlin o strae.

Ma an Da an da black coo
Ma an Da an da black coo
Ma an Da an da black coo
Oot wi a windlin o strae.

Traditional bairns' song.

Few people ever come out to Foula. We get a handful of visitors
in summer when the weather is settled and they can depend on
returning to the mainland of Shetland the same day. Some of
the more adventurous may stay for a week or two but for most of
the year a stranger is a rarity thanks to the island's reputation
for being cut off from the rest of the world for up to a month at a
time. So to most people Foula is an unknown island, "out of this
world" and almost forgotten. But to the forty or so people who
live here it is our home—the loveliest of all islands. It is a place
of distinctive qualities with a lifestyle of its own.

Foula lies out in the Atlantic 14 miles west of the mainland of
Shetland. It is only 3½ miles long and 2½ miles wide, but it is
bigger than it looks since its hills rise to 1,373 feet. It is big
enough for us to be able to walk all day and still not cover the
whole area but small enough for us to be familiar with every
corner—the ideal size for an island.

The essence of Foula is her hills. Rising in sheer abruptness
from the lowland they sweep in a rhythmic silhouette to the
north—Hamnafield, the Sneug, the Kame and Soberlie. The
Noup is a small hill, 800 feet high, at the south end of the isle
and separated from the rest by a glacial valley. These hills are
the background to our life. Golden and ethereal in the early
morning sun, dark blue and lowering in a storm, russet-red and

far away in the pink autumn haze, white with drifting snow they rise high and sheer into the sky, grey and bitter in the cold of winter. Always our hills are changing, always our eyes are drawn to them and always we are refreshed by them.

But our isle is really only half an island, for the west side has been cut away as though sliced by a giant's knife, leaving a sheer rampart of cliff rising to 1,220 feet at the Kame. These awe-inspiring cliffs which the Foula folk nonchalantly call "da banks", once played an important part in life here as sea-birds and their eggs were a big part of their diet. Fortunately these days there is no need for the men to go risking their lives "cloorin (clawing) through da banks" for a handful of eggs or birds—one can get a tin of meat out of the cupboard instead. Sea-birds are closely packed in noisy crowds on even the narrowest ledges—kittiwakes, guillemots, razorbills, puffins and fulmars. The puffin or Tammy Norie, as it is called in Shetland, was once so abundant here that it gave rise to the old Shetland nickname for an inhabitant of Foula—Foula Norie. Much of the cliffs are so steep that not even a bird can find a foothold and some parts are overhanging. These cliffs are of sandstone and their smooth faces are striped with the pinks, oranges and creams of the different strata. In contrast the rocks on the east side of the isle are metamorphic—mainly schists and microgranites—and there are many tiny geos or inlets in the relatively low cliffs.

Foula has no harbour which is a pity for the island would otherwise be an ideal centre for fishing. Many an islander in his daydreams has excavated out a harbour—the answer to all his problems. The only landing place—"the Voe", as it is presumptuously called—is on the east coast and is a mere 150 yards long. At the head of the Voe is our sole sandy beach, a tiny scrap of sand and rotting seaweed, where the small boats are hauled ashore. In 1914 a pier was built on the north side of the Voe, a small concrete structure with a strip of concrete above it where the island's mailboat stands out of reach of the sea. Scattered round the Voe is a handful of crofts of which seven are still inhabited. This could be called the centre of our community since here, too, are the school and the post office. A couple more crofts lie to the north, and the other populated area is the Hametoon at the south end of the isle where there are five inhabited houses. In all this makes fifteen households with thirty-seven inhabitants at the time of writing of whom ten are children.

Situated on latitude 60 degrees north, Foula lies directly in the path of the weather systems that cross the Atlantic from west to east and make it one of the windiest parts of Britain. The wind after blowing unhindered across the open sea is suddenly compressed when it hits the great wall of the Foula cliffs. Pressure builds up until it is forced up over the top and flung down the other side of the hill to form whirlwinds and vertical gusts or flans. The grey stone houses seem to crouch, heads down and shoulders hunched as they make the most of the available shelter. Wooden sheds are tied down with iron stays set in concrete blocks, while in winter everything movable is weighed down with stones. The land is bare and windswept for no trees can survive here.

Across the exposed stretch of sea between Foula and the mainland the tiny mailboat crosses once a week in summer taking three hours each way. With no proper harbour the boat must be lifted out of the water and pulled up onto the land and this necessity limits its size. It is small and low—only 35½ feet long—and it seems much smaller as it disappears out into an awkward sea on a bleak winter day, ploughing into waves twice its height. In winter when the days are short and the weather is at its worst, weeks may go by without the boat being able to cross, making Foula Britain's most isolated inhabited island. But isolation is only a state of mind. Some people panic when isolated for only a day because of snow-drifts, they could not face the awful prospect of being cut off for as much as a week. But we don't care. It is nothing to us whether one week, two weeks or four weeks. Our lives are orientated about our island—we can get on happily without the rest of the world. So isolation is a word that has a different meaning for us.

From this misconception springs the idea of a brave little population defying isolation. "Brave, romantic, noble islanders", well-meaning outsiders call us. On the other hand there are those who see only the small infertile crofts and the scruffy houses, the poverty and dilapidation. They wonder why anyone should choose to live here and decide that the islanders are unco-operative, lazy, inefficient, conceited and condescending. In reality we are none of these things—just ordinary people, a mixture of good, bad and middling.

Like all other seafaring people the Foula folk have always been strong individualists. This is the greatest difference between them and the islanders of St Kilda with whom they are sometimes compared. The St Kildans were landlubbers with a close-knit co-operative society based on fowling, living side by side in a crowded little street—an extraordinary idea to anyone here, where the houses tend to be on the outer edges of the crofts as far apart as possible. In 1930 a total evacuation of St Kilda took place—an event that will never occur here. Excessive dependence on one another is a bad thing and makes an island very vulnerable. So we stand on our own feet and go our own ways. Our pride in our island might be mistaken for conceit. One may insult a true islander or even insult his family, but one should never insult his island! And if we are condescending we can be excused—isn't our island the best in the world and should we not pity all those poor folk who have to live elsewhere?

Who knows when man first settled on the isle? Evidence shows that he has been here a long time. By 2000 B.C. Neolithic man had several settlements here, his round-house sites still visible under the green turf while stone axes and fragments of pottery have been excavated at various sites and the remains of a burial cairn serve as a bül (resting-place) for sheep. In time the Neolithic gave way to the Bronze Age with its burial cists and cinerary urns which are sometimes dug up by the islanders working on their crofts and always carefully re-interred. One big stone stands by itself on the side of the valley. Perhaps it dates back to these distant times, though nothing is known about it other than the fact that it chews its cud once a year on Nuer Night like any horse on the hill, as such stones are wont to do.

During the eighth and ninth centuries the Norsemen set sail from Norway to plunder Britain. Shetland became a convenient half-way base and was soon populated by Norse settlers to whom most of the present-day population can still trace part of its ancestry. Each small inlet, each rocky baa, each dip and rise in the hillside, still retains its Norse name, as does the island itself which was originally "Fugloy"—island of birds.

Old Norse, or Norn, was spoken on the island right up to the end of the eighteenth century. Due to its isolation the language was a purer form than that spoken elsewhere, and we are told that the Norse jarls sent their sons to Foula to learn the old language. They lived at Nordahus—now only a collection of ruins. From the Norsemen, too, came the udal law under which each man possessed his own land, subservient to no-one. With the right to live his own life and state his own views—rights, some might complain, we still possess!

In 1469 Shetland was pledged to the Scottish crown for 8,000 florins when a Danish king found himself short of money for his daughter's dowry. The next century was marked for its oppression under the Scottish tyrant Earl Robert and his son Earl Patrick, with their extortionate and often illegal taxation. In the following centuries with the immigration of Scots and the growing disregard for the Norse law a change in the Shetlanders' way of life took place. From a society of middle-class farmers and fishermen owning their own land under udal law, they changed to mere tenants living in abject poverty on crofts that became increasingly smaller. Due to its isolation Foula at first fared better than the rest of Shetland. The islanders retained their udal status, at least they believed they did for they still held their original title-deeds written in the old Norse tongue. However, according to local tradition, one of the Scotts of Melby, a ship's surgeon, visited the isle towards the end of the eighteenth century. Because of his professional standing, the islanders trusted him when told that their deeds needed to be restamped due to a change in the law, and he persuaded them to hand the documents over to his safe-keeping so that he could take them to Edinburgh to be altered. That was the last the Foula folk ever saw of their deeds and all attempts to obtain justice failed. Much of the rest of Shetland had already been taken over by the in-comers from Scotland often as a result of pretty dubious dealings. In Walls a man called Laurie Umphray had three crofts at Setter, two of which belonged to his elderly aunts. One day when Laurie was off at the fishing, Scott visited the aunts and conned them out of the deeds, giving them meal in exchange. He thought it a joke worth bragging about that he had made them eat their land. Laurie declared his intention of going south to Edinburgh to reclaim his deeds, but Scott warned him that if he did so and was unsuccessful he would have him "thrown out upon the knowe", whereas if he complied he would make him factor of Foula and give him one of the best crofts there. So the Umphrays, Laurie and his son John, came to Foula to the croft of the Gravins, though not in fact as factors. To make room for them the elderly occupant of the Gravins, Magnus Georgeson, was put out and ordered to live at Bloburn. They said the shock turned him witless.

As in the rest of Shetland the lairds and, later on, their factors, were all powerful. Conditions of tenure ensured that the islanders sold their catch of fish to the landlord, who paid them with meal and other necessities, the price of which was fixed so that the islanders were in permanent ever-increasing debt. Eviction was an ever-present threat for anyone who did not submit.

However, the distress of the Clearances, carried out in much of the Highlands and Islands, did not occur here; the landlord and his factors found the rewards from the tenants' fishing endeavours far more profitable than any investment in sheep would have been.

Not until 1882 was a commission set up to investigate the conditions of the tenant crofter. The minister here at the time was my husband's grandfather, Robert Gear. Originally he was a helmsman at the Greenland whaling but after a mishap to his ship he and some of the crew rowed to Iceland in their small open boat, a journey of several weeks, after which he suffered from rheumatism and was obliged to take up a less arduous career and so came to Foula. When the islanders heard that the commission had left for Shetland, Robert Gear and Andrew Robertson, who had been chosen as the spokesman for the island as he was not afraid to speak up, both set out for Lerwick, assuming the hearing would take place there. They stayed overnight in Walls, but in the morning Andrew Robertson refused to go any further, saying that he had been given notice of eviction by the landlord's factors. Robert Gear borrowed a horse from the minister of Walls and rode to Lerwick alone, but there he was told the commission was sailing direct to Foula. So he galloped back to Walls, returning the horse in such a lather of sweat that its owner declared he would never lend him a horse again. He then engaged Johnie Jeromson to row him the eighteen miles back to Foula. As they pulled clear of the land they sighted the sails of the factors' boat leaving from Reawick heading for Foula too. He was afraid that the factors would arrive first and the hearing be finished before he could state the islanders' case. But Johnie Jeromson's crew were fit and they arrived at the isle just in time to state their case, which was very different from that put forward on the landlord's behalf declaring his tenants were well satisfied with things as they were.

Later the factors tried to take their revenge on him. His annual debts for goods purchased from the only shop, which of course belonged to the factors, generally amounted to the same as his stipend of £20. The following year, however, he was charged exactly double and believing he would be unable to pay, the factors sent in the bailiff to have him rouped, i.e. to put him out of his house and auction off all his belongings. But he had been expecting something like this and sent his son running to the Hametoon to ask one of the Cruglie men to come with the extra money as previously arranged. When the bailiff held up the first item to be auctioned, a small creepie (stool) Muckle Johnie o' Biggins took it away and set it aside firmly saying "Na, a bairn would need that to sit upon." The auction proceeded with not a thing sold for no bids were forthcoming. Suddenly the door burst open and the man from Cruglie, normally a mild-mannered man, roared out "Put that down or there will be bloodshed." Thereupon the bailiff slipped the article as though it had been red hot, and readily accepted the offer of the money and of two young cows in payment of the debt.

At last in 1886 the Crofters Act was passed; fair rents were fixed with security of tenure, thereby lessening the landlord's power over his tenants. The landlord-tenant relationship still continues but most of the estates are not managed at all and apart from an occasional visit in summer and the annual taking of the rents the landlords do not play much part in most Shetlanders' lives. It is very rare for a Shetland landlord to put any of the money he receives as rents back into his estate.

One would have thought that with the removal of oppression all would go well with the island. But it was not to be for the population could never be supported by the land alone. The land was poor and crops were often flattened by the severe gales before the grain ripened. The men had to find work to supple-

ment their meagre gains from their tiny crofts. Traditionally
the Shetlander was a fisherman who crofted in his spare time,
and this was still the case in Foula. Some of the best fishing
grounds in Shetland lie off the island and even in the hardest of
times a household with one or two able-bodied men was always
able to keep going. But when the age of sail came to an end and
larger powered fishing boats equipped with trawls came into
use, Foula, because it lacked a harbour, was not able to partici-
pate in the great fishing boom. Families left the island and as
the population declined crofting became more important in the
island's economy. One croft could not provide a living, but several worked together as a unit could. For a while the men turned
to lobster fishing to earn the much-needed extra money. Previously unexploited, lobster catches were high and at first the
islanders did well, but with the decline in white fish catches, due
to overfishing, big boats from the mainland began lobster fishing around the island, and in a few years lobster catches dropped
to barely economic levels.

Hardship is a recurring theme in island lore but it does not
dominate the tales of our forefathers. Many an interesting or
amusing incident was told and retold until all knew them by
heart, and they would be passed down to become part of the
island's spoken history. Such was the accuracy of the telling
that sometimes conversations have been passed down in detail,
often with the tellers impersonating the actual voices of the
original participants who died before their fathers were hardly
old enough to remember them. Particularly enjoyed were short
sayings notable for their wit or aptness of phrase or even the
absurdity of the situation. For instance there are three different
descriptions of falls down a steep slope—"Screechy-bung,
scrush-scroosh-scrool" was said of a cow coming to grief on
Hamnafield. "Head up, feet up, head up, feet up, head up, feet up
and bumble in the burn" was said of an old wife from Leraback
who tumbled down the Brugs. "Skry-eye, outle, outle, outle,
outle" was said of a man from Bloburn falling from the top of the
Bruistins. Some anecdotes described events important in the
island's history, some gave an insight into a man's character
while others have come to be used as proverbs. One favourite
often used to deflate a braggard is "Ya boy, put up dy hand an'
tak doon Hamnafield". That was said originally by Jimmy o'

Shoadels standing in the doorway of the Brae (now our lamb-house) nearly a hundred years ago, yet I can visualize the occasion as though I had been there to hear it myself.

2

A Summer Day

A'll rowe mesel in til a skerry
'Wey doon ida sea;
A'll rowe mesel in til a skerry
An lonsome A'll no be,
Wi da shalder, da scarf, an da scorie
Freendly, aye freendly wi me.
Oh, my Tammie Norie
Wha could be lonlie wi dee?

Harry Kay.

Unfortunately, contrary to popular belief, we do not spend our time sitting in the sun plunking a guitar, or wandering through the hills crying "Dear peerie lamb" to our sheep. The same mad rush that pushes on the rest of the world is just as relentless towards us. Time and tide wait for no man, certainly not for an islander. Summer is short here and winter stretches for seven long months, so we must pack a seemingly endless list of jobs into our few months of reasonable weather.

One fine summer morning I was pottering about the house doing some clearing up and casting an occasional glance out to sea where my husband Jim and his cousin, John Andrew, were fishing. Now and then I popped outside to fetch in an armful of peats from the peat stack, or a pail of water from the well, and stood for a moment to gaze at the sunny hills, dappled with drifting shadows of the small white clouds that formed unendingly above the isle. I listened to the cries of the tirricks (terns) nesting on the back of the Taing and the wild haunting call of the allens (Arctic skuas) that wheeled and swooped in the blue summer sky. I breathed in the scents of peat reek, of new-mown hay and of sun-ripened heather berries (crowberries) and wondered if anywhere else could be as beautiful as this isle?

Out on the Shaalds the boat was rising and falling gently in the swell. Jim let out his line, paying out about fifteen fathoms, then sat jigging it gently in his hands. Almost at once there was a tug, another tug, another, until the line was being pulled this way and that.

"Boy, I doubt dere's ane or twa fish aboot."

He quickly pulled the line in hand over hand; down through the water he could see the white flashes of fish, struggling on the hooks. Deftly he lifted them on board and winkled out the hooks, flinging the fish into an empty box. Every hook had been taken. Quickly he flung out the line again and soon he was hauling in another catch. They were piltocks (two- and three-year-old saithe), the commonest fish around here, grey-black in colour with silver bellies. Sometimes we ate them fresh, but mainly they were used for lobster bait or salted and dried for use in winter. As they were plentiful at this spot the men drew enough to last for a couple of days, then steamed back to the shore, gutting the fish on the way. A crowd of maalies (fulmar petrels) and bonxies (great skuas) followed in their wake, squabbling over the guts. Occasionally a tiny stormy petrel would flutter over the waves picking up the oily scraps of liver.

The boat nosed its way in between the skerries and baas that lie scattered higgledy-piggledy off the rocky coastline. Now occasional painted corks and buoys came into sight bobbing up and down on the sparkling water. Jim steered towards one, marked with his own identifying colours, while John Andrew held the boat-hook ready and hooked up the rope. He pulled steadily coiling the rope in the bottom of the boat. The creel itself came slowly into sight and with a quick heave he lifted it into the boat. It was empty except for some crabs that scrambled over the bottom trying to get out. They had eaten the bait until only a small tatter of fish was left. Some held onto the meshes or backed into a corner and wedged themselves in, but John Andrew pulled them out one by one and chucked them for'ard out of the way. My husband made another sweep and began hauling the next creel, while John Andrew chopped up some new bait and fastened it in his bait string. There was a lobster in this creel. As soon as it surfaced it flapped its tail frantically trying to get up enough power to shoot off backwards into freedom. Carefully avoiding its powerful claws, my husband gripped it over the back and manoeuvred it out, taking care not to force it in case it should slip a claw. He twisted rubber bands round its claws rendering it harmless and laid it carefully in a fish box.

The next creel contained an unwelcome occupant; a large black sleekie (conger eel) lay coiled round and round inside.

"Go on, you black deevil, get oot o dere," said John Andrew as he removed it and despatched it. It lay writhing on the bottom of the boat for a while after its head had been cut off. Sometimes they catch other fish in the creels—funny-looking peddal fish (lump suckers), spiny "maa's glugs" and gaping plukkers, brightly coloured wrasse, golden brown butter fish, and an occasional blind hoe (spotted dogfish). Starfish are numerous of various varieties from little familiar pink five-armed ones to big sun stars with numerous arms. Skadman's heeds (sea urchins) are common as are crabs of several kinds including the "fleeing crab" so called because it flies or rather swims through the water.

When the creels were rebaited they set them again, sweeping in alongside a baa and throwing over a creel as they passed, just avoiding the sea as it broke dangerously over the hidden rock, or gliding into a narrow geo, slipping the creel and reversing out again in a hurry before the swell could carry them ashore. They worked their way "sooth alang", hauling creels, rebaiting and resetting. As the sun rose higher the boat seemed to catch the warmth and hold it. Along the rocks black scraggy-looking skarfs (shag) stood in groups stretching their ungainly wings out to dry. Others flew, always in small groups of two or three, long necks outstretched, wings beating rhythmically, going somewhere.

"I wonder quaar aa yon skarfs is gyaain?"

"Dey! Dere no gyaain anywhere. Dere just making oot dere busy just like some folk does."

The tide was running hard off the South Ness, setting up a rank of short steep waves, leaping and jumping up glittering in the sun, some curling over and breaking with a splash. Jim, standing in the stern at the helm, braced his legs to keep balance, eased down the throttle and the boat slipped through them, rushing up to the crests of the waves, to crash down the other side.

They had a dozen creels set off the back of the Noup, in a big semicircle. Here the long swell rolled in to the cliff face, rising and falling against it, revealing a glimpse of bright pink rock, with bands of white barnacles and clinging fronds of dark brown shining seaweed. Towering high above them rose the cliff face, with its jagged overhanging shelves, its smooth banded sweeps and whitened ledges crowded with lungwees (guillemots)—small black and white upright figures packed in rows from which there came a continual coming and going and a deep resonant "kirr kirr" as the birds nodded and bowed to their neighbours. Other ledges were plastered with kittiwakes' nests from which came an unending clamour, echoing out across the sea. In places the edge of the cliff tumbled down in steep grassy slopes and jumbled grey boulders, and here grazed small groups of sheep having climbed down to seemingly inaccessible ledges to crop the grass right at the very brink of the high sheer drop. On these grassy slopes nested the leeries (shearwater) whose strange wild laughter can be heard at night at the Hametoon. They are very talkative birds, the returning bird calling out to his mate when he lands and she answering him from the depths of the burrow. They are among our favourite birds, so gentle and inoffensive, yet they often fly hundreds of miles to fetch food for their chicks. So far, yet they return unfailingly to their own small island and find their own burrow in the dark of the night.

One particular jumble of boulders is known as the Tieves' Hol. Two Orkneymen in trouble escaped north in their boat and landed unseen at the back of the Noup where they lived undetected in the shelter of the boulders. At night they crept down to the Hametoon and stole any food they could find including sheep. One night the Biggins folk were having tatties and fish for supper and set the kettleful out on the dyke to cool. The thieves were unable to resist the tempting smell and made off with the lot, and after this they used the muckle kettle to cover up their fire during the day so that the smoke would not be seen. One day however they both fell asleep and the kettle tipped off, so that some men fishing off from the back of the Noup spied a wisp of smoke halfway up the slope. The thieves were caught and kept captives until a boat came to take them away. The men would tie them up when they went off fishing, but while they were away their wives would take pity on the captives, release them and get them to churn butter and help about the house.

There is a great sense of peace here, with the wide unlimited ocean stretching before one, and the isle, high and solid, a guardian at one's back. The first creel they hauled here had two

lobsters in it. Although they had shared the creel amicably
enough underwater, as soon as it was pulled up they attacked
each other and were only separated with difficulty. One of the
other creels had two lobsters also, one inside and another clinging on outside.

"Watch! Tak it up peeriewise."

John Andrew hauled until the creel lay just below the surface
then leant over to grip the lobster, but at the last moment it
realized its danger and with a rapid flick of its tail scooted off
down into the deep water below.

"Put in some mair bait and hoove o'er da creel. We'll maybe
catch him da morn."

The next few creels were empty.

"Dere's naething here. We'll try setting dem aff Granny Geo.
Haul du da hindmost wan and we'll get out o here," shouted my
husband, eyeing a wave as it broke over the rocks nearby.

"Dwine! I doot he's fast on da bottom."

"Tak a turn o da burrope roond da thole pin." John Andrew
wound the rope round the steel pin that served as a rowlock for
the oar. As the boat steamed slowly in a circle, the rope tightened and creaked with the strain, slipped suddenly a few feet
then brought up again.

"Right. Try him noo."

John Andrew gave a quick steady pull. "Yon's him free. Here
he comes—the bruks o him onywye!"

The creel looked as though an elephant had sat on it, the thick
wire rods were squashed flat and the net was frayed and torn.

"I doot yon wasterly gale dis weekend didna do him any good!"

Seven lobsters lay carefully packed in the fish box as they
steamed back to Ham Little, a small round cove in the cliffs,
where their stock boxes were kept moored. The boxes were
overgrown with green and brown algae and water lapped in and
out of the cracks between the boards. The lobsters would live
happily in them until they were shipped to Lerwick to be sold
the following week when the mailboat should cross again to the
mainland. Here the tide had washed in some large exotic jelly-
fish—big orange and cream-coloured Chrysaora, trailing long
yellowish tentacles, and a few Cyanea of an unusual deep
purple-blue colour, as big as soup plates. They floated through
the water pulsating gently. Sometimes the currents bring other

varieties like the fragile little Aglantha jelly-fish, like pointed pixies' caps, or quantities of small ctenophores or sea gooseberries that light the breaking waves at night with their pale green phosphorescence.

While the men were hauling their creels I turned my attention to the barrel of salted piltocks that stood outside the porch window. They had been in the pickle for three days so it was time for them to be taken out and hung up to be dried. I fished among the brine and pulled out fish after fish, stiff now and a dark, dull grey, no longer slippery but wrinkled and shrunken. I tied them together in pairs by the tails and hung them out to drip. Later they would be hung in the ceiling to dry for winter use and their fishy, salty, smell would linger through the house for days. There were several big lürs (pollack) among them too, which were split and dried flat, and one or two hoes (dogfish) which would be pinned open with wooden pegs. Their strong rather oily taste would provide some variety in our winter dinners.

In mid morning my husband came home expecting another breakfast—or perhaps it was lunch—then he was off again to work on the small airstrip which was being made on the Santoo, a flattish stretch of land opposite the chapel. The Foula folk were doing the work and had raised half the cost of the expenses while the Highlands and Islands Development Board would provide the other half. A party of IVS workers had been here the previous summer helping to clear away the big stones and rocks and breaking them up to fill up the hollows. Now the men were clearing away stones and clay, lengthening and widening the strip which would be used by a small Islander aircraft for emergency flights and charter trips for summer visitors and visiting officials.

Meanwhile the sun had evaporated the wet dew, so I hurried down to the Brae to work in the hay. Hay is almost the sole winter feeding available for our livestock as little other feedstuff can be imported in the winter. When few winter days allow the boat to cross, human foodstuff must have priority, and considering the severe exposure here very little grain or root crops can be grown. Some kale is cultivated—a special tough hardy Shetland variety that takes two years to grow to a usable size. Scattered about the lowland, often in the most unlikely places are small stone circles called planti crubs. Here the kale seeds are sown and here the young plants manage to survive the winter. The following spring the plants are transplanted to the kale yards which again have stone dykes to shelter them.

In the old days the people could break out new crofts if they so desired, draining a chosen area and carrying innumerable kishies (back baskets) of earth from other parts of the island and sand and seaweed from the beach, to convert the poor moorland into fertile soil. But after the Crofters Act was passed this concession was withdrawn. So we are limited to the crofts that were already in existence, and they are small, averaging six acres. The hay is short and of poor quality—in fact many of our summer visitors when asked politely to keep off the hay, look at the short rough grass and ask, "what hay?" Most of it is not accessible to a tractor, so that it all has to be worked by hand—a time-consuming and frustrating job. But the number of ewe lambs we can keep to maintain or increase our flocks depends on how much hay we can make, so we toil away at it one, two or even three months according to the weather.

The Brae is one of the more unpromising crofts on the island, exposed to every direction and drenched with salt water in the winter. It is little more than a deep peat bog girt by rocks and low cliff and cut up into small strips or rigs up to fifty yards long, but only three or four yards wide. In between the rigs are the remains of the old deep drains or stanks with which the old folk attempted to drain the water-logged ground.

Picking up the old wooden rake, I walked up and down the rigs raking over the swathes of hay, turning the wet green underside up to the sun. The ground squelched under my feet and I had to be careful not to tread accidentally on the hay and get it soaked. In places the water lay an inch or so deep and the hay floated on the cut stubble. All morning I walked up and down the rigs, the rake going out automatically turning the hay as I went, until I began to feel like nothing but a two-legged hay turning machine.

As I worked my thoughts turned involuntarily to the old folk and the days when the meagre croft land was all used for growing bere (a variety of barley) to provide meal for the people, and corn for the precious kye, and very little land could be spared for hay. Sheep were far less important in the island's economy then and some crofts were only able to keep a handful. To supplement their hay, the men went up into the hills and cut the rough grass growing there and carried it home on their backs—"going to da tek" it was called—or climbed down the banks to cut sinna (sheep's fescue) a fine sweet grass which was much appreciated by the animals. The best place for sinna was the Little Kame, an outjutting green nose half-way down the Kame. On a calm winter's day the men would row off to the foot of the great cliff and climb up to where the prized grass, grew over 500 feet up. There on the sloping ledge half-way between the sea and the heavens they would crouch to cut the grass with a handhook and pack it into bags which were then lowered to the boats far below. Outsiders consider Foula a place where time stands still. This is just an illusion. We may be behind in the march of "progress", but times have changed and I for one am grateful.

Although the work was tedious I enjoyed hay-making down at the Brae. The sea was just a stone's throw away and I could see the glistening brown fronds of seaweed waving gently in the water and watch the tirricks (terns) diving for sand eels for their chicks. And all around me were flowers, yellow, blue, white and pink, filling the air with their scent. The hill stood back, remote and high, keeping watch over the Voe, round which were scattered the old grey croft houses sleeping in the sun, with wisps of blue peat reek rising lazily from the chimneys. The bairns picked flowers and tunnelled through the old stanks (ditches) overgrown with trowie ferns and clumps of floss (rush), but the Voe inevitably attracted them like a magnet and I had to keep shouting at them to keep back from the edge of the banks, as they crept nearer and nearer fascinated by the boats berthed at the pier just opposite.

Far out to sea I could see a small dot steaming up for the Isle—Hansie with a load of tourists likely. Shortly after the *Hirta* arrived in the Voe and there was some confusion whilst Hansie awakened the fishermen and persuaded them to put to sea leaving him room to lie alongside the pier and disgorge his load of tourists. And a motley collection they were! Three of them got as far as the head of the pier where they sat down and, as far as I could see, fell asleep. Another group made it to the Ham hay and settled down in the middle of the best rig to have a genteel picnic, with a white tablecloth laid on the grass and numerous plates, cups and goodness knows what. Four more of them wandered up to the Haa and stood in a row, noses pressed to the window, gaping in. A small band of "Intrepid Explorer" types set off for the hills, backs bent with heavy rucksacks—well they at least might appreciate the isle!

By now I had turned more than half the hay and it was nearly dinner-time, so I went up to the house via Ham Little. A Painted Lady butterfly danced along the cliff edge and I pointed it out to the bairns. Butterflies are rare visitors here. I stood there a moment listening to the "pui pui pui" of the baby dunters (eider duck) and the "gloop-gloop" of the sea echoing in the small caves, while the children poked around in the rock pools. I would have liked to linger here but my husband would be home soon expecting his dinner. Up at the house I flung some tatties in a pan, poured a lot of paraffin onto some peats and set the pan on to boil. Cold roast mutton from yesterday, a tin of peas—yes, everything was under control. I had just laid the table when I heard the rumble of my husband's tractor outside the house. He came in and collapsed full length on the sofa, his face flushed with tiredness and streaked with dust and sweat, and a minute later was fast asleep. This gave the tatties time to cook anyway.

Dinner over and down to the hay again, bairns in tow, to rake another rig—and another and another. The sun was high by now and hot. I could almost see the hay steaming in the heat. My hands turned hot and sticky and my shirt clung to my back with sweat. Well, I mustn't complain. A day as fine as this was a rarity and usually a bad spell followed in its wake. But somehow I never had time to appreciate the fine days—all I saw was unending hay! The dogs started barking and I looked up and saw a couple of tourists mincing in my direction.

"I say, Cynthia, just look, how cute!" one of them cooed fluttering her green-tinted eyelids.

"Oh, that is interesting!" exclaimed the other enraptured at the sight of my rake. "Do let me take a photo!"

"You lucky people! I do envy you so. No nasty machinery like we have back home."

"Oh yes?" I said sweetly, picking the skin off a burst blister.

I saw them five minutes later strolling up to the front of our house where Cynthia carefully took a photo of the wheelbarrow piled high with empty tins and all manner of old rubbish that we had never got around to throwing over the cliffs. Then they both peered in through the but (living-room) window where no doubt the sight of the dirty dinner dishes still on the table drove them into fresh ecstasies over the simple life.

Whilst I was so occupied a few puffs of white cloud had appeared beyond Soberlie to the north, and looking south I saw some similar pretty white plumes of cumulus. Mentally running up to the top of the hill and looking out to the west I visualized a wall of rain clouds advancing on my hay. Perhaps it was only a shower! I grabbed the rake and rushed around raking the hay up in heaps. After my initial enthusiasm had worn off and I was plodding along scraping up a meagre heap of hay off a huge nearly bare patch where not even the cotton grass was growing, another tourist appeared and stood watching me, one of the "Intrepid Explorers". I could picture the contents of the huge rucksack—spare clothes, emergency rations, first-aid kit, perhaps even a bivouac tent in case he was caught in a storm and had to sleep roped to the hillside. He took out his pipe, stuffed it with tobacco and took a few puffs.

"I say," he remarked conversationally, "Lovely day!"

"Yes, isn't it!" I responded politely, eyeing the gathering clouds to the west, "But I think it's going to rain soon."

"Oh, do you think so? Is that why everyone is working in the hay?"

I nodded, carefully scraping up the hay in a circle round about him.

"That's where mechanization would pay off. I cannot understand why you islanders don't co-operate more and buy a hay baler."

"Oh yes." I vaguely replied watching with fascination as the water from the bog slowly seeped up round his hob-nailed boots and lapped at the lowest eyelet hole.

"No initiative!" I thought I heard him mutter as he squelched off.

The advancing cloud spread itself across the sky and stretched out long fingers towards me. I could smell the rain in the air, cold and raw. I had to hurry. I ran from heap to heap gathering up the driest hay in my arms and putting it up in coles (miniature haystacks). The first cole looked fine, round, even, tapering to a nice high peak; the second had a bulge on one side and the top was slightly squint; the third teetered omin- ously downhill and shed handfuls of hay about itself. I was just bedding down the stead of the fourth one as the first tendrils of rain swirled misty white before the dark hill. The wisps gathered into a white curtain which swept down towards me. The hay! I leapt at the heaps in a frenzy of activity. As the first drops hit me I suddenly remembered the fish hanging on the fence to dry. Yelling wildly at the bairns to hurry, I ran up hill to the rescue, over the stanks (ditches), through the bog, under the fences.

I grabbed the pairs of fish and hung them on my outstretched fingers. How many fish can a hand carry? Twice as many, if it's raining. Weighted down, I fled for the house and dumped them in a heap on the table. A few more trips and fish and bairns were safely inside and I sat down to watch the rain. Only then did I find out how tired I was. My arms ached, my back was broken and someone had nailed my feet to the floor. And then I noticed that the fire was out and the water pail was empty.

The evening was grey—grey sky, grey sea, grey isle. The hill rose cold and silent, waiting—waiting for a new day, or a new era, I could not tell. The rain had cleared now but the hay was still lying damp and limp. Reluctant to leave it lying for yet another day, which would involve turning it all again, I put it up on racks, tapered step-ladder like contraptions which we use for hay-drying in difficult seasons. We often use them and they take out much of the tedious frustration of hay-making in our uncer- tain weather.

I was sitting in the middle of a clump of rür, a tall reed grass which was brought to the isle long ago to be used for thatching and now grows on all the crofts, patterning the heads of the rigs, marching down the stanks, encroaching on the old yards—the waving whispering rür that softens the starkness of the land. And as the fluffy plumes of its seedheads whiten against the sky and the evening air is filled with its soft rustlings, we know summer is at its height. Only a few roofs are thatched now but we still find good use for it since, properly arranged, a sheaf on top of a hay cole will keep out even the heaviest rain. So I was sitting cutting armfuls of it with a hand-hook and tying it up in fat sheaves. Above the sighing of the wind through the rür came the rhythmic purr of the mower as my husband cut another batch of hay, the sound of the engine picking up then faltering, picking up, faltering, over and over, due to the rough ground. Only the midges and the sharp stubble of the cut rür kept me awake.

At last the day was over and we crawled thankfully into bed. Could it be only this morning we were down on the beach—it seemed like a hundred days not one. And tomorrow was yet another day. Sometimes I longed for a week of gale and rain.

3

The Crü

Lugs prunk
Een bricht,
Tail athin a curl,
Paw lifted,
Head hich,
Waiten fur da whistle.
Black fur
Windblown
Keen to geeng again.
On gaird
At du crü
My dog Glen.

J. Eunson.

Although the crofts are so small, the hills provide a large area of rough grazing, which forms the scattald or common land on which about two thousand sheep are kept. Unlike most of the scattalds on the mainland ours is unregulated, i.e. there is no limit to the number of animals one is permitted to graze on it so that a couple with a young family may have several hundred while an elderly body living alone has only a handful. The sheep are all pure-bred Shetland sheep, small, agile, hardy and of independent mind. They are a very ancient breed of sheep, and are well known for their soft wool which may be of any colour ranging through white, brown or moorit, to black. Formerly the cow was more important in the island's economy and every croft had a byreful of kye, from three or four to over a dozen, and these were grazed on the scattald during the day, coming home to be milked at night. It's strange now to look at the hillside dotted with grazing sheep and hear the old folk speak of the days when herds of kye wandered there. A few sheep were kept for wool which they spun and knitted into clothing for themselves, with some to sell, and the lambs provided a little meat. It was not until the war, when moorit wool fetched a high price as it was used for khaki, that sheep became more important, and now, with the availability of tinned milk, the kye have nearly disappeared and crofting is entirely based on sheep. The hills are completely unfenced, and although the sheep keep to their own home areas, rounding them up takes a lot of co-operation and energy, hence the tendency to regard in-comers to the island under the terms of "can he run?"

"We're going to da Fleck crü da morn at eleven o'clock, if he's weather," announced Ken as he passed by one summer day on his way to the lobsters. The word passed through the isle. The next two days were wet and windy, but Saturday dawned bright and clear.

"Wake up, it's a crü day!" I shouted in my husband's ear.

"It would be," he muttered and tried to go back to sleep, but as he had to tend his creels before going to the crü I bullied him into rising. In the cold early morning sun he set off to the Voe accompanied by a sleepy-eyed John Andrew. I popped back to bed and snoozed until a more reasonable hour.

Crü is the name for both the rounding up of the sheep and the enclosure they are driven into. On this occasion the sheep from the scattald known as the Fleck at the north end of the isle, were to be sheared. Everybody who was able, from seven to seventy, would go and help although most of the sheep belonged to Ken. Unlike more domesticated breeds Foula sheep do not form flocks when disturbed but tend to scatter in all directions, each individual sheep making its own escape, which makes the rounding up of them very difficult to say the least. The crü is a small round enclosure with a long wire fence, the stjagi, as a flank on one side and a natural boundary such as a cliff or dyke as the opposite flank.

By 11 o'clock Jim had returned and he sharpened up the sheep shears while I hunted out bags for wool. Every now and then one of us would go to the door and survey the scene, but everyone was carrying on as normal. Joan was out kittying on the hens to come for their feed, the yaps of dogs announced the kye were being driven north the road, the purr of Ken's boat came from north by the Taing. While we were having an early lunch around 12 o'clock we saw the first signs that the crü was on— Davie was hurrying to the shop with Kimmy lolloping at his heels. Next the contingent from the south arrived and Bessie, Edith, Frances and half a dozen children disappeared into the

schoolhouse. Visitors are often puzzled by island timing; sometimes 11 o'clock may actually mean 11 o'clock or perhaps 12
o'clock, or on the other hand it might mean after Ken comes
ashore from the lobsters or when I've finished turning my hay.

Loading up dogs, bairns and bags we set off to the schoolhouse
where everyone was drinking cups of coffee and chattering
nineteen to the dozen, while a tangle of dogs and children
swarmed over the floor. The phone rang. It was Jessie to say Ken
and Jock had left for the back of the Kame half an hour ago. So
the confusion gathered itself together and packed onto the
tractors and trailers.

Arriving at the North End we piled out and after a short
discussion on battle tactics we dispersed to our positions. My
husband and I set off up Codlefield making for the Kame, climbing slowly, dogs at heel. Ahead of us stretched the Oxnagate, a
dark green line running diagonally up the steep smooth side of
the Sneug. This was the path along which the islanders used to
drive their kye over to Waster Hivda, a green grassy headland
at the back of the isle.

"How long since they drove the kye up here?" I asked.

"I don't know, but I mind dem saying it was da Gossameadow
folk at were da last anes to do it. Peter Manson's first job as a boy
was herding da kye over on Watsness, so da folk here were likely
still doing it den."

"Did someone stay with the kye then all summer?"

"Aye, dey had to watch dey didna stray ower da banks. Likely
dey had a peerie felly hoose over on Waster Hivda," Jim explained.

"It's a wonder the track still shows so noticeably if they only
drove them up and down once a year!"

"Well, after a', folk have been driving kye alang here for Guid
kens fu lang. Hundreds o years. Du minds, dey used to hide da
kye in da byre o Waster Hivda to keep dem safe from raids in da
days o da Vikings, and dat was a while ago!"

I thought of the folk climbing up here, chivying their oxen
before them—old beasts plodding up patiently, young ones stub-
bornly stopping every second step to tear mouthfuls of green
scrunchy woodrush or kicking up their heels and setting off in
the wrong direction. So long ago, yet they felt so close I could
almost stretch out my hand and touch them. The same sun

shone on their backs. The same hills looked down on them.

Half-way up we sat on a boulder and rested. Below us lay the Fleck, a smooth green plateau with a cluster of small lochs, bordered along the northern edge by the great Nort Bank, the 700 feet sheer cliff that stretched without a break for almost a mile.

Now we parted company as I was to stay here, whereas my husband had to go on further up. I crouched expectantly on the high hillside, young Bluey at my feet whining quietly with suppressed excitement. Around me floating, sweeping, swirling, a myriad bonxies (skuas) kept watch over their territories, their solemn "kak kak kak" echoing through the hills. Behind me rose the Sneug, a wisp of mist playing round its summit. In front the steep green slope stretched up to the Kame and swept down to the Nort Bank, along which the sheep would be driven, close to the cliff edge which would form one flank, a running line of dogs and people the other. Below me I spotted Ann taking up her position near the Clay Pool. Bessie, her head popping up occasionally, was hiding behind a hummock further down. Above her, Francie sat silhouetted on the ridge keeping hold of her dog Tibby. My husband, with old Dandy Dog at his heels, had already disappeared over the ridge to reinforce Ken and Jock in their job of rounding up the sheep.

Faint shouts and barks came over the ridge. They must be having some trouble with the sheep over there and no doubt we were in for a long wait. The sun shone warmly on my back, I relaxed, snuggled down into the green-scented woodrush and idly watched a small black speck, a trawler, drift across the pale blue sea out to the north. A score or so of sheep grazed along the edge of the Kame—small brown and white dots. No other sheep were in sight. I closed my eyes. A fly buzzed happily round my head, something was crawling up my leg, but I couldn't be bothered to look and see what it was. Ah, this was the way to spend summer!

The shouts sounded a bit louder. I opened one eye and noticed with surprise that Francie appeared to be jumping up and down waving her arms. Strange! Wondering what all the excitement was about I staggered to my feet. My left foot had developed pins and needles so I bent down and rubbed it. This appeared to throw Francie into a frenzy and suddenly I realized that she was trying to attract my attention. Glancing hurriedly around I saw no sheep but I was unable to see immediately above me because of a bump, so I scrambled up the steep face, Bluey bounding ahead ears pricked—work at last. Just in time the sheep saw him, snorted indignantly and halted, eyeing us malevolently. It was the contingent from the cliff edge that had been grazing so peacefully but which were now on their escape route to the Gillings, headed by Bessie's old White Horny, last year's fleece trailing down to the ground signifying that she was a veteran escapee.

"Good dog, Bluey. Caa them!" I shouted.

The sheep turned and fled back along the slope to the Kame, Bluey in hot pursuit.

"Peeriewise, peeriewise! Bluey come back, heel! you bad stupid dog! Heel!" I shrieked in vain.

Paying not the slightest attention Bluey sped after the stampeding sheep who were now making straight for Bessie. My heart sank, they would get by her. But no—here comes Roy, lolloping lackadaisically along, head turned sideways, sniffing the grass and pretending to ignore the sheep. Suspiciously they slow down and eye him warily. Roy crouches menacingly and fixes his eye on old White Horny. Deciding discretion is the better part of valour she turns and runs back to the cliff edge, the others follow and they settle down to graze again. I heave a sigh of relief and settle down in the sun again. Bluey shame-facedly creeps back to my feet but I ignore him. This time however I keep a close watch on the grazing sheep in case they try to break by again. They stir restively and make several abortive attempts to escape, but now a chastened Bluey works better and between us we keep them under control.

The first signs that the men are coming up from the back of the Kame are shown by our Shetland ponies as they pause in a bunch then gallop full tilt down the steep grassy face right along the very edge of the cliff, manes and tails flying, hooves pounding, mares whinnying to their foals. I can hardly bear to watch, expecting any minute to see one skid and plunge over the thousand-foot drop. Twenty-one, twenty-two, twenty-three—one missing! No, here she comes now, over the top, lazy old Flossie, last as usual.

Now the first sheep are at the top of the Kame and pour down

over the side, the air filled with maaing and baaing. A man
stands silhouetted on the summit, watching them. It must be
Ken. Then my husband appears along the ridge with Dandy
hurrying up the stragglers. He waves and shouts to us to move
further over to the foot of the Kame where the sheep are gathering in a baaing mêlée. I run down, Bluey at my heels, to
reinforce Ann and Davie. Out of the corner of my eye I see
Francie having trouble with a bunch of sheep determined to get
by her to the Sneug. They split up into twos and threes and leap
by above and below her. Some of those fiends from the back of
the Kame, I surmise, wondering how many of ours are among
them. The sheep at the foot of the Kame break past Ann and
Davie and set off along the cliff edge. Bessie sends Roy out in
front of them to try and still them, but they only stand a few
seconds and then stampede off again.

"Hurry up! Da sheep is getting too spread oot," yells Bessie to
the folk running down the side of the Kame behind the sheep.
But they are exhausted after running all the way up from the
back of the Kame trying to take the obstinate stragglers with
them. Ken, red in the face, shirt dark with sweat, utters something unprintable, picks up a particularly stubborn sheep and
flings it towards the main bunch, but immediately it leaps
round and bounds off. Sheep are now trying to break by in all
directions but people and dogs head them off again and again.
Some jump down the rocky faces in over the cliff edge, knowing
they will be safe there. Ken calls back Kimmy to leave them. We
all set off, running flat out, along the Nort Bank flanking the
sheep who appear to be possessed by demons. The dogs run
backwards and forwards covering the gaps between their owners who signal first one way then the other. In the days when
there were fewer sheep, dogs were not used to round them up,
but were mainly pets used only to chase livestock off the crofts in
summer. The first working sheepdogs here came from Sum-
merside, Walls, on the Shetland mainland, where my husband's
great uncle worked with them.

Now I am able to pick out individual sheep. There's Essy
Face's daughter—my, her lamb has fairly grown! Good heavens,
there's that old ewe off the back of the Sneug, the one that gave
me so much bother during the lambing—she seems to have lost
her lamb! Not much wonder, poor peerie runt! Who owns that

bright sneedled lamb? It looks unmarked. That moorit ewe of
Francie's . . . no, that muckle ewe of Ken's is answering it.
There's a little sean (late born lamb)—hope it's not ours. Better
watch that old ram back there, he's going to make a break for it.

"Bluey—caa it—peeriewise!"

"Look out, dere breaking by afore dee!" yells Bessie.

A large bunch splits off, running like mad away from the
edge.

"Fetch them, Bluey!" Out shoots my arm. It's Old White
Horny again! Annoyance speeds up my tired legs. I'm darned if
I'll let her get by. Bluey overshoots them, bounds through the
middle scattering them in all directions, then races in circles
round about them.

"What the—is that—dog doing!" screams somebody.

"Don't ask me!" I shriek back, wondering how it was that such
a wise dog as Dandy could sire such an eccentric puppy as Bluey.

However the sheep are as baffled by Bluey's tactics as I am
and they stop in a tight bunch, then trot meekly back to the
main flock. The sheep are all more or less under control again as
we slog up the short rise to Soberlie, running as fast as our
gasping lungs and leaden legs allow. I pause a second to get back
my breath and admire the view. Another very steep green slope
drops on the north side in a sheer cliff, which falls down to the
stacks off the North End. Seven hundred feet below us lie the
ruins of the old crofts of the Nort Toons, strung out inside the
perimeter of the old boundary dyke with sun and shadow marking out the old disused rigs.

The sheep move more slowly now as the folk coax them down
the steep face, cautiously keeping away from the cliff edge with
its dangerous unexpected indentations. In places the slope is so
steep that some folk slide down on their bottoms while others
hold onto the slippery close-cropped grass with their hands. At
the bottom the sheep collect in a confused baaing group on the
little headland of Est Hivdi.

"Fetch them, Dandy!" orders my husband.

Dandy sweeps round them in a wide circle shifting them
forwards, calmly and in control, a pleasure to watch. Kimmy
dances ahead of them, preventing them from going ahead too
fast.

"Press dem doon to da back o da dyke!"

We chivy them down, dogs running tirelessly, half crouching eyeing the sheep. People now stretch all the way to the end of the stjagi. The sheep move forwards in fits and starts along the back of the dyke. Every now and then a particularly daring sheep leaps through the line of dogs and people and sets off up the hill to freedom for there is no time now to retrieve a straggler. The sheep make one final bid to escape at the end of the stjagi but are confronted by Jock and his three dogs and are forced towards the crü the only way now not blocked by people.

"Watch oot! Dere going to turn back. Run doon on dem!"

A solid wall of people and dogs run down behind the sheep, shouting, barking, flapping jackets, waving sticks, jumping up and down. Young Hempie, at his first crü, gets confused and is caught up in the midst of the sheep and is borne towards the crü, yelping, tail between his legs. The sheep pay no heed to him now. They reach the mouth of the crü and balk, realizing they are trapped. Pandemonium breaks loose. Sheep spring in all directions. Folk grab them and fling them back, shove, push, pull, force them into the crü. The children squeal with uncontrolled excitement. Francie aims a kick at a defiant old ram. Mima trips up an escaping ewe with her stick. Ken drags two in by the scruff of the neck. Quickly the spare coil of wire is unrolled, posts are hammered in and the entrance to the crü is blocked off.

"Look out. Dere jumping over da wire!" exclaims Mima as Old White Horny leaps out over the back of the crü. Davie flings himself at her and grips a corner of her enormous fleece, but the wool comes away in his hand and she leaps and bounds away.

"Dwine just tak dee, du auld grise!" yells her owner and flings her stick at the triumphant ewe in a parting shot.

The sheep, several hundred of them, stand panting, sides heaving, the light of battle still shining in their eyes. Some of the wilder ones are frothing at the mouth and some of the people look as if they might do likewise. Ken and my husband have collapsed flat out soaked in sweat, and Bessie's face has taken on an unusual purple hue while Davie gasps for water.

Lying in the warm sun we slowly recover. I rise and go over to the crü to scrutinize the catch. Well-known faces peer back at me, brown, white and black. There are woolly faces, smooth shiny faces, ones with white spots or dark eye patches, old wrinkled faces with grey hairs showing round the mouth, young setnins (one-year-old sheep) faces almost unrecognizable now that they have lost their lamb features. Beside me Mima and Bessie are discussing a ewe.

"Na, Na, yon's no da daughter o' Auld Ringy Legs daughter. Yon's Young Moorit Ringy Leg's daughter. Du kens, it's her dat had da twins last year."

"Lass, I thought dat was wir Auld Bussy Faced Ringy Leg's daughter."

The menfolk are discussing the success of the crü. "How many got by dee boy?"

"A score or so won by me at da Blue Holes. Near caad da dog over da banks. Last I saw dey were making for da Sneus like da devil was ahint dem," explained Ken.

"So dey would, da b—s!" Jock was never one to mince words.

I drag myself up to the tractor and fetch down the bag with the shears.

"Grip me a ewe, and I'll get started."

Jim lifts a ewe out of the crü and after a short struggle I manage to get her legs tied up. Unlike most sheep, mine never sit placidly on their bottoms whilst being clipped. Even with their legs tied they still manage to wriggle energetically. Clip, clip, clip go the shears as I run them through the ewe's wool. The ewe glares at me balefully out of the corner of her eye, grinding her teeth with what sounds like suppressed fury. Some of us still cut off the wool with knives—old-fashioned bread and butter knives with faded yellow handles and the blades worn to a point by sharpening. Earlier on in the summer when the new and old fleeces were still separate the wool could be rooed or plucked off by hand, but by now the new wool had grown up through the old fleece fastening it on quite firmly. This natural separating of the old and new fleeces in the Shetland sheep has been ascribed to various causes, from genetic factors inherited from their primitive ancestors to unusual hormone balance caused by eating seaweed. However I believe it is caused primarily by a prolonged break in wool growth due to the severe winter conditions here.

We all take part in the clipping regardless of whether or not any of our own ewes are in the crü, so we know that we will eventually get them all finished. The fleeces are tossed onto different piles one mound for each owner. Some ewes have lost nearly all their fleeces and only have a few tufts left, whereas others have enormous fleeces trailing to the ground and solid rolls of wool under their chins.

Clip, clip, clip—we are tiring now and clip almost mechanically. The floor of the crü becomes churned up with deep mud and muck; the men slither and slip as they attempt to grab the elusive sheep and hand us struggling armfuls of muddy legs. Clip, clip, clip—my forefinger develops a large blister, my hands are dark with sheep's grease and with sweat out of the wool, my legs are becoming cramped as I crouch over the sheep, and everything seems soaked in their strong, pervasive smell. In the shelter of the dyke Mima has been coaxing the primus into action and brewing tea. We are glad to stop when she calls us to come and eat, and rubbing the dirty grease off our hands on handfuls of wet sphagnum moss, we tuck in gratefully to piles of bread and marge.

Revived, we clip the rest of the sheep with renewed vigour, but still they don't seem to be getting any fewer. The dogs provide us with a diversion by launching into a full-scale battle, whirling round in a tangle of teeth and tails. Half a dozen angry owners pounce on them shouting and laying about them until the contestants skulk away much subdued. In the excitement a half rooed ewe escapes and sets off up the hill, trailing her fleece behind her. Now there is nothing quite like a crüful of folk and dogs all going after one lone ewe. Suffice to say that after a lot of running and shouting, commands and counter-commands, the ewe jumps back into the crü of her own accord. No doubt she feels safer there.

Finally the last ewe has been clipped and we pack the fleeces up into the bags. As usual there is a shortage and we are faced with the problem of how to get all the wool packed, but eventually the last scrap is shoved in. The lambs in the crü are examined and any unmarked ones have paint smeared on their heads or ears. Before we go to this crü again, some of us will go to the hills to identify their mothers. Finally Mima shouts.

"Have you aa finished wi da sheep, folk?" and the wire across the crü entrance is opened. The sheep pour forth and fan out over the hillside with a confusion of baaings and maaings as mothers look for their lambs. We stand in the evening sunlight watching them disappear over the top of the hill.

4

The Sea Around Us

O Lord abön, hadd Dy grit haand,
    Afore da daylicht dees,
Ower aa at ploo dir lonlie furr
    Trowe Dy wind-scordet seas.
O Lord, I pray, look kindly doon
    An haad Dy haand ower aa,
Till my lang-santed hert wins back
    Whaar winds shall never blaa.

Laurence Graham.

At the end of last century the island supported the amazingly large population of 267, with 38 children at the school. Whilst the crofts produced some of their food, some meal, milk, butter and perhaps a little mutton, the fishing industry produced their cash with which they bought material for clothes, leather for shoes, flour and oatmeal, salt, sugar, tea, luxuries such as tobacco and whisky for Yule, and most important of all, their boats and fishing gear.

In a good year a man could earn £10 in the summer season and perhaps £1 or £2 in the winter. So a house with several menfolk going to the fishing could manage despite the system whereby the landlord and his factors had sole monopoly of fish sales, and paid the tenant fishermen in kind with goods from their shop. Households with no men going to the sea, a widow for example with a young family, were wretchedly poor and would have starved if the other islanders had not helped them with gifts of food.

The best fishing grounds were off at the Far Haaf, which lay 40–60 miles away out to the north-north-west of the isle right out near the edge of the continental shelf. The sixerns, the traditional six-oared boats used in Shetland during the last century, rowed out until, it was said, the Nort Bank (700 feet high) lay like a linn (piece of wood) on the far horizon. The men were usually away from three to four days and fished continuously, only taking occasional naps on rota. They carried peats to keep the fire going in the muckle kettle (very large pot) and here they boiled fish and brewed a pot of tea. They also took their ferdi meat with them, usually a single big thick biddy (oatcake), which was all the bread they ate during the whole time they were away. They fished with great lines—lines with hooks every three fathoms and a buoy at each end. Each man was responsible for providing his own line and keeping it in good repair, although the fish caught was pooled together and the cash shared out equally at the end of the season.

Big adult ling up to nine feet long and large halibut were caught off at the Far Haaf, using sleekie (conger eel) as bait. Sleekies abounded in the deep water overshadowed by the cliffs around the isle, where they lurked among the waar (seaweed), and being greedy were easily caught with a line baited with piltock. Then they were strung up from a line and left to go sour for several days. The line was usually tied below the Orkney Man's Gaet at the foot of our toon (croft) and the smell coming from the rotting eels was said to be something! Such was the activity about the Voe in those days with men coming back late at night from the eela (inshore fishing) and others going off early in the morning to the haaf, that the birds never touched them.

Cod and some ling was caught with hand lines at the Hame Sea which lay much nearer home up to ten miles off the isle. The men used two types of fishing gear at the end of their hand-lines—the spreader and the rikker. The spreader was made from lead shaped like a flat iron with a length of wire passing through a hole in its centre bearing a short length of line with a hook at each end. The rikker was a long heavy weight with several hooks dangling from it. Cod were taken most easily with bare hooks used for only one day after which they became dulled and useless. The most popular hooks were of the Mermaid brand Kirby Bend type which, it was said, had a poorer quality galvanized coating which shone white under water.

Haddock were caught on the Sand, a stretch of sandy bottom extending for a mile out from the Voe and on another much bigger area off the north end of the isle. They, too, were taken by handline and a spreader baited with limpets. Limpets gathered from rocks in the shade were preferred as bait. They were normally gathered before sunrise and the large numbers of men going to the fishing put a big demand on the limpet population. One man, Johnnie Manson of Bloburn who was a noted crags-man used to climb down the Nort Bank to the rocks 700 feet below just to collect limpets in the shade there. The collected limpets were immersed in the burn for two days, until they came out of their shells. This was considered to be the very best bait for haddock. When time was short the limpets were leeped, (that is placed in hot water) but they didn't fish so well.

Adult saithe, big heavy fish, 2–3 feet long, black above and silver below, were found where the tide was strong, the current carrying a plentiful supply of food. They were caught at the end of the summer for salting for the winter. They too were caught with a spreader but instead of limpets a large piece of white cloth was used as a lure. The men would choose a really fresh breezy day and would sail along the edge of the tide rank "going like da Melashun" (the Devil), trying to throw the spreader out to the side into the rank—an exciting and somewhat hazardous performance.

The ling and cod were split open, salted in vats and dried in the sun on the rocky foreshore. Some folk made their own "beaches" for drying them. The bare stony patch above our house up at the clothes line was probably one, and there is another made of flat stones over at Mogle that my husband's father and uncle made. Two rectangular holes were cut out in the rocks below the shop to make a convenient place for washing fish before salting. When dried, the fish was sold to the landlord or his factor, who had the monopoly, and it was exported mainly to Spain. Long ago, it is said, the islanders would sometimes sail and row south to Orkney, to barter a load of fish with the inhabitants there.

Fishing so far away from shore in the unpredictable weather that occurs here even in the summer could be dangerous, but there were never any major disasters such as those experienced by some of the other parts of Shetland. The Foula men learned to read the weather well and if it looked unsettled they went to the Hame Sea instead, from where they could quickly run to safety. Very occasionally a boat did not return, the crew having ling-ered behind to get the maximum catch. Returning home heavily loaded in freshening weather even the great expertise of the fishermen sometimes did not bring them safely to shore. Other dangers awaited them away out at the Far Haaf. During the last half of the eighteenth century and the beginning of the nineteenth, up to the end of the Napoleonic Wars, the press gang harassed the whole of Shetland, keen to get hold of the islanders who were well known for their seafaring skill.

Fish were abundant round the isle then. Small cod could be caught from the rocks "at the craigs", in certain spots. Soon after my husband's grandfather's arrival on the island, he took his waand (fishing rod) one evening and went to the craigs. Walking north along the banks looking for a suitable place to fish from, he saw two Veedal wives down at the Smell Geo fishing with unusually thick waands, so he climbed down to see why and found they were catching lovely big codling. He tried fishing himself and caught two, then the next tug broke his waand, so he took himself home to fix up an extra strong waand for himself. Nowadays you would be lucky to catch a sillock (baby saithe) there.

There was many a superstition connected with going to the fishing. In common with the rest of Shetland a special set of sea names was used at sea, most of them old Norse names such as *yunsie* for hen, *fitlin* for cat, *rakkie* for dog. Some are more recent like "beni hoose" for the church (house of the benedictus), and "sprickled fellow" for trout, "hairfish" for seal. Some subjects were simply not spoken about at all, for who could say what ill luck the old sea gods might bring? And of course if you should chance to meet an ill-footed wife on the way to the boat you need hardly bother going further, as nothing brought worse luck— unless perhaps, cats in the büddie (the fish basket).

One fish they did not like to catch on their lines was the stane biter (catfish), a big ugly fish with a faceful of teeth, caught only very occasionally. It was supposed to signify that it would be the last season that crew would fish together. My father-in-law told of the time he caught one when he was crewing with the Niggards men, Davie and Robbie. Its teeth were so powerful it had bitten half-way through the lead rikker—hence the name stane biter. He remembered what the old folk said, but dismissed it lightly as mere superstition, but the next year found him and Robbie south, and long years of fighting in the First World War were to intervene before he returned alone to the isle. The War Memorial bears Robbie's name along with four others.

By the beginning of this century fishing at the Far Haaf was becoming uneconomical, and thereafter the islanders went mainly to the Hame Sea for cod in the smaller fourerns or four-oared boats. The cod they caught there were known as "gaain" cod—fish that migrated south in large numbers at the beginning of the summer until by autumn they were about ten miles to the south-east of Foula. They were greenish-grey with big bodies and small heads unlike the resident or "grund" cod which were yellowish with big heads and small thin bodies. Hand-line fishing was carried out here commercially until shortly after the First World War. Then some of the young islanders left and settled on the Shetland mainland where they were able to fish in larger decked boats which used more profitable modern methods. Some went further afield, to Australia and Canada, like so many others from the poorer regions of Britain.

In 1913 the school roll dropped to twelve and by 1927 it was down to only six. A similar population drop occurred over most of the outlying parts of Shetland, although it is very interesting to observe that islands such as the Out Skerries, Whalsay and Burra, where fishing is still the most important occupation, did not suffer this severe population decline, and still support thriving communities. They were lucky—unlike Foula they have good natural harbours.

The end of commercial fishing left Foula with only its crofts but the island was never self-supporting agriculturally. The land is too poor, too exposed and too far away from the market. It was a very rare year, one in fact to be remembered, that the island was able to grow all its own meal. Usually the home-grown meal lasted only four and a half to five months and the rest had to be bought. And although every house had several milking kye, there was no milk in winter when fodder was scarce, nor did the salted butter last until spring. Meat, too, was a great rarity, for kye were too valuable to be killed and the number of sheep kept was low. The biggest flock numbered fifty while some houses had none, and the average was only about half a dozen. The economy then was very dependent on the fishing. Not only did it bring in cash, it also provided the main part of the island diet. Very rarely was a dinner eaten that did not consist of fish either fresh or dried.

Up to the end of the last century the landlord's factors, the Garriocks from Reawick, had the monopoly of all the island's trade and the islanders were threatened with eviction if they dared to sell their fish elsewhere. Anyone unlucky or unskilled at the fishing was miserably poor. Some of the North Toon folk, being hard up, practised the false economy of using the same hooks over and over again, carefully rubbing them clean for re-use. But this removed the white galvanized coating that made the hooks so attractive, so they were less successful at the cod fishing. As a child, I can remember old Jeannie o' Banks, who was blind eating only a tiny portion of the food she was given. "Eat you it," she would insist, "I'm had plenty," so accustomed was she to eating less than her fill. Another family was so poor that my father-in-law remembered seeing the bairns eating bruinies (thick oatcakes) made out of soft peat dug from the side of the burn. A real bruini in one hand and a peaty one in the other, they took a mouthful first from one hand then the other. On protesting about this to their mother, he was told, "Mony a good dinner have I eaten oot o' da broo o' da burn."

At the end of the last century, with the passing of the Crofters Act, the Garriocks' monopoly over the island was broken. The shop was run by an islander and for a short time, as long as the fishing held out, the islanders were able to lay up a fair amount of money in their kists.

In some ways, despite all the progress that modern times have seen, the isle was relatively less isolated then than it is now. Superbly at home on the sea, the islanders thought nothing of sailing over to the mainland on a mere whim, and they would sometimes row over to Watsness, 14 miles away, just for an evening visiting friends, or to do a bit of courting, and their friends would pay them return visits. There was a continual coming and going as men served in the Merchant Navy; boys went to the whaling or the herring fishing and girls spent their summers in Lerwick gutting fish or went south as maids in service. When they had earned enough back they all came to the isle. In the days of the line fishing sixerns (six-oared boat) from the mainland came here for the summer fishing, some of the crews living in the little stone böd or booth at the head of the baa. Later cattle dealers came with their boats to buy and ship out kye, and the big fishing boats from Shetland and Scotland

called along to get islanders to complete their crews. Because of
this interaction with the outside world, the islanders were never
inbred like the populations of many other small isolated communities. It was common enough for an islander to bring back a
girl from the mainland as his wife or for a family from a less
favoured district of Shetland to come and settle on the isle.

The Foula men knew the sea well. Without a compass they
could navigate to the Far Haaf or to Orkney in thick fog, and
return safely back to the isle. Like other Shetlanders they could
read the "Midder Dye", the deep underlying swell that always
runs in the same direction towards the shore, regardless of the
surface motion caused by the wind. Round our isle it ran from
the north-west down towards the south-east end of the mainland, and it runs there yet for those that have eyes to read it.

During the winter, the island was completely cut off as the
boats did not cross then but isolation did not matter for the
islanders bought their winter supplies when they sold their fish
at the end of the summer.

A regular service first came to Foula in 1879 after my
husband's grandfather had written to Queen Victoria. He received a reply from Disraeli himself assuring him that they
would be given a mail service. It was run by the landlord's
factors and crossed once a month from Reawick, though in the
winter it seldom crossed and the islanders sometimes had to go
in their own boats to fetch supplies. Robert Gear wrote again
asking for a more frequent service, once a fortnight, and pro-
posed that it should be run from Walls, which is much nearer to
the isle than Reawick. The contract was put up for tender and
given to a Walls man, Johnie Jeromson, but as the islanders
came to use the service more and more it was decided to increase
it to once a week during the summer and before long the contract was given to the islanders themselves. Six men formed the
crew, Magnie Manson being the skipper, and the other five all
hailed from the north end of the isle.

The first boat they used was hired for £6 a year from Mrs
Trail, an adventuress who settled in Foula as factor for the
landlords, after the demise of the Garriocks. She had to provide
a new sail every second year, but she still made a good profit as
the value of a boat then was about £20. The crew of six shared
£3 each trip as payment from the Post Office. Expenses were

low as there was no insurance, engine repairs or fuel so they were able to earn a good wage by going in the boat, and it was an important boost to the economy of the island where no other local employment was available. More than one family was able to remain on the island because one of their menfolk went on the boat, when otherwise poverty would have forced them to leave. The boat only lasted eight years as the skipper drove her hard, seldom missing a trip regardless of weather. He was a man with a great eye for the sea and could predict exactly how a wave would act and how much the boat could stand. In rough conditions he didn't bother to steer the boat dry. Spray came in all the time and the men had to bale regularly, but he never took a heavy lump of water on board. One day nearing the Walls Sound with a fresh wind behind him and a fully reefed sail, the boat was fairly skimming along.

"Shake out a reef," he said, as he wished to get in before the weather worsened.

The boat gained speed till her gunwale was nearly awash.

"Right, boys, I wonder how she would stand up to full sail."

She came up the Sound with a huge bow wave and a great wave pressing out from the side well above the level of the gunwale, going like the Sunse, they said, and Magnie at the helm grinning from lug to lug.

But many a day they had to row instead, each man at an oar. With a good tide and the boat light they could reach Walls in four hours, but with a hard tide and a heavy-laden boat the round trip sometimes took them twenty-four hours. By tradition they only used to take half a biddy (thick oatcake) to eat on the journey. At the end of each journey the boat was pulled up on the beach, but without an engine it was not nearly so heavy to pull up and down by hand as a motor boat is today. In fact at one time three forty-foot herring boats belonging to some of the islanders were kept on the beach. For a year or two they did quite well at the herring which used to be plentiful in season round the isle, until one of the boats lying at anchor in the Voe, was caught unawares by the first gale of the autumn. The sea took her and smashed her up. She was insured at the time and for long years after it was impossible to obtain insurance for a Foula boat.

The second boat lasted just six years. The third boat, the *Advance*, was bought with money lent by Jimmy Isbister, nick-

named Jimmy Cody, the first Hametoon man to have a share in
the boat. Jimmy Cody also bought a Gardner engine for the boat
and went south for three weeks on a special course to learn how
it worked, this being only the second motorized boat on the west
side of Shetland. She was still running when we were bairns but
since then her hull has lain on the beach and our own bairns
used to play at being fishermen in her.

In the old days there was no pier. Passengers and goods were
landed onto the rocks on the north side of the Voe at Tushkarig,
and kye were loaded on at the south side where a boat could lie
alongside a straight face of rock. As long ago as 1883 Robert
Gear petitioned for a harbour and eventually after twenty years
of campaigning the government agreed. Then followed more
years of disagreement between the government and the landlord over lease of a suitable bit of land, which the landlord
refused at first to consider, wishing to own the pier himself.
Finally in 1914 work on the construction of the pier was started.
A one-hundred per cent grant was given to a contractor who
employed island men to do the work. Local material was used,
some of the shingle being ferried by boat from the back of the
Smell Geo. With the First World War looming ahead the para-
pet was provided with a firing step.

The fishing was still profitable at this time, those fishing
earning slightly more for their summer's work than those working on the pier who got 4d an hour. The men on the pier used to
watch for the boats returning from the sea, for they could tell the
size of the catch by how low the boat lay in the water and if a
typical catch was more than three hundredweight there would
be less men on the pier the next day—the others would be off at
the fishing too.

For reasons best known to themselves, the officials planned
the pier so that the only skerry in the Voe lay along the outer
side and end of it, thus preventing boats from lying alongside
except on the inner side. Presumably it was cheaper and easier
to build it out to the skerry and to be honest many a less
practical pier has been built in Shetland. In fact, as someone
once remarked, the only trouble with Shetland piers is that the
top of the water is too near the bottom of the pier.

Even after the building of the pier, the old *Advance* still had to
be pulled up on the beach after each trip, but in the early fifties

the mailmen purchased a new boat, the *Island Lass*, and davits were erected on the pier so that she could be lifted up out of the water onto the pier and pulled up the slipway by winch. The davits were worked by hand chains. Two men stood on deck pulling down on the chains over and over again until they turned tired and the next two took their place. It's a sound I'll never forget, the continuous rasp, rasp, rasp of the chains. Imperceptibly the boat would be lifted out of the water inch by inch until it was hanging above our heads, then it would be swung in over the pier and lowered onto the waiting cradle. The winch was also worked by hand. Four men took the big handles and swung them round and round. First one pair would stretch their arms and strain forwards, and then the two partners opposite— push and pull, push and pull. It took over four hours, to get the boat up out of reach of the sea. Next mail day the whole process had to be repeated in reverse. In winter this wasted precious hours of daylight and always meant that the men had to face another long spell of work when they finally arrived back home again. The men grumbled about it for years. After the loss of the *Island Lass* the County Council removed the old davits and winch and put in a power-driven crane and winch, and I must say that this has been one of the few real benefits that we have received from the government in recent years. No more the long hours of pulling chains and pushing handles—the boat is lifted up quickly by crane, swung in and lowered onto the cradle, then whisked miraculously up to the top of the slipway. True, the crane is positioned so that the boat cannot be launched or lifted at low tide, but we can't have everything.

The mailboat crosses every Monday or the next fine day thereafter. In the summer she usually manages to cross once a week, but in winter it is another matter. Then fine days are rare and all too apt to deteriorate quickly. Thus it sometimes happens that the boat crosses to Walls safely but is unable to return that day so that the crew have to wait on the mainland for several days, or sometimes weeks, for a chance to return, while their families try to cope amidst storms and blizzards without them. While away from home the men stay in a small wooden hut near the pier at Walls where they while away the tedious days of waiting by yarning and looking at the weather. One wall of the hut is lined with three old-fashioned box beds or wooden bunks, built one above the other. On one occasion a particularly heavy sleeper fell out of the topmost bunk but much to everyone's surprise only his temper sustained any damage.

The *Island Lass* ran for about ten years. Built with a double diagonal construction she was a good boat handling well in awkward seas—a fact that was to stand her in good stead one never to be forgotten winter's night. It was in the month of March, well known here for its treacherous weather, and the boat had been unable to return to the isle the night before, due to the weather. It was still windy next morning but in the afternoon the wind moderated although the sky had an ominous look and a heavy swell was running from the north. The mailmen were behind with their quota of mails for the year required from them by the Post Office, so against their better judgement they decided to attempt the return trip. It was dark as they neared the isle. The wind had increased to gale force, and the swell was running in big heavy lumps. Only the blinks of a hand torch flashed by someone ashore showed where the Voe was. Suddenly, without warning, a blinding blizzard swept down from the north driven by a Force Ten wind. The folk waiting on the shore for the boat were appalled to see the boat's lights blotted out in flying snow and spray. A while later, away to the south, they saw through the snow the red stars of a distress flare—the boat, miraculously, was still keeping afloat. Then followed a long distressing night of waiting during which there seemed little hope.

Meanwhile the crew of the *Island Lass* put out a sea anchor and while the boat drifted they worked frantically at the water-logged engine, swamped by towering waves which broke continuously over the boat. Peering through the darkness, they could see little difference between the white snow above and the flying spray below. They were unable to tell where they were for no reassuring blink of light was visible. Four hours later the boat was still holding its own in tumultuous seas. By then the snow had partly cleared, and they could make out a light on the island. But although they had succeeded in starting the engine, whenever they attempted to drive the boat towards the isle she would dive right through the breaking waves which threatened to sweep away the wheelhouse. The men were drenched and chilled to the bone and two were near collapse with the cold. But help was nearby. An Aberdeen trawler heading for shelter from fishing grounds away out to the west of Foula spotted the stricken boat, and eventually all the men were picked up safely and the boat taken in tow. But alas the tow rope broke within minutes and the storm swept her away down towards Orkney where she was spotted next morning, full of water and minus the wheelhouse, but still just afloat. Attempts to take her in tow again were unsuccessful and she sank.

The present boat is a small ex-RNLI lifeboat. Unfortunately before she could meet the Board of Trade regulations the original engine had to be replaced by a Perkins diesel, despite the crew's objections. Too light for the boat, the engine broke down after only two crossings and its performance has continued to be unsatisfactory ever since, so that one member of the crew has to spend much of each crossing crouching in the fumy engine room nursing the engine to keep it going. How many summer evenings have I sat on our cold stone doorstep, binoculars held steady against the door jamb, scanning the pale pearly grey sea for a small familiar black dot. How many bright spring days have I peered out over a sea of dancing, glancing white waves for the one constant splash of white. In Hairst, in the humin (dusk), I stare out at a darkening sea, hearing the swish of the increasing wind rustling in the dead rür, willing the boat to hurry. On black winter nights I stand in despair, blinking, blinking, with my pocket torch, my imagination for ever conjuring up answering signals out of the corner of my eye, so faint they disappear when I turn to look at them.

The boat has none of the usual modern navigational aids, no radar or decca. On a black night or a day of thick fog they steer by the compass, negotiating the complex of tides by experience. Making a landfall somewhere on the long stretch of mainland is relatively simple, but finding the isle again is another matter. A few degrees off course due to an incorrectly reckoned tide and they will find themselves happily heading out for Greenland, but during all the years the boat has been running only once did they fail to find the isle, when a cargo of gas cylinders had affected the compass.

When the mailboat was first run by the islanders themselves the crew received £3 a trip between them from the Post Office. Expenses were low and this represented a good week's wage.

Now, some seventy-five years later, although expenses have increased manifold, the wages have not kept pace and some years they have had no returns at all for their work. From being an important boost to the economy the mailboat has become a sore burden to those that have to run it, and it says much for the calibre of the island men that someone is still willing to volunteer to do so.

For twenty-four years the Post Office has refused to give the mailboat a rise, on the grounds that the country's postal service is making a big loss. And as everyone is always glad to point out it is more expensive to deliver a letter to Foula than anywhere else in Britain. When the *Westering Homewards* was purchased ten years ago the mailmen were told that they would receive a rise, but there followed years of being fobbed off by one government department after another. Finally the local County Council granted them a small subsidy of £500. Their final application for a rise from the Post Office received the following answer: "Since we are now expected to run our services economically, I cannot hold out any further hope of further financial assistance from the Post Office"—yet it was announced that for that year the Post Office made a profit of three hundred million pounds.

In July 1978, the crew of the mailboat asked the Post Office for termination of their contract. By January 1979, when their six months notice were completed, it had been twenty-five years since the Post Office had given them a rise. The service is now run by the Shetland Islands Council, who are better able to bear the financial burden.

Islanders are often accused of being apathetic. Small wonder. Apathy is a condition caused by banging one's head against a brick wall too often.

5

Time for Reflection

Come up ta da hill wi me, dearie,
A'll shaw dee da sheep an da kye
An da horses cropin da lubba,
An da böls whaar da gimmers lie;

James Stout Angus.

But it was not all work. Many a fine Sunday we spent wandering over the isle, ostensibly perhaps to check up on our sheep or Shetland ponies but, more important, to catch a glimpse of our elusive summer. Two of our young horses had been missing for several weeks, so we set off for the hills for a final search. In time we learnt the hard lesson that inevitably a certain number of our horses disappear, gone over the banks like many another animal. Sometimes it isn't easy to equate the sight of one's bonny peerie filly impaled on a rock at the bottom of a 400-foot drop with a percentage annual loss. But we have come to accept it, just as we have learnt to accept the high mortality rate of our sheep fending for themselves on the wild exposed hills. Only the passing of an islander is different. This is always an irreparable, unconsolable loss—part of us torn away each time. But sometimes, looking into the future, I wonder if we will accept even this too in the end, with the wisdom that comes with old age.

We went south along the road to where the little grey stone church stands on the tail of Hamnafield. Built relatively recently by the Congregational Church, it was known officially as the Baxter Chapel. The original church, belonging to the Church of Scotland, now stands roofless at the south end of the isle. It is the second oldest kirk in Shetland and was built on the site of a much older church dating back to the days of the old Norse. The churchyard is still used as the island's burial place. In summer a neglected tangle of unpleasantly rank grass and dockens testifies to the strong belief in the importance of the soul rather than of the body. Grave stones are very rarely used. During the times of the great religious revival, when the

Church split into various different sects, services were also held
in a big barn up at Hamnabreck, and in what is now known as
Jeems Henry's Hoose, a little square stone enclosure in under
the hill.

In the old days the Church was very authoritative and played
a big part in the islanders' lives. Any troubles among the people
were brought before the church and much remonstration and
sometimes punishment was given out. The old parish records
give an interesting glimpse of what it must have been like; a
young girl, who was being scolded for her wrongdoings, shocked
the elders by being "observed to hide a smile behind her hand";
another entry tells of a married couple "remonstrated for living
in a hellish state of animosity one towards the other"!

Leaving the church behind us, we climbed up along the ridge
of the hill, stopping now and then to breathe in deep lungfuls of
honey-scented air that wafted up from the close springy carpet
of purple heather flowers, and to pick mouthfuls of small black
juicy heather berries, or crowberries, that grow in profusion
everywhere.

To the south-west of the church are the remains of an old
dwelling known as Cru Kaitrin. According to legend, Kaitrin
dwelt here about three hundred years ago, and she is said to
have owned a part of the isle. The man she was going to marry is
said to have been captured and sold to America as a slave, so she
decided to sell her land to someone on the mainland. On her way
out, unfortunately, the boat capsized and she was drowned in
the Banks Sound. The land round about Cru Kaitrin has been
scalped bare of soil. Perhaps she left no relatives who could
legitimately sell it so that no-one could claim it without dispute.
Instead the other islanders may have carried away the fertile
ground to replenish their own land.

Further up the hill is another much older site, known now as
the Laamus o da Wilse, a sheep's shelter built from stones from
an ancient ruin. It may have been a look-out place dating back
to Pictish times or earlier for the ground round about is full of
bits of old pottery and burnt stone. Now the east face of the hill
dropped very steeply away, almost sheer below us down to the
Mill Loch which lay blue in the sun. Along the ridge here are the
remains of a stone and turf dyke which was built long ago to stop
the cows from falling down the steep face.

From the top of the hill the view was like an aerial photo-graph, the isle lying spread out below us like a multicoloured map. Behind us to the north rose the high steep slope of the Sneug with a wisp of white cloud catching the top, and the Kame like a duplicate peeping out behind it. And all round stretched the sea. A slight swell rolling in from the north, patterned the surface with ripples, and being caught by the point of Strem Ness was swirled round into a fan shape so that the rank there was breaking white. The low land was gold and purple amber in the sun, edged with bright green along the shore. The road running the length of the isle through the middle of this low land was a thin white ribbon—a long walk. The tiny Voe was a small nick in the coastline where tiny white and blue boats bobbed at their moorings. Every detail of the croft land was clear, each little rig and each drain dividing the ground into innumerable little strips while the houses stood scattered round the edge. Outside the toonship the ground was scarred with the black cuts of peat banks, and with bare patches where the mould had been scraped off for bedding. The burn meandered along the foot of the hills, taking a twist here, a turn there. Here and there along its banks were the small stone circles of the planti crubs. Casting my eyes southwards the crofts there, at the Hametoon, were less cut up, lying fertile and vividly green in the sunshine. How small an area of our isle was actually tamed! How puny our efforts seemed from up here with only a few meagre green patches scattered here and there over the island.

Over at the Santoo we could make out the windsock fluttering beside the airstrip. A plane was expected shortly so we lay in the sun waiting. Around us the bonxies circled, old ones kaking, young ones uttering their long drawn out whistle. The echo of dogs barking drifted up from the houses below us, and the distant irritating rattle of a generator disturbed the silence.

By and by Jim nudged me, "I hear her noo."

After a few moments I caught the purr of an engine to the south and soon we could make out the small speck flying in over the sea. The plane turned and circled in towards the airstrip and from our vantage point we were looking right down on top of it. We watched with interest as two figures got out; who could they be? They set off at a brisk trot along the road lying far below us, past the church, down to the Post Office where they paused for a

moment—but Harry was not there on a Sunday. They walked
past the school, with a brief glance down to the pier, then they
turned and quick marched back to the airstrip. There was a
revving of engines and the plane departed again leaving us in
peace.

We left the summit behind us and walked along the ridge
towards the Sneug. Here was a domain belonging solely to the
bonxies who soared in hundreds in the sky above us. Individuals
defending their territories swooped like miniature bomber
planes at our heads with a roar of wind through their wings as
they dived. Usually they aim for a close miss, and very rarely do
they actually hit you. But that is quite often enough as they are
big birds with a 4½-foot wingspan. We ignored them unless
when they skimmed so close that our hair lifted, and then we
raised a hand to make the bird sheer off.

Now the ground fell away steeply on both sides of us leaving
us poised in the sunny sky, the soft wind gently caressing our
faces, and a lightness in our feet. The vegetation was different
here on the top of the Sneug where the scrunchy green woodrush
and moss gives way to short, sparse arctic-alpine varieties,
remnants of the vegetation of the last Ice Age. I imagined the
vast ice sheet as it crept slowly westwards flowing out over the
sea to our island, diverting and piling up against the steep
eastern faces of the hills, squeezed through the deep valley of
the Daal like toothpaste out of a tube, leaving only the tops of
the hills rearing up above the ice, bare, windswept and frozen.
Glacial erratics, stones mainly of granite carried from far away
by the ice, are scattered all over the island up to a height of
about 500 feet.

The Ice Age ended 10,000 years ago and belongs to relatively
recent times. Sitting on the top of our little world, leaning
against the old lichen grown cairn, we pondered long on the
origins of our isle long before the Ice Age. The steepness and
abruptness of the hills make a big contrast to the lower rounded
hills of the rest of Shetland as though one of the ancient mythi-
cal gods had flung it up in a moment of high spirits.

Could our minds reach so far back, back to the first be-
ginnings—back to the times when the ancient Caledonian
mountain chain was uplifted to form the hills of Scotland and
the backbone of our own Shetland Islands stretching out to the

north. These same ancient rocks were then eroded and worn away into sand that was deposited grain by grain, to form the Old Red Sandstone of Devonian times. We could almost visualize the bare eroded mountains, the vast stretches of desert, the inland lakes and warm shallow seas repeatedly advancing and retreating. And one tiny scrap of this ancient world was to remain as our island!

It was strange to sit here at the top of the steep green grassy slope that fell away so dramatically to the east and wonder if it was once a cliff face chiselled and whittled away by wave action, or if the high plateaux of the Fleck and Ourafandal were once beaches at the foot of cliffs—some other sea, some other time. It was easy to look back into the past, a hundred million years, but how hard it is to see the future, even one year ahead. But we knew some day, long after man was gone from here, the last little bit of our isle would be washed away by the sea and the long, long struggle would be over. And we knew it was right that this should be so.

Erosion is a continuous process, a little bit here, a small rock there, sometimes imperceptible but sometimes carrying away a familiar landscape. One of the biggest falls in recent years occurred in the early 1950s in the spring of the year when a green slope at the back of the Noup known as the Shitleens slipped away from the rock face and plunged 500 feet to the foot of the Noup in a jumble of rubble. The sound of it falling was heard all over the island like a rumble of thunder, and further occasional bangs and crashes occurred throughout the summer. On another occasion a crü which was perched on the very edge of the banks vanished overnight, leaving a raw brown scar where they had been rooing sheep only the day before. In the late autumn of 1969 after a severe north-westerly storm we were saddened to discover that the Broch, one of the prettiest stacks at the North End, shaped in the form of an arch, had fallen leaving only two jagged rocks behind.

The horizon of sea now lay higher than the tops of Hamnafield and the Kame, giving us the impression of being perched on the top of the world. On top of our world. Stretched out to the east across a wide expanse of sea, floated the rest of Shetland, a fairyland of gold and blue as the little isles and voes caught the sunlight—a fairyland however that wove its magic spells in vain for we do not hanker after it. Far to the south we could see a low dark blue hump—Fair Isle. We looked at it with mild curiosity. Since being taken over by the National Trust for Scotland its population has increased considerably. At first the increase was caused by in-comers from south who appeared to come and go at rapid intervals, but now, at last, we hear young islanders themselves are beginning to return. The standard of living, we hear, is far above our own, housing being improved with help from the Trust. But we do not hanker after it either. It is not our island.

"Is yon Orkney o'er yondrew?" My husband pointed further round the horizon to where a faint blue smudge floated—a far-away island or perhaps only a small wisp of cloud?

"Hand us da muckle glasses." He peered through the binoculars.

"Perhaps it's the hills of Scotland? Can't you see Ben Hope or something from up here?"

Strange to think of all that land lying down there, out of sight—round the corner as it were. All those people! All that mess and muddle!

"I'm thirsty," I announced. "Let's see if there's any water in the waters of the Sneug."

We climbed down the ridge towards the Kame, scrambling over big grey outcrops of sandstone.

"Here it is!" My husband pointed to a small saucer of rock hidden under an overhanging outcrop. Like a small stone basin it held the water that had seeped out of the rocks above. Cool sweet water. We drank our fill. The water is believed to have special healing powers. Perhaps minerals are dissolved out of the rock and vegetation above it. It was discovered little more than a century ago. One of the Dykes men lay ill of what was known as da cruels—big open sores which were possibly a form of TB. He had little hope of recovery but one night one of the North Harrier men had a strange dream. He dreamt his aunt came and told him of a particular place up near the top of the Sneug where he would find water to cure the dying man. Three times the dream was repeated that night and the third time his aunt threatened that if he did not do as she told him, he would suffer for it. He rose and went outside, and looking up at the hill soaring up before him, he saw the place she had spoken about.

Impressed, he went up the hill first thing next morning, found the spot exactly as described in the dream and carried down some water to the dying man, who eventually recovered completely.

On the ridge between the Sneug and the Kame there is a conspicuous small green hump used by the bonxies as a club where they gather to display. Their droppings over the years have altered the composition of the soil allowing fine green grass to grow there. There are several main clubs on the island and since the rapid increase of the bonxie population many smaller ones are being formed—"soap boxes" used by only two or three birds at first but soon by dozens. The sheep and ponies appreciate the improved grazing and brave the swoops of attacking bonxies to reach the sweet grass. This day the horses were there, grazing peacefully in the sun. As we approached, the mares raised their heads and whinnied a welcome while Jacob, the stallion, came prancing towards us, the sun gleaming on his strong red body and the wind ruffling his flaxen mane. Nostrils flared, neck proudly arched, he let out a shrill whinny of anticipation—perhaps we had brought another mare to add to his harem. But no, nothing doing! So he consoled himself by nibbling at my bare toes and poking his nose into my husband's pocket. The mares converged on us from all directions, pushing and shoving each other, breathing down our ears, chewing our hair.

"I see dee, du's a braa bonny horsie," said my husband, dishing out sheep's nuts to all and sundry.

"Look, here's Charm come for some." One of the small foals had cautiously approached and was sniffing my hand. "Try her with a nut."

"See, peerie horsie, yon's braaly good. Thinks du would du eat some?" The foal gave a sniff at the proffered delicacy, then rolled back her upper lip in an expression of utter disgust. Old Flossie took advantage of this and snaffled the nut in a twinkling.

"Du is a hocken brute, Flossie!" He gave her a shove. "Yon was da hidmost nut du ate!"

Watching the ponies eating their titbits made us hungry.

"How about some of those lettuce sandwiches?" my husband asked presently, looking hopeful. Now if there is one thing he is very attached to it is his lettuces, particularly if they are crisp and juicy, oozing with salad cream, so I rescued the bag from the inquisitive hairy noses that were snuffling at it, and handed a sandwich to him. Immediately Primrose, who was the pushing type, made a grab at it.

"Oh no you don't," he exclaimed, taking a large bite out of the sandwich and holding it out of reach behind his head. "Clear off Primrose, this is my sandwich."

Whilst his attention was occupied, Flossie who was standing right behind him, eyed the tempting morsel with relish. Delicately she reached out her upper lip and tweaked out a lettuce leaf. She munched it with interest and sneaked all the rest, leaving him only the plain bread and butter. "Not bad" her expression said as she licked the drips of salad cream off her nose.

From here we made our way out towards Nebbifield where we would get a magnificent view of the Kame. As we approached the cliff edge the uplifted wind wafted the special smell of the high cliffs to us.—It is a scent with many ingredients—the sun shining on the old worn sandstone, the strong fishy tang of the birds' droppings which stain the crowded ledges white, the overgrown scurvy grass whose leaves as big as cabbages hang from the ledges, and the close cropped sea-pinks along the very edge where the sheep lie chewing their cud. It is the smell of summer and the high banks.

We sat down carefully near the edge and gazed for a long time. Before us the Kame dropped 1,220 feet down to the sea. By peering over we could see where the foot of the great cliff plunged sheer into the water. Much of the cliff was bare—it was so smooth and steep—but wherever there was a tiny ledge a maalie (fulmar) nested, so the cliff was dotted with small white spots each accompanied by a little clump of vegetation. Thousands upon thousands of maalies circled round and round and round in the air, soaring and gliding in the up-draught. Some, more curious, floated motionless only a few yards out from the edge of the cliff where we sat. Wings tipped up, breast puffed out, tail cocked, feet spread, braced against the wind they observed us placidly. An occasional norie (puffin) whirred past, his coloured beak packed with a row of sand eels. How relatively few of them there are now. Many of the burrows along the cliff edge were deserted and the ledges where they used to pack in myriad rows were almost empty. I looked down to the small green pointed ledge of the Little Kame more than half-way down the cliff where the green was dappled all over with their small burrows. There were still a few hundred nories there, I could see their white tummies catching the sun as they turned in flight, a continuous twinkle against the dark green grass, but where were the clouds of midge-like dark specks that used to circle unendingly round and round? Perhaps the maalies are partly responsible as rapidly increasing they have taken over many of the nories' former sites. Through the binoculars I could even see them sitting at the entrances to their burrows on the Little Kame. No doubt the nories were as anxious as we were to avoid being spewed at by disturbed maalies. We at least can wash this revolting oily mixture off, but for a norie and most other birds it means certain death.

There was a sudden whirr of wings as a frantic norie fled by, the zoom of a bonxie swooping after it—down, down, down they fled until my eyes could no longer pick them out against the far-away background of sea below us. Echoing up from the rocks below came the distant croon of a seal, and a tiny wren burst into clear liquid song, clinging to the steep rock face then flitting away and disappearing into a cool hidden crevice where it had its nest. Another norie circled round and landed on a narrow ledge just near us, the sand eels drooping from his beak like a silver moustache. He bowed up and down once or twice then shuffled sideways up the ledge and scuttled out of sight into his hole.

All to the north and west stretched the sea for hundreds and hundreds of miles, the waves rolling in unceasingly against the cliff rampart in infinite unending motion. Watching the eternal surge and hush of the sea we were lost in its timelessness—a hundred thousand years before us, a hundred thousand after we were gone, so it would keep rolling in.

Poised on the top of a high cliff there is a peace not found anywhere else: a vast space, an eternity of sea and sky, a freedom. Sit here and scan the distant horizon where sea and sky meet in a far silver line, let your mind roam free; here you will find a glimpse of understanding of life, of its eternity, formed from a million myriads of mortal fragments, a million upon

million of livings and dyings, creatings and destroyings, buildings up and wearings down,—a grain of sand, a wave, a bird, a
man, an island, all add their small part to the eternity of the
universe.

6

Hairst Days

You dönna see da Simmer pass,
  Rose-red wi laamer een;
You see a glöd o blue and gold,
  A glisk o white an green
Onlie da Sooth wind sees an seichs
  Ta tink at shö is geen.

Vagaland.

One day at the end of August we woke up and found it was
autumn—hairst we call it in Shetland. Hairst always seems to
come like this. One day it's summer, green and blue, flowers
everywhere then next day suddenly it's autumn, the green has
faded, the sky has a pinky tint, the sea turns darker and the hills
seem to grow higher. The last of the summer visitors leave and
we are sorry to see them go. We all go down to the pier to wave
goodbye, feeling rather deserted, and sad because this is the
final sign that summer is over. But now the island is our own
again. It seems to grow twice as big. There is room to roam over
the hills all day and see no one—no bright orange and red spots
converging from all directions. No need now to stop and make
intelligent conversation when you are trying to get on with your
work; no need to explain the same thing for the umpteenth time.
We settle down into our comfortable ruts again with a sigh of
relief.

At the end of the month there came a fine spell and I finished
the last batch of Brae hay. It was with great satisfaction that I
tied down the final cole—thank goodness that lot was finished.
The rigs that had been cut first were already turning green
again contrasting with the bare yellow stubble on the recently
cut piece. The coles scattered haphazardly over the rigs looked
like small African huts with their topknots of rür. The wild
flowers were having a final fling before the onset of winter, the
uncut areas of the crofts sparkling with the yellow dandelion-
like flowers of hawkbit and the bright purple-blue heads of

scabious, while on one small patch the creamy white variety was predominant. Albino flowers occur quite commonly here— white scabious, campions, ragged robins, squills, heather, to name but a few. Flowers occupy a special place in our lives as we take notice of such and such a clump here and that little plant over there. In some cases we can even remember when they first appeared in Foula—"Mind when yon unken weed came in wi da hens' wheat? Or was it wi da budgie's seed? And did du hear tell o yon floo'er like a muckle high spootie drum dat grew on da beach ae year and da auld folk said it came oot o' da sheep dip? Dat was da year wir auld blue coo died o da milk fever. And du kens yon peerie mintie white flooer abune da Lerabeck well. It was Beenie fetched it hame ae year when she was walking back frae Lerwick, when she was working at da herring."

The first day of September my husband took his creels ashore. By late afternoon they were piled up in an orange heap on the head of the pier, the blue ropes coiled up carefully inside each one. They smelt of the sea with fronds of seaweed still tangled up in their meshes and an occasional small crab scuttled out and dropped over the side of the pier. In the evening he fetched the tractor down to the beach and the men pulled Jock's and Ken's boats ashore and shourded them up with blocks of wood up in their winter noosts, tying them well down with thick heavy chains at both ends. Next day Bobby, Eric and Rob took their boats ashore too, and the Voe looked bare and empty. Only our own boat still swung and bobbed gently at her moorings, casting a blue reflection on the water.

We were hoping to get a few more fish to salt and dry before laying her up for the winter, but the wind suddenly freshened from the north-west overnight, till it was gusting up to a full gale, setting up a nasty swell which curled in around the head of the Taing. Out in the Voe the blue boat swung uneasily at her moorings, twisted as the in-coming run (swell) tugged at her, pulling her towards the jagged rocks. My husband, watching her antics anxiously, decided he would have to take her ashore before the next low tide, and the other men came down to the beach to help. He waited until the run retreated again leaving the Voe half empty of water, then he and John Andrew picked up the dinghy and ran with it down to the water's edge while

Harry and Ken paid out the courlene rope tied to the stern. The next run came in, advancing up the Voe in a foaming creamy crest, the severe wind whipping off the froth and spinning it out through the Voe in a sheet of white. It advanced to where the two men sat waiting in the tiny cockleshell of a boat on the bare wet sand.

Suddenly the boat was snatched up by the steep wave, reared upwards, plunged down, swirled round and almost tipped upside down. John Andrew struggled with the oars and almost lost one as the boat twisted violently, then the worst of the waves were past to go rushing up the beach where the men stood holding on the rope. The wind whipped the little boat out through the Voe midst a sheet of flying spray, but the bright orange rope kept a safe link with the land. My husband caught a hold of the blue boat as she swung round, and in an instant they were on board and had lifted the little dinghy in beside them. He started up the engine and waited for a while as the boat swung violently round and round, then when she stilled for a moment he pointed her in the right direction straight for the beach. John Andrew then slipped the mooring chain, and the boat swept up the Voe on the crest of the run, engine going full speed ahead and the men on the beach pulling as hard as they were able on the orange rope. The next run caught up with the boat and snatched up her stern, and for one horrible moment she stood right up on her nose, but then she grounded safely on the beach and was stranded as the run went out again. After that it was simply a matter of pulling her up the beach with the tractor and making her fast and snug in the noost.

"Next fine day we'll have to hird (carry home) the Brae hay," I declared when the weather looked like improving. Because of the soft wet ground and the innumerable ditches we are unable to use the tractor for fetching the hay into the yard in front of the lamb-house, so we must carry it on our backs in the traditional manner. A suitable day dawned shortly afterwards and we hurried down to the Brae. I untied the coir from the first cole and my husband doubled it up twice and knotted the ends to make his carrying rope. He lifted off the top portion of the cole and dumped it onto the middle of the string causing a mass of disturbed earwigs to scurry away hastily to safety. We gathered up the ends of the string, and crossed them over to the top of the hay. Now the theory is that we both pull as hard as we can to tighten the burden so as to make it easier to carry. However since my husband is twice my weight and more than twice as strong as I am, I usually get pulled clean off my feet and collapse on top of the burden.

"Try again," he said, "and this time—pull!"

I pulled with all my might, nearly wrenching my arms out of their sockets.

"I said pull!" he exclaimed.

"I am pulling," I retorted, about to turn blue in the face.

"Push down with your knees on top of the hay."

I tried my best but my legs weren't long enough. He gave a gentle tug and the burden rolled over and deposited me on the ground whereupon he gave up and twisted the ends of the string together as tightly as he could.

I bent down, gripped the string under the burden and lifted as he heaved it onto his back and set off for the lamb-house looking like a walking haystack with only his feet in sight. Sometimes I carried in a burden too. The rough string cut into my shoulder and always seemed to be tangled up in my hair while the hay got heavier and heavier and I wondered if I would ever get there. I must have been a funny sight as I plopped into ditch after ditch on my way across the rigs. My husband was lucky as with his long legs he easily took them in his stride. As we carried in the hay we slowly built up the dess, shaking out the lumps of hay to form the large oval shape, our hands automatically putting dry hay to the centre and any damp stuff to the outside. The dess was going to be huge as we had to fit fifty odd coles into it. Every now and then we climbed up onto the hay and trampled it down firm with our feet. The bairns thought this was great fun and bounced and leapt up and down on top of it shrieking with glee. They excavated burrows in it to hide in, took off their boots and lost them in the middle and slid off the sides—no wonder it looked a funny shape.

Each cole brought back a memory of the summer. This lovely vivid green hay was made that hot day we all wore shorts and got so sunburnt—see the clover flowers still pink and sweet-smelling. That brown, washed-out stuff lay through all that rain at the end of July. That coarse yellow lot I put up that day after the south crü and it came a gale and blew it over because I was too tired to tie it down. Back and forth we went carrying the burdens of hay. The strong pungent sweet smell of green hay filled the air. When the dess reached above our heads I had to stay up in it and build while my husband threw up armfuls of hay.

However, despite our efforts, we did not get it finished that day, for after dinner the wind started to increase from the south, a murky haze spread across the sky and soon the first heavy drops of rain arrived. Hastily we flung up enough hay onto the dess to make a temporary rounded top and with a struggle arranged the big polythene tarpaulin over it. The bairns held down the flapping corners while we eased the big net over the top and my husband tied on the big stones called yard fasts on to the net at the ends and round the sides. By now it was raining heavily, so we hurried up to the shelter of the house—thank goodness for polythene.

After a week or two came another fine day, when we had nothing else on the agenda, so we removed the net and poly-thene sheet, flattened out the top of the dess and set to hirding the hay with enthusiasm. With the weight of the stones hanging on it, the dess had settled considerably but it was still a monster, far bigger than any we had built before. My husband now had to use a ladder to fling up the hay and I began to feel rather insecure perched so high in the sky. Worse, the top began to develop an alarming wobble.

"Crofter's wife breaks neck," I imagined the newspaper head-lines.

"More likely 'Crofter smothered under collapsed dess'," said my husband, eyeing the monster suspiciously—it appeared to be swaying in the wind.

My husband passed up the edge of the polythene sheet with a long plank of wood, and by leaning forwards as far as I dared, I just managed to grip it and then pulled it up over the top of the dess, inching gingerly backwards until I slid down the far end with a rush and landed in a heap on his shoulder.

"I mind Dad saying da folk here always tried to get da hay and corn biggit into da peeriest number o desses and screws. Den dey bragged during da winter as to how well da animals were doing on so little fodder," Jim remarked as he struggled to get the big stones hung up.

"Maybe this was because their neighbours would come borrowing if they thought the folk had more fodder as themselves," I suggested.

"I've heard tell dat some of da auld folk used to steal fodder oot o other folk's yards when dey were ill-off in da winter. Du kens Peti (Peter) Jamieson dat bade in wir hoose. Well, ae dark winter's night he went over to Veedal to steal some corn oot o der yard. He tied da sheaves up in a burden and lifted it up on his back, but ane o da Veedal men heard him and came oot, and crept up behind him and cut da string o da burden wi his peerie pocket knife. Da corn fell to da ground whereupon Peti turned roond and came after him wi a muckle tulley. He reckoned he was lucky to escape wi his life!"

The young boys used to get up to all sorts of pranks when they went out in groups in the autumn nights, and quick-tempered Peti Jamieson was one of their favourite targets. One night some of the womenfolk had gathered in his ben end to caird wool, as was the practice then when such tedious work was done in company to make it more lightsome. Young Magnie o Lerabeck and Uncle Peter came by the house and decided to liven things up, so one belled neeps down the lum while the other watched the fun in through the window. Supper was cooking on the fire and one neep after another splashed into the pot destroying the entire meal. Peti, in a right temper, ran out shouting, but the boys ran away in the dark and hid at the head of the Brugs. They heard Peti dadding down the road to the burn then stomping up to the Ham yard where he looked round the stooks and cairnies. Suddenly he flung open the Ham door, stuck his head in and bellowed at the astounded womenfolk sitting quietly knitting by the fireside, "Are there any devils here?"

A yapping of dogs announced the approach of Harry on his way to the craigs.

"Man, he's a pretty fellow," he exclaimed walking round the monster of a dess.

"Aye, he's truly no peerie."

"I mind ae year da folk o Broadfoot biggit a bra muckle wan."

"Did they have any trouble with it?" I asked anxiously.

"Na, na," Harry reassured me, "But ae day late on in da hairst dey saw thick white reek (smoke) pouring from da top o it. When dey lookit at it, it was heating up in da middle, almost o'er hot to touch. So dey had to tear it all doon. Dats da trouble wi green hay, it wants to heat up."

I eyed the monster with alarm—was it about to erupt into a volcano?

By the time he had finished adding weights my husband had over a ton of large stones hanging round the dess. "Yon ought to be OK for eenoo (now). I'll put on more weight afore da winter gales start."

It was evening now but the moon was rising out over the sea, shining a path of rippling light across the dark water and casting long mysterious shadows over the rigs. By its light we scraped up the steads of the coles, nasty slimy stuff like silage, but after drying on racks, the horses were clean daft for it. The evening quiet was broken only by the hush of the sea breaking on the Cletts, an occasional chatter from a disturbed snipe, and a muttered curse as someone tripped over a lurking cole pin for the umpteenth time. The bairns gathered up the sheaves used for cole heads, even the youngest toddling along with a sheaf far bigger than herself. It was long past their bedtimes by the time we finally staggered home, exhausted, aching, bits of hay sticking to our clothes, our hair full of hayseed and the smell of hay still lingering in our noses.

Every morning for the next few weeks we went down and worriedly examined the dess, feeling its shaggy sides with our hands like a mother fussing over a feverish child. We discussed its symptoms like two learned doctors attending a wealthy patient—was it running a slight temperature at the north end? It certainly seemed to be sweating a lot for condensation formed on the inside of the polythene sheet. But luckily in the following week, came a strong cold wind from the north and the symptoms subsided. After each gale the dess settled down a bit lower due to the wind rocking it and the weight of the stones, but it remained "The Monster".

Unlike the indigenous hay, our reseeded ground up at Harrier produced a second crop of grass in the autumn, though only grudgingly after generous applications of fertilizer. I hated working with this hay—it seemed one long toil from start to finish. The sun no longer had the power to dry up the sodden lumps of wet grass and all too often after I had dragged the bairns all the way north, the clouds would roll in from the west and heavy showers of rain would sweep across the island. The nights were drawing in rapidly now. Long after darkness fell I would still be banging in cole pins, tying down the hay with innumerable whups of coir, and tightening up the previous coles that the wind had blown slack. Then followed the long slog home through the dark, trying to keep the bairns cheerful by pointing out the stars and the moon glinting behind the black clouds gathering over Hamnafield. There was no sound now but the hush of the wind and the gurgle of the burn. The birds have gone for the winter leaving the moorland empty and desolate. No allens (Arctic skua) wheel in the sky, crying out their hearts—or ours.

The sound of the wind is the sound of winter, moaning, wailing, shrieking, sighing, always present. The contouring of the island has such a violent effect on the wind that every house has its own particular airt or direction of wind which is especially bad. Ours is north-west and a few hundred yards away at Lerabeck it's due west, while Ham gets it bad in a southerly gale and yet all these houses lie in one small part of the isle.

As the equinox came nearer we began to feel a bit nervous, wondering what nasty surprise it had in store for us. Sure enough at 6 o'clock on the evening of the 22nd September when I switched on the radio, a voice announced brightly, "There are gale warnings for sea areas Hebrides, Bailey, Fair Isle, Faroes and South-east Iceland." A few minutes later we were given more detailed information—"Fair Isle—north-west storm Force Ten imminent, rain, visibility becoming poor." We went outside for a look. The sky to the east was still clear, but a nasty looking band of cloud, dark grey and dappled was drifting across the sky from the west, its edge straight and clearly defined, almost as though someone was drawing a curtain across the sky. The gale did indeed look imminent. Once the cloud passed over us it would be here.

We hurried to secure everything from the wind, placing stones on barrows and tubs, gathering up loose bits of wood and fishboxes and rolling barrels into shelter before going down to the lamb-house to secure the hay. As darkness fell, the wind increased and swiped at us as we crouched in the lee of the coles, fumbling with the coir and pins in the dark, trying to get the ropes as tight as possible. With the wind came the rain, lashing in our faces. The bairns were glad to shelter inside the lamb-house, and fell asleep on a heap of cornsheaves. Across the valley we could see an occasional blink of light—Lizbeth was out tightening down her coles and stooks of corn. Now there's a knack to banging in a cole pin in the dark—you shove it in at an angle with one hand then after a few taps with a stone it docilely subsides into position, unless you're like me and end up balancing the pin between your feet, gripping the torch by your knees and bashing several or all of the aforementioned with the stone. It's just the same with the coir. Those who know about such things assure me that the neat roll uncoils to give four separate balls of string. Why then do I always finish up with a cat's cradle which doesn't seem to possess one end let alone four? Then of course we've all met those bags of animal feedstuffs that one has to attack tooth and nail to open. You're just finally hacking it apart with an old screwdriver when your husband comes by and demands to know what the – you are doing with his best chisel. Then he tweaks an end of a thread and it simply falls open.

The torch comes into its own at this time of year with its long dark nights, and the inevitable jobs that must be done like tying down hay, searching for a lost animal, going to the well or fetching an armful of peats. Sometimes in midwinter we run short of batteries and try to economize by going without our blinkies—and I can vouch for it that there is no experience more traumatic than tripping over a black horse on a dark night. The name "blinkie" arose from the habit of only switching it on occasionally for the merest blink in order to save the batteries. It's easy to recognize a stranger at night from the way he shines his blinkie all the time. Before the days of such new-fangled inventions the folk took a glowing peat with them when they went out at night and if they had to go far they called in at a house halfway and got another one. I mind the Bloburn folk telling how as bairns they used to watch the small glöds (glow) of light come bobbing along up the road when they were having a cairding, and the red spunks (sparks) flying if it was windy.

That night we were woken by the noise of the wind and lay listening to the rumbling roar of the approaching gusts or flans and the slam as they hit the back of the house—we could feel the jolt jarring the bed. Then the air was sucked out of the house making our ears pop with the sudden change of pressure as the

wind swooped over the roof, leaving a sudden quiet before the
next flan. The noise of each approaching flan was like the roar of
an aeroplane. I can sympathize with all the people who live
within earshot of busy airports. However they have one advantage over us—the aeroplanes do not keep crashing into the back
of their houses. "Don't you find it awfully quiet in the winter?"
ask the summer visitors!

Lying snuggled up in bed, the blankets up round my ears, I
thought of the hay coles up at Harrier. A north-west wind is very
severe up there. Building up against the great barrier of the
Kame, the flans tear down from the Fleck in gigantic whirlwinds of such strength that I have seen them tearing up frozen
snow from the ground and whirling solid lumps of it hundreds of
feet into the air. And how many times have I watched them pick
up my hay in a high twirling column of green or brown, spinning
it away out over Crougar and out to sea. With every flan I braced
myself against the impact until, drifting into sleep, I, myself
and the hay became confused and merged into one single being
desperately resisting a wind that was determined to tear it from
the ground.

Eventually morning came. The first thing we did when we
awoke was to sit up and look out through the window and assess
the damage. Over the sea the fierce wind was carrying the
surface of the water in a white swirl of spindrift, and small
whirlwinds swooping off the head of the baa were tearing up
water spouts and skimming out to the south-east. And all this
seen through a flying curtain of rain or cloud, or was it spray?

Later when it moderated we went up to Harrier to assess the
damage, worried in case one of the roofs was torn for, if unat-
tended to, the next gale could remove the whole roof. Long
before we got there I could see that many of my coles were gone
and where there should have been a neat row there were only a
few untidy heaps of hay. Close inspection showed that the wind
had taken four coles clean away, having torn the cole pins right
out of the ground. But for the bare patches on the ground and a
few wisps of hay caught in the wire netting fence you wouldn't
have known they had ever been there. The rest of the hay had
been blown over and was soaked through, but we bundled it up
on racks, tied it down thoroughly and hoped for some drying
weather. Three days later came another hard gale from the

north-west and the wind fairly sorted through the racks. Somewhat daunted, I scraped up what hay was left and wheeled it with the stone-barrow up to the fence by the road where there was a bit of shelter, and built it into six muckle coles. Next morning the kye discovered it and flattened down the fence and what they didn't eat they trucked into the mud. Which no doubt all goes to prove something—make hay while the sun shines!

7

First Catch Your Lamb

Simmer is lowered her pretty white sail
An pooed up her boat ida tapmist noost
Cauld winter is caerdit his oo ower da sky
In doon ida shörmil da waar lies laek roost.

Stewart Smith.

By the end of September it was time to take in the lambs. The best ram lambs would be shipped out to the mainland to be sold, the poorer ones would be killed to be eaten fresh or dried for the winter, and most of the ewe lambs kept to "set on" as breeding ewes. After some discussion we decided to go first to the Wasten crü.

Next morning was a typical autumn day, sunny but with a noticeable pink haze round the horizon and a fresh wind from the south-east carrying the salt tang of the sea and the hush of the waves. A plume of pink mist hovered over the top of the hills, for ever forming and re-forming. The pink tinge heightened the effect of the autumn colours, painting the moors and hills red russet and gold, burnishing the red burra and glinting on the tiny flames of the leaves of the clowie flooers. As we went south along the road in the tractor, redwings flew up in drifts out of the heather, filling the air with their "tsee tsee"—the sound of hairst. Mingling with the redwings were groups of dapper grey and chestnut fieldfares, another very familiar species of autumn migrants that delight us with their chattering "chuk chuk chuk".

Most of the breeding birds had already left us. The cliffs now rose bare and stark, the ledges empty without the hordes of noisy kittiwakes and lungwees. Only the maalies still wheeled and soared. They remain all winter but only come ashore to their nest sites on fine days. The skarfs stay too, often the only birds to be seen on a stormy winter's day. But the cliffs in the autumn provide refuge for many small migrants. Warblers, whitethroats and robins fluttered in their sheltered crannies searching for the last of the flies. How out of place the robins looked—no Christmas card birds these. They were shy and timid as they flitted across the stark rocks. Tiny goldcrests, like little green mice, hugged the shelter of the banks and broos; sometimes we could count up to a score of them creeping among the long grey lichen on the ruined walls of the old croft houses. Flocks of brambling patrolled the rigs searching for seeds among the brown withered stalks, accompanied by an occasional chaffinch or two. In the garden a couple of dunnocks skulked under the bushes. Sometimes one would stay with us through the winter, and once one individual caused considerable interest by remaining into the summer singing with great melody from a fuchsia bush every morning. Redstarts are regular visitors, flashing their chestnut tails from the tops of fencing posts and stone dykes, and so are the little blackcaps darting among the bushes and scolding the cat with a sharp chirr.

Before us stretched the Ufshins, a steep narrow slope that runs across the cliff face from the end of the Daal to Waster Hivda. We crouched in a spread-out row up along the nearest edge of the slope, watching the far end anxiously for signs of movement. At last we could make out a small upright silhouette appearing out of the mist at the far end of the Ufshins—Jock was coming with the sheep. We watched with our hearts in our mouths as he ran, sure-footed as the sheep, along the narrow lower gaet (path), cliff above him, cliff below him, but his eyes only on the sheep which his dogs drove in front of him. One slip and he would plunge to instant death on the rocks hundreds of feet below.

We stood up and advanced on the on-coming sheep, driving them down the steep slope to the crü perched right at the very cliff edge. After a rest to regain our breath, we carried the lambs up on our backs and laid them, with legs tied together, on the flat green, well away from the edge. The ewes were then released and driven away into the Ufshins in the opposite direction. Now the fun began. The lambs had to be driven home through the Daal as the ground was too boggy for the tractors. Each lamb had a specially made piece of rope about 18 inches long called a shacklin put on it, joining one of its front legs to the opposite hind leg. Each of us collected a bundle of shackled lambs around us, sitting them up on their bottoms, closely packed together.

"Right, du had better slip dem."

At Jock's command we quickly set all the lambs up on their feet. They immediately erupted in all directions. Because of the shacklins they were unable to run fast, but not realizing this they jumped forwards, brought up suddenly, then leaped backwards, sidewards, round about like demented firecrackers.

"Look out!"

A lamb with too long a shacklin set off at a brisk run for the Noup.

"Fetch him, Dandy."

"Shorten his shacklin, boy."

My husband tied a knot in the rope to make it shorter and let the lamb go again. It shot off rapidly backwards in a series of hops towards the cliff edge. Immediately several of the dogs rounded it up and, overwhelmed, it lay down and refused to budge.

"Go on, you brute." Ken picked it up and pushed it towards the main group, but it sat down on its bottom with a hurt look on its face and wouldn't shift.

"Poor peerie mite, lengthen its shacklin," Mima said sympathetically.

He untied the knot and stood the lamb up again, whereupon the "poor peerie mite" raced off for the Noup like a jet propelled rocket.

Eventually the chaos sorted itself out and the lambs discovered that if they went at a sedate pace they could walk all right with the shacklins on. We drove them slowly along the Daal, pushing the more stubborn ones that lagged behind. The mist crept ominously lower, the sky darkened and a light rain began to fall. A skein of geese flew across the grey sky to the east, circled round and landed on the South Ness. We moved in fits and starts, with frequent halts as the stubborn lambs became more stubborn. Some of them lay down and refused to go so we took their shacklins off them, whereupon they gained a new lease of life and kept us busy heading them back to the main group. Wet and tired we got them home as dusk was falling.

"Fleck crü da morn, folks," announced Ken.

We groaned.

Every reasonable day we went to a crü and the numbers of lambs down on the crofts slowly increased. Each mailday a batch of up to seventy lambs were shipped to the mainland to be sold. Only islanders like ourselves can really appreciate the anxiety and the hard work that makes an apparently simple event a major achievement. It involves sitting up late at night to catch the Shipping Forecast and if it sounds hopeful, rising before dawn to peer into the darkness for the slightest signs of worsening weather. More forecasts follow, phone calls go back and forth and neighbours come with messages from the mainland—"No, Jack says they can't take them till Monday"; "Yes, Benji says it's too late for them to go south with the steamer"; "No, Harry says he can't keep them in his park till next week, it's full of heifers". Finally a decision and you run yourself silly after a handful of the most obstinate lambs ever. Sweaty and bad-tempered, you finish loading them and wait impatiently as the others arrive, only to watch the wind freshen out over the sea and the sky to the south turn slimy. No go! You slip them loose, and watch them lose condition as you wait for the next fine day.

Every possible day from September to November the boat crosses with lambs, but in a stormy autumn only two or three trips may be possible and inevitably some of the lambs cannot be shipped out. Again this highlights the weak spot in the island's economy—the lack of a harbour. Although the natural harbour is poor, the present pier is a pitiful effort for the 1980s. It could be improved with money—money which the government is not prepared to invest in the island and without which its economy must inevitably be shaky! Some day things will be different, when the powers that be realize how ridiculous it is to have an island without a proper harbour.

Our lambs are sold to local Shetland slaughterhouses or are shipped south to Aberdeen by steamer and sold there. So many are now sold in Shetland, that arrangements for sale must be made in advance—an impossibility here because we never know when the boat may be able to cross. Hence we are either dependent on the buyers to make a special concession for us or we must try to find someone on the mainland who will look after them for us until they can be shipped south. To add to our problems freight charges are excessively high—on average a quarter of the lamb's price goes to pay this. The animals sometimes lose weight in travelling and may end up at Aberdeen, after two boat crossings and two journeys by truck, in such poor condition they no longer make the grade and are sold as rejects.

It is only during the past couple of decades that lambs have been sold from Foula. Before this they were slaughtered at home and eaten fresh, or salted and dried for the winter. Wool then was fetching high prices—as much as 10 shillings a pound—so the sheep were bred mainly for wool, their lambs being incidental. The rams were put to the ewes late in the season so they did not lamb until June. This was supposed to be better for the ewes, but it meant the lambs were small, not being fully grown by autumn. Now with wool prices in Shetland so low, lambs to be sold for slaughter play a much more important part in the economy of our island. Over most of the rest of Shetland the original sheep have been crossed and recrossed with all manner of breeds, but during the past few years demand has been growing again for good Shetland lambs for breeding and, since the sheep here have been kept pure bred, the island has been able to cash in on this market. But the much larger numbers of sheep kept per household makes their management considerably more difficult, especially when the increase is linked with a big drop in the human population. Gone indeed are the old days when every single lamb on the island was in from the hills by Martinmas.

We selected out the poorer lambs, which could not be sold, and killed them for our own consumption. Now we gorged ourselves with succulent roasts and stews—no dainty carved slices or a single chop on a plate for us. Our favourite was juicy boiled mutton with freshly baked bannocks washed down with cupfuls of brü—the stock formed from the meat, or crisp roast chops with tatties dipped in the fat and juices. The roast pan was set on the table and everyone helped themselves to potatoes which they dipped in the pan. Not so long ago when the folk here were poorer, dinner was often only "tatties and dip", there being no meat left but only a little fat, melted butter or fish liver oil, or sometimes only brine in which the tatties were dipped. In a more extreme case the menu consisted of "tatties and point", when the dip was finished and the potatoes merely pointed towards the middle of the table. Tattie soup was another dish we enjoyed in the hairst. Mutton, potatoes, kale, turnips, and onions all simmered together to form a thick mush, which

Foula croft house.

The author's children.

Foula from the north.

Unloading the mailboat.

Opposite: The view from Summons Head.

Fulmars taking fish offal.

Opposite: The Voe in a storm.

Hauling up a lobster creel.

Rossies Loch and hills.

Hamnafield, the Sneug and the Kame.

Bloburn and Harrier.

Ham Voe from the top of the hill.

Looking along the Nort Bank to the mainland.

makes a very satisfying meal. The lambs' stomachs were emptied, thoroughly washed, turned inside out and stuffed with a dough to which fat, onions, raisins and spices had been added, and after boiling the resulting puddings were cut into slices and eaten fried. Some folk skin and boil lambs' heads to make potted head, but I must confess that the sight of a pair of boiled eyes staring reproachfully at me when I lift the saucepan lid does not appeal to me. The fat we rinded (that is melted it down into lard which lasted us the whole year), or we salted it to use for making puddings in the winter from pudding skins preserved in jars of brine. Sometimes the old folk used to clean the intestines or reddings by turning them inside out, and plait them into a rope which they hung in the roof to dry. Later on bits would be cut off and used for making soup.

My husband usually killed the lambs in batches and Harry often came over to help him. The selected lambs were shut up in the lamb-house before dusk fell and after teatime they would go down there, light the Tilley and set to work. Here, as in most parts of Shetland, the sheep skins are not flayed in the normal manner by making a cut right down the middle of the belly. Instead the flayer sits on a chair holding the dead lamb on his lap, and after inserting his fist between the skin and meat, he works it round about pushing the skin loose. After a few minutes he is finished and the whole skin is then pulled back inside out. This method is known as buggy flaying. By the end of the evening there would be nine or ten carcases hanging from the roof and two large basins full of livers and fat. I heard the men chuckling and joking to each other as they clumped into the porch after one session.

"Well, we fairly cured yon poorly fleckit lamb du fetched doon frae the Fleck last week," announced my husband with a laugh.

"What!" I shrieked leaping off the sofa in horror. "You didn't shoot her did you?"

For some reason she was unable to walk and I had to carry her all the way down on my shoulders. She had lain in the lamb-house since then being doctored with every concoction we had, but still she made no attempt to get up.

"Na, she took ae look at Harry coming in wi twa headless lambs, jumped up and shot oot through da door like da very devil himsell was ahint her."

"Ya, man, she surely thought we hadna done dem muckle good!" laughed Harry.

And we never did discover what had ailed her.

A couple of evenings later my husband sawed the carcases in half along the backbone, then it was my turn. Cutting the lambs up into quarters I laid them in a large tub, covering up each layer well with coarse salt. Five days later I removed the quarters from the tub. They had turned silvery and were wrinkled due to the salt they had absorbed and I had to fish for the bottom pieces, up to my elbows in brine. I hung them up to drip for a while and then carried them up to the house. The old folk always declared that salted meat would be ruined if the wind blew on it, but I carried up many a bit in a flying gale without noticing any ill effects. The meat was hung from a special rack on the ceiling where it continued to drip for several days, catching us un-awares when we forgot and walked underneath. As it dried the meat gradually changed colour until it was yellowy white out-side and a very dark rich red inside. This dried salt meat is called reestit mutton and is a great favourite with Shetlanders around Christmas and New Year. Usually eaten cold with bread, it has a strong smoky taste—something like bacon only better.

Our fish was also dry and ready for eating. Boiled in the same saucepan as the potatoes, which absorb the salt, it was eaten with melted margarine and was rather like a cross between a kipper and a piece of wood—an acquired taste, perhaps, for some people, but one which we appreciate greatly. It is satisfying on a stormy winter's night when the wind and rain batter and lash the house to glance up at the roof at the rows of dried piltocks and reestit mutton—enough dinner to last us all winter no matter how hard the wind blows.

Several folk here now have deep freezes and they are becom-ing very popular all over Shetland; in fact they appear to have taken the place of the old tub of brine. Previously much of the surplus meat was wet salted, i.e. kept in brine all winter, parti-cularly if a cow had been killed. In the old days too, when salt was harder to obtain here, meat, known as vivda, was cured simply by direct drying either above the fire, or, more com-monly, in a skio, a small stone hut with gaps in the wall through which the wind blew. None of the old skios remain although the walls of one form the upper corner of our garden dyke.

October was the time for getting in the rest of our winter supplies. Bags of flour and oatmeal toasted in front of the fire on chairs in case they had got damp on the boat; cupboards overflowed with boxes of margarine, sugar, milk, coffee, jam and other basic essentials; hundredweights of animal feedstuffs were stored away in the lamb-houses and byres in old barrels that had been found washed up along the banks. Paraffin was one of the most important essentials as bleak indeed have been the winters when there was a shortage of fuel and no light. Inevitably something or other is bound to run short but we take such things in our stride, having more to worry about than whether we have sugar or only syrup in our coffee.

The last big dearth occurred in 1962 when there was no incoming mail for eleven weeks and the isle was without supplies of margarine, sugar, tea and coffee or any tinned goods, and very short of flour. Although the headline "Last Foula rabbit shot and eaten" was a bit of journalistic exaggeration, meals were monotonous and meagre. Potatoes for breakfast, dinner and tea washed down with only water and perhaps half a bannock without margarine or jam as a treat became monotonous after a while. Fortunately there was still a little salt fish and dried mutton.

Hearing of the island's plight a Prestwick Pioneer plane bravely attempted to fly in supplies. As there was no airstrip then, they decided to make a trial run first to find out what weight of foodstuff they could land with safety. Unfortunately on landing the plane bogged in and damaged its nose leaving the crew stranded on the island to be supported on the ever dwindling supplies. Many a long struggle the airmen and islanders had before the plane was finally able to take off again. By this time the mailboat had managed to cross to the mainland to bring in the long-awaited supplies.

What I miss most in winter is a regular supply of bread. Once a week in summer the boat brings in our large box packed with bread. Lovely and fresh at first we gobble it up in delight but by the end of the week it has turned hard and sawdusty and our appetite has waned somewhat but at least I don't have to bake during the summer. In these days of health food fads, "back to mother nature" and "the good old days", when the pinnacle of culinary success in the ideal housewife, apparently, is the ability to bake her own bread just like great-grandmother did, it might seem odd that I hate, loathe and detest baking bread. In fact the only pleasure I derive from it is giving the dough a good bashing, stabbing it to death with a fork and bunging it in the oven, where, with a bit of luck, it will be cremated. But then perhaps it's because I *have* to do it.

Baking isn't the only old-fashioned pleasure we indulge in. I shall gloss over the delights of not having a flush toilet. The lack of running water is always a big problem in midsummer when the well dries up, but by this time of year it is overflowing. Having to nip out every now and then for a pail of water has become a way of life—the "snyirk" as you lift the old wooden lid, the "swittle" as you fill the pail, the "K-nyk" as you lay back the worn stone weight, a glimpse of the dark hill brooding in the mist and the great grey waves rolling by from the north.

In an island as boggy as Foula it always seems ironical that so many of the houses have no dependable water supply and suffer severe shortages in the summer months. The young islanders, who complete their education on the mainland, grow up expecting flush toilets, baths and washing machines. But still Foula is one of the few remaining places with no water scheme. Water is only one of the amenities lacking here that others take for granted in this modern world. Modern houses, roads and communications are some of the others. Any other place so deprived would surely have lost its population long ago.

8

Ponies for Sale

In October ee nicht he came on ta blaa
  Wi a odious tömald o rain,
Da spöndrift cam in ower da aest sea-waa,
An drave trowe da yard laek da moorin snaa;
Neist moarnin my peerie white flooer wis awa,
  An never wis seen again.

James Stout Angus.

Next morning the wind had shifted to the north-west, it oobed round the house wailing tales of snow and ice. Although the sun was shining brightly, a large lump of cumulus cloud was building up over Soberlie, looming up in a tumbling tower, brilliant white where the light caught it—a cloud of snow. Throughout the winter whenever the wind went up to the north, the big white clouds would build up along the horizon, billowing up more than a mile high in the sky, hanging over the isle, sweeping past us to the east, with a flurry of hail silhouetting the big black lumps of the waves. And as the short winter days drew to a close the low sun would paint the cloud tops a vivid crimson, the only colour on a slate grey canvas. I sniffed the frosty air appreciatively, winter was getting nearer, I could smell it.

It was time to fetch down the ponies from the hills in preparation for selling their foals at the annual sale in Lerwick. The sharp cutting wind blew through us as we struggled up to the Fleck. Come up here on a summer evening and you'll find a peaceful bowl of vivid green, embraced securely by a sweep of smooth steep green hillside, like a safe familiar garden of childhood. Now there's nothing but the bare grey hills of winter. Come up here during a severe winter's gale and you will hear the crash and rumble of the wind roaring through the stones on the hillface so high above you, like the thunder of a tremendous sea about to overwhelm the whole world, and you will feel fear.

The horses were sheltering up over the back of the Kame, in

the small hollows by the burn that caught the sun, trying like us to pretend it was still summer. But the summer scents were gone. Even the sea smelt different, not of warm shingly stones and seaweed glistening in the sun, but of bare black rocks, starving sheep and missing boats. And the bonxies were gone too. People often ask us if we feel lonely here, particularly in the winter; they even daub the isle "the Lonely Island", but it is a feeling we experience possibly less than they do, secure as we are in our own community of people—our own people. But when the birds leave at the end of the summer, during the first few weeks after they are gone, then we feel loneliness and experience a sudden ache of desolation. But how can you explain to an outsider what it feels like to sail west and find the high banks empty of the kirring lungwees, to step outside the door and see the Santoo bare of tirricks, to climb the hills and hear no bonxie's whistle.

Back home, the horses were delighted to be let in through the gate and immediately started munching at the grass—a treat after the rough hill grazing. At first we got muddled as to which foal was which but after a bit we got them sorted out.

"Chinook's the one with his mane standing up on end."

"Who's this then?"

"That must be Charm, June's filly foal."

The bairns were equally delighted to find the horses back again and wandered unconcernedly among them. The youngest had to be forcibly restrained from climbing up Rose's tail, but then turned her attention to the more intriguing pastime of poking her finger up Flossie's nostril, while the boys were fussing over Carina, their arms round her neck and whispering in her ears. That night we lay listening to the clumping of the horses sheltering round the house, a nice friendly sound. Next morning a thumping and banging right in front of the window woke me up and I sat up to look outside. Flossie, old greedy guts, was leaning over the garden fence making a good meal of my few remaining flowers. I banged angrily on the window pane. She turned her head and looked at me, gave a smirk and neatly plucked the last remaining white rose.

Now began the time-consuming job of taming all the foals. We approached them carefully, speaking softly, and held out our hands with a little maize. Thanks to their instinctive curiosity, they at last approached us cautiously.

Flossie's foal, Caramba, braver than the rest, stretched out his neck, touched my hand with his nose and gave a tentative sniff. A flake of maize blew up his nose. Startled he sneezed and jumped backwards and in a panic the foals all rushed back to their mothers. But after a few days they became accustomed to us and by the end of the week would come when we called, for a handful of maize and a petting.

Every day we studied the weather anxiously but the gales continued. North-west, south-west, south-east, the wind blew round and round restlessly. A fine day is essential for shipping out the foals, as they fall down if the sea is rough. The pony sale occupies only one day—that year the 19th October. If we were unable to get the foals out by then we would not get them sold as the prospective horse dealers only come up to Shetland for a couple of days. Besides we did not have enough extra fodder to keep them ourselves over winter. To add to our worries the horses were rapidly eating up our grazing. Now we knew the truth of the saying "to eat like a horse"—not to mention a score of horses.

On the evening of the 8th October the wind fell away. Was this just a temporary lull while the wind changed direction, or would it be a day for shipping them tomorrow? We listened to the weather forecasts. The Shipping Forecast said "South-west Force Five, drizzle, poor visibility," whilst the regional forecast informed us that "tomorrow will be bright and sunny and the moderate northerly wind will continue."

"No very helpful."

We slept uneasily, wakening up every now and again to listen for the wind. The sky was already lightening in the east when we rose.

"Do you think it'll be a day?" I asked as I sleepily poked the ash out of the fire.

"Couldna say. Dere's a tremendous noise in da sea." He consulted the calendar and did some calculations in his head, "Weather tide turning just about eenoo. Some braaly big lumps coming in to da south. Still he'll maybe moderate through da morning."

By nine o'clock the sun had moved further round and we were able to study the sea better. The wind was scrapping up small

white waves and big uneasy lumps marked the edge of the tide
rank.

"No, I doubt hits no weather," my husband stated. "I'll ging
o'er and phone Ken and tell him."

I spent the rest of the day riping tatties, turning over the
stony earth with my spade and flicking out the tatties. The
bairns enjoyed this and eagerly gathered them up and put them
in an old fish basket my husband had found along the banks last
winter. Our potatoes are black skinned with a dark purple
centre, an old variety we prize for its mealiness and sweet nutty
taste, but they are hard to see, and often the bairns pounced on a
dark stone or lump of mud by mistake. Ordinary potatoes such
as the Kerr's Pink we find insipid and watery. We favour the
more colourful varieties like the Black Tattie, the old Red Tattie, and the big nobbly Blue Hearts. The oldest tattie grown here
was known as the Yam, a long potato tapering to one end with a
red purple skin, which was said to be the original variety introduced here in the mid eighteenth century. The fresh wind blew
through the meshes of the basket and when the tatties were
dried I tipped them into the barrels in the shed where they
would be stored during the winter. Some folk still keep their
tatties in the old tattie cros—big wooden boxes built into the
byres.

The wind had died down again by the time my husband came
back from Harrier where he had been repairing the fence which
had been torn when the burn flooded. Perhaps tomorrow would
be a suitable day for shipping the ponies.

We rose at dawn to a clearing sky and by eight o'clock the
wind had moderated. We drove the mares and foals down to the
Brae, and unsuspecting they walked into the lamb-house without any trouble. All, that is, except old Flossie who took the
opportunity to make a meal of one of the hay desses and only
shifted when I stuck the maize bucket under her nose and my
husband shoved from behind. Now began the tricky business of
putting the halters on the foals. Approaching Caramba carefully with a handful of maize, my husband slipped the noseband
over his nose, then whilst Caramba was occupied with the maize
he gently eased the halter over his ears and tied the chin strap.

"Dere noo, peerie horsie, yon's no sae bad, is it?" he soothed
him, "Right, let's try Chinook next."

We got Chinook backed into a corner and tried the same procedure. But he took one sniff of the halter and decided some direful treachery was afoot. Rolling his eyes, he reared and leapt forwards. Jim flung his arms round his neck and tried to get the halter on, but Chinook was too strong for him and went bucking and rearing across the lamb-house while he hung on grimly. The foal's squeals were punctuated with thuds as various parts of my husband's anatomy hit the low roof. At length they both subsided in a heap at the far end.

"Well thank goodness we're not breeding carthorses!" I comforted him.

Ken in the meantime had lowered the mailboat into the water and had made the deck ready for the horses by tacking on sacking to stop their feet slipping. John Andrew, Eric and Davie arrived to help us lead the ponies to the pier. Taking a foal each, we set off for the gate, or rather some of us did. Davie shot off in the opposite direction hanging onto the end of Chinook's tether, Eric and Caramba were having an argument with a hay cole, whilst Charm was winding her tether round my legs with surprising effect. After a bit of reorganization however, we got them through the gate and down the path to the bridge.

This was no mean feat as on occasions like this the path becomes a treacherous slide with a steep drop on one side. Reaching the bridge the foals took one horrified look at the drop showing between the slats under their feet, and flatly refused to cross. The only thing to do now was to set our shoulders against their bottoms, dig in our heels and shove, progressing across in a series of bucks. By now they had realized they were being separated from their mothers, and on reaching firm land again they set off in a panicky gallop with us running wildly behind trying to steer them towards the pier.

By now the tide had ebbed and the mailboat was already lying five feet lower than the edge of the pier and moving in and out uneasily with the swell. Jim jumped down onto the deck to catch the first horse, which Ken and John Andrew grabbed and eased over the edge. It landed safely on top of him. The other horses were lifted down and he tied their halters to the sides of the wheelhouse. Back we went for the next batch, leaving Davie in charge of those on the boat. It was after twelve o'clock when the last foal was safely on board. By now the foals had recovered from their alarming experience and were standing quietly. The rest of the cargo was quickly loaded, the boat's ropes cast off and away she went. The foals found the sudden instability under their feet very frightening, rolling their eyes and sweating, they hauled against their halters, and it was with great difficulty that my husband calmed them down. Reaching Walls after three hours, they were then transported by truck to Scalloway where friends would kindly look after them until the day of the sale.

I went back to the lamb-house and let out the mares, who whinnied for their foals but eventually agreed to be driven up to the yard quite docilely. I went into the house and collapsed onto the bed, exhausted. A heap of dirty clothes, the week's washing, looked me sternly in the eye. Wearily I rose.

Well, we don't have a washing machine. We don't have running water. We don't even have a sink. I'm just grateful that there is plenty of water in the well at this time of year. I often wonder how our county councillors who have denied the island a water scheme for so long would feel if they had to do the family washing with a well that dried up every year between May and September. I stoke up the fire and put the muckle pot on to boil, settle down onto the sofa, arrange two or three basins on chairs in front of me, switch the radio on to what promises to be a good thriller and I'm all set. The only disadvantage of this method is deciding the strategic moment to run out to the well for another bucket of water or to hang out the next batch of washing. One may miss a vital clue and may never know the significance of the missing left shoe. Later on one is apt to return to find that the heroine has apparently murdered the hero, and that there are three new voices. As the row of washing on the line gets longer the plot thickens and one becomes completely baffled. But all is revealed in the end—the original play finished half an hour ago and one has been listening to a repeat of the weekly serial.

Next day when my husband returned home with the boat we put the mares out to the hill and the place seemed very empty without them. We now looked forward to the day of the sale and wondered how our little horses would get on. My husband was going out with a fishing boat in time to attend both the Lerwick sale and the sale up in Unst the day before.

"I'll maybe buy twatree peerie foals up there if I see any-thing," were his parting words.

"Well, just don't get carried away. Mind we've a lump of lambs to feed all winter," I cautioned.

Jim had promised to phone as soon as the Unst sale was finished. I bundled the children who were half asleep by now into their jackets and boots and we struggled over to the phone box. The wind was from the north-west and it was bitterly cold. It tugged and pushed at us so that the bairns kept falling over in the dark and my blinkie was only a small red glow since we were short of batteries. A smell of hay came from the grass burned dead by the frosty wind. The hill rose up before us, black and forbidding against the dark sky. We reached the shelter of Andrew's boathouse just as a shower of hail launched a vicious attack on us and we crouched in the darkness, huddled together until it passed. I would have been content to sit there in that little calm for a while listening to the wind howling past us, but perhaps Jim was already trying to get through on the phone. We struggled on across to the fence, through the gate, down the steep road, over the bridge across the burn and up the other side to the phone box. I pulled out the big nail that was always poked through a hole in the side of it to keep the wind from blowing the door off and we packed ourselves into the small space—dogs too—glad to get out of the wind. A few seconds later the bell rang—it was Jim. The Unst sale had gone quite well and prices were a bit higher than last year so the breeders who had foals to dispose of at the Lerwick sale were quite hopeful about tomor-row.

"Did you buy any?" I asked.

"Only one, a peerie black filly with white feet. I'll maybe buy another da morn if I see a good small one."

That night I dreamed of prize-winning horses of exotic colours.

The next day found me again in the tattie rig wondering how the Lerwick pony sale was going. By phoning time the weather had deteriorated and sharp showers of hail lashed the island. Picking a lull in the storm I ran over to the phone box with the bairns. What was the news, I wondered. The next shower was looming overhead and I could hear the first few hailstones peppering the roof of the kiosk when the phone rang.

"Hello, is that you?" I shouted into the phone. Jim's voice came through amidst a background of crackles. The hail shower was upon us and the kiosk seemed to shake with the wind as though it was about to take off.

"How did you get on at the sale?"

"Mumble, mumble, crackle, crackle," he replied.

"I can't hear, you'll have to shout, there's a bad shower on."

"Mumble, mumble, crackle, crackle."

"Louder!"

"Crackle, crackle, buzz," came the reply.

Trust the phone to play up at the critical moment. Well I would just have to wait until the shower was by.

Eventually the sky cleared and the moon came out again. After I'd done a bit of explaining the operator got us connected again. The line was a bit clearer this time; gone were the snap, crackle, pop to be replaced by a discreet but penetrating supersonic whistle. This did not bother us for we are all well accustomed to the idiosyncrasies of our telephone system.

The first telephone link with Foula was established during the First World War, the cable being laid only two or three days after war was declared. In those days a main shipping route lay out to the west of Foula and the cable was connected to a look-out hut built at the back of the Sneug. It was reputed to be the best look-out in Britain. The phone was kept in repair for a few years after the war but the cable was frequently broken by trawlers and so the system was disconnected. Some of the old posts that had carried the cable up the hill became posts for the old Brae fence, now pulled up and re-used as our hay racks. Only one post still remains standing up alone on the site of the hut. In 1936 a wireless link was provided from Foula to Huxter on the Shetland mainland. Calls were transmitted every four hours during the day but not at all at night. Later there was a link to Sandness Post Office, calling twice every hour, at the hour from Foula, and at the half hour from Sandness.

In 1954 the public telephone was installed with a kiosk outside the Post Office. This was a big step forward and provided a very welcome link with friends and relatives on the mainland and a ready access, though a somewhat expensive one, to shops and offices, doctors and vets, engineers and lawyers, previously only contacted by prolonged correspondence.

It transpired that my husband had bought no less than five foals altogether. Prices were again poor and good quality horses were going for relatively little. They were easy enough to buy— a far harder problem was how to get them back to Foula. My husband could only arrange for someone to keep them in the meantime, whilst getting a lift back to the isle himself on a passing fishing boat.

9

Shortening Days

Hail sheetin doon wi a nort wind ahint it,
Blottin oot laand an sea frae da scene.
An iron coortin closin aa thing:
Winter has come to da islands ageen.

Jack Renwick.

Now the days grew shorter. The change to Greenwich Mean
Time when the clocks were put back gave us a nasty shock as our
already too short day finished even sooner. Now dusk fell at 4.30
p.m. and by the end of November we could no longer see to work
indoors by four o'clock without the light of the Tilley lamp.
Struggling away with the hay on a summer evening I looked
forward to the long dark evenings, curled up on the resting chair
reading a good book perhaps—or simply doing nothing at all.
But somehow it never seemed to work out like that, and the
darkness caught us tightening down our hay, fetching home
lambs from a crü, salting meat, baking bread—always something to be done.

In November we take our ewes into Harrier to put them to the
ram. Anxiously we waited for a reasonable day to go to the crü,
and finally we set out on a bitter squally morning. At first all
went well. We took up our positions, my husband, Davie and I
climbing up into the Bruistins where most of the sheep were
sheltering. The ram was easy to pick out, bright fleckit with big
curling horns and he ran from sheep to sheep sniffling hopefully,
but when we tried to move the sheep on towards the Gillings he
led a bunch in a determined break for freedom. They got past
Davie in spite of his running and yelling fit to burst, and
stampeded madly towards me. Bluey met them like a streak of
lightning so that the ewes took one look and turned tail back to
the main bunch, although the ram stood his ground, head lowered menacingly.

"Good dog, caa him peeriewise!" Bluey tried his best, but was
met each time by a vicious butt from the angry ram. When I

reached him he tried to box me too, but I gripped his horn, turned him in the right direction and gave him a push. Nothing doing. He dug in his hooves and refused to budge. I tried dragging but to no avail. Davie was sounding more and more frantic, so I gave the ram a parting biff on the nose and set off at a run to catch up with the others. We gathered the sheep at the head of Yelper's Burn, where they stilled for a moment then poured down to the floor of the valley. With a bit of difficulty we kept them going down alongside the burn, managing to control several massive attempts to escape first on one side and then the other.

Now we had the ewes safely in Harrier, all we had to do was find the ram. This turned out to be more than a slight problem. Word reached us that a bright fleckit ram had been seen outside the Hametoon dyke going with some of Edith's ewes the morning after the crü—he had obviously set off to look for a new harem. But the weather turned so bad we were unable to look for him. South-west Force Nine, the wind shrieked like a banshee through the telegraph poles, and pounced down on our little house shaking it angrily and hammering the roof with rain.

Next day the wind eased slightly and we searched the Nort Wilse and the Bruistins, presuming the ram had gone back home again. Up there conditions were very severe. The tussocks of sphagnum moss were frozen so they crunched under our boots, icicles hung from the overhanging peaty banks and the Sneug and Hamnafield were powdered grey with snow. Up on the plateau of Fandel we could hear the wind roaring through the boulders on the high hilltops above us, making a noise like heavy breaking sea. Were these the friendly hills where we wandered barefoot in the summer? Then it would have been quite easy to cover all the ground on a search for an animal, but now in these conditions it appeared a hopeless task.

We had intended to pension off the old ram this year—"Fine reestit chops!" I said with enthusiasm—but now it looked as if he would have to be reprieved. We packed our best green hay into him and tempted his appetite with nuts and maize. I thought he looked like a genial elderly gentleman with his wrinkled old face and his mild eyes, but he soon had the end of the hay rack where he was tied battered to pieces. We took him up to Harrier and he bounded off among the ewes, delighted to be free, and he soon established himself as boss amongst his wives, and indeed seemed to have gained a new lease of life.

Our next worry was the new foals we had bought. When would we ever get them in? Eventually it was a fine morning so everyone bustled around and after a couple of hours the mail-boat set off, heavy laden with empty barrels, calor gas cylinders, the last of the bags of wool and a small batch of lambs. I stood at the door watching it disappear into a small black dot. When would it be back? Already the wind was freshening from the south, blowing chilly in my face, and a yellow haze spread over the sun. By midday the wind was scrapping the sea white and the first heavy drops of rain began, just "skeeting oot", but a forerunner of the continuous heavy rain which a strong south-erly wind usually brings. There followed days of gale as the wind tugged unceasingly at our little house as though de-termined to uproot it, days of phoning, days of emptiness, days of listening to the weather forecast.

But even gales come to an end eventually. After the wind had blown from the north-west for several days the temperature dropped enough for hard frost to set in one night. The clouds cleared away, the stars twinkled and winked, the Northern Lights danced and flickered in an arc to the north. By next day the restless sea had become subdued and tame, although there was still too much swell rolling in from the north for the boat to be able to come in to the pier. All day phone calls went back and forth and Mima kept popping over with bits of news.

"They would leave after dinner if the sea was still modera-ting."

"They had loaded up and gone over to the steamer pier for mair stuff."

"They doubted they were o'er heavily loaded to tak the peerie horses."

"They've heard a bad forecast: south-east increasing to Force Nine."

"They werna coming after all."

Well they finally left, very heavily laden with over 5 tons of winter supplies at 4.30 next morning, accompanied by a friendly fishing boat the *Bairns' Pride*. The frost still held, the moon was shining brightly, as bright as day, when they arrived at the isle. John Andrew came down to the pier with the tractor and helped unload the boat and take the stuff round the houses. By the time they had finished and the boat was safely up on the slipway again the forecast had come true, the frost "slipped" and the day deteriorated into "a day o' dirt" as the Foula folk succinctly describe a day of lashing wind and rain.

We were disappointed we had not managed to get in the little horses, but as it was, they had also had to leave some of the animal feeding and barrels of fuel. My husband was determined that the next fine day he would make a quick dash across to fetch the foals without wasting time taking anything else. But once again the wind blew round and round, gale after gale. Even when it moderated the sea was still too rough. Finally we asked the pilot of the Loganair plane if he would be willing to fly in with them—this would be the first time livestock had been flown to Foula. We spent a frenzied evening phoning, getting it all fixed. The pilot agreed and arranged transport to the airport while the vet agreed to give them tranquillizers. They would come in next day—if it was weather.

I dreamt all night of horses prancing up and down the airstrip, but by morning the familiar thud of the wind hitting the house woke me up. No weather for the plane. My husband rose and went over to phone, undoing all his arrangements. That evening he phoned again and fixed it all up for the plane to come on Monday, the pilot's next available day. But Monday dawned—a true "day o' dirt", south-west gale and driving drizzle. The plane would come on Wednesday—but on Wednesday the mist dropped a thick curtain down over the island. Friday—but by Friday the wind had backed north-west bringing fierce squally showers of hail and sleet. We were quite surprised when Saturday arrived for the wind had moderated, the showers were lighter—it was a day for the horses at last. The sun was rising over Durga Ness turning the hills into gold and blue, casting long shadows behind the dykes and banks. My husband went out to take some photos—well it's not that often the sun shines at this time of year. He rushed back in and grabbed his rifle.

"I'll get him this time!" He cautiously poked the barrel of the gun round the doorway. Our friend the crow was sitting on a fence post wondering whether it would be safe to partake of some tempting old fat I had laid out specially as bait for him.

"Bang!"

The porch shook with the sound of the explosion. The crow lifted into the air fluttering and turning, the wind caught him and lifted him up over the valley, then dropped him straight down to land in a small black heap right outside the Ham door.

Jim went out again to take his photos. The sun was rising higher, sparkling in all the little pools of rainwater, drying up the sodden brown grass. A few minutes later he rushed in again, this time grabbing his binoculars.

"A waxwing!"

The bird was sitting in the fuchsia bush uttering a high shrill whistle—a pinkish chestnut bird with a noticeable crest and bright white, yellow and scarlet wing tips.

"Keep the dogs and bairns inside and I'll take a photo of him."

"Where's Bluey gone? Blast! The fool dog's run off when you shot the crow."

If there's one thing that scares the wits out of poor Bluey it's gunfire. I rushed outside shouting, "Bluey—Bluey" in a high-pitched yodel. The waxwing took offence and flew off. My husband muttered darkly as he sat down to his overcooked breakfast. I finally found Bluey cowering in a corner of the lamb-house.

"You are a fool," I remonstrated.

Bluey wagged his tail in agreement.

When I returned home I was met by a large pool of golden liquid oozing over the porch floor. I traced it up the leg of the table, then along the shelf. One of the bairns had sabotaged the plastic drum of horse shampoo.

"Hurry up! What'n da sad sight have you been doing? We'll miss da plane!" my husband looked agitated.

I grabbed a sponge and basin and started mopping. The result was dramatic. The shampoo erupted into a glorious bubble bath and the more I mopped the more the bubbles increased. Bubbles overflowed the basin and slithered down the wash-stand, bubbles carpeted the floor, bubbles nestled among the pot plants, bubbles started floating up to the ceiling.

"Come on, hurry up, dear!"

"OK. I'm just coming!" I gave a last swipe at a drift of bubbles, threw down the sponge in defeat, exited smartly through the door leaving the situation to sort itself out. It was obviously one of those days.

The wind was still gusting south at the airstrip and we watched with some alarm as the plane came in to land. It gave a few lurches as the wind hit it, but landed safely.

"Quick!" The pilot stuck his head out of the window, "I think one's fallen down. Open the back door!"

My husband yanked the door open, bits of horse seemed to stick out in all directions. One of them had fallen down onto its back and the others were standing astride it. Hastily we pulled them all out and they seemed none the worse for their flight, although they were still dopy from their tranquillizers. Two bays with bright red-tipped coats and black manes and tails, a skewbald with big soft eyes and a friendly face, a plump little brown with white feet and a tiny black with an independent air. I eyed them with approval, they looked like our sort of horses. It was the last day of November, six whole weeks since they had been bought.

December. Now we struggled to get everything finished before the winter really set in. Fine days were rare and we waited for them anxiously. When they arrived everyone was outside trying to get as much work as possible done before the next gale. We scoured the hillside looking for any of our lambs that had escaped the crüs; sometimes we could drive them down to the Harrier crü with the dogs, but other times it was a case of catch and carry. The bright fleckit ram turned up again one day, standing outside the Harrier gate waiting to be let in. Better late than never I supposed.

Our sheep had to be drenched for otherwise after the wet autumn, liver fluke would cause problems. After caaing them into the crü I stood at the entrance, legs astride, drench gun strapped onto my back, while my husband grabbed a hold of them and shoved them between my legs. Poke the nozzle of the gun in their mouth, squeeze the trigger, release them; poke, squeeze, release; poke, squeeze, release—simple. The only snag was that the ground was very muddy and with some of the more obstreperous sheep I was liable to find myself sprawling on my face, whilst sheep leapt over me, escaping to freedom.

The sheep also had to be dipped otherwise keds and lice would get the upper hand, which would not only result in loss of condition, but also cause the sheep to tear out their wool because of the irritation, and a half naked sheep does not have much

chance of surviving the winter. We used a small portable
wooden dipper, like a large wooden bath tub with a long
draining-board we call the dreeper, on which the sheep stood
and dripped, the dip running back down into the dipper. This
was a long tiring job and we were all already exhausted by
driving the sheep off the hill to the crü. Each sheep had to be
picked up and submerged in the dipper, to which it usually
objected violently, kicking in all directions and spraying us with
the foul-smelling dip. It was then hauled out and pushed onto
the dreeper, where it stood with its legs sagging with the weight
of its wet wool and an offended look on its face, though some of
the more awkward ones refused to stand up at all or else leapt
defiantly back into the dipper causing a tidal wave. On days like
this we were grateful for the moonlight as we often did not finish
till long after darkness fell.

The days were very short now. The sun rose at 9.30 in the
morning when I was busy getting our oldest boy off to school. A
brilliant orange ball, it appeared above the dark headland of
Durga Ness, to the south, and described a low arc across the
south horizon. Usually we only had a glimpse of it before it hid
behind the curtain of cloud that generally covered the sky. Even
at its highest the shadows it cast were long evening shadows.
Every dip and bump was emphasized, each little tussock was
picked out by its long blue shadow, giving the crofts a golden
and blue dappled effect. At 1.30 p.m. the sun sank behind the
tail of the hill, plunging us into the shade, but still shining
tantalizingly golden on the Back of the Taing. We were reluctant to light our lamp until the last possible moment, trying
to draw out the day longer, but by 3 p.m. it was impossible to
work indoors without it.

But the moon shone at night, shone with unbelievable brightness. Is it due to the reflection off the surrounding sea, or does
the moon always shine brightest in the place one loves best? The
isle was flooding with its silvery golden light and turned into a
magic isle. I could pick out each withered stalk of grass, each
peat bank, even the very stones on the top of the hill. Small
clouds drifted by the moon casting mysterious shadows; a sudden shower brought a pale silver moon rainbow arching over the
valley. If there is a pot of gold at the foot of an ordinary rainbow,
what might one find under a lunar bow! I wandered out to the

point of the Brae and stood watching the sea which was patterned with the shadows of every little wave. The waves rolled
in, breaking into dancing white froth. The dark rocks twinkled
with hoar frost; walking over them was like walking through
the Milky Way. The moon shone high in the sky above me;
perhaps this is what made me feel exhilarated—the comparison
with the lazy old sun, who could hardly be bothered to rise at all.

10

Midwinter Foys

Here we ir met ta wylcome in Yöle;
  Up wi a licht fit an link hit awa, boys.
Send fir a fiddler, play up da Foula Reel;
  We'll skip it as licht as a maa, boys.

Traditional Foula song.

We celebrate Christmas or Yule on the 6th of January because in 1752 when the calendar was reformed the Foula folk still adhered to the old Julian calendar, not approving of the high-handedness of shifting all the days twelve days back. New Year's Day or "Nuerday" correspondingly falls on the 13th of January. This custom has nearly died out in the rest of Shetland, but there is never any question of that happening here, despite pressure from nearly every missionary and school teacher that we have had since the calendar was first changed. The custom has been ascribed to everything from backward old-fashionedness to downright heathenness, but in reality it is simply a declaration of independence, a refusal to conform with the rest of the world and it gives the island a sense of identity.

December 25th passes as any other ordinary working day, apart from the carol service held in the evening. Round the time of the shortest day and longest night it often comes a fine spell of weather which enables us to finish the remaining odds and ends of work before the Yule celebrations. So the 25th might find us drenching our lambs, much to the horror of the teacher's young boy who came to show us what Santa had brought him.

During October and November we rack our brains over Christmas presents. Christmas shopping is difficult enough under ordinary conditions, but imagine what it's like trying to buy anything without seeing it first.

Armed with long lists we go over to the phone. The shops in Lerwick are busy.

"Hello, is that Andersons?"

"Yes, can I help you?"

"I'd like to order a pair of ladies' leather gloves."

"Hold on, I'll put you through to the other department."

"Hello, I'd like to order a pair of ladies' leather gloves."

"A pair of what?"

"A pair of ladies' leather gloves," I shout into the phone. This sets the dogs barking madly; Penny opens her mouth and yells, and Ross knocks the rest of my phoning change onto the floor.

"Hold on and I'll put you through to Miss Barclay."

"Hello, I'd like to order a pair of leather ladies' gloves—ladies' leather gloves."

"Hold on a minute and I'll look and see."

"Excuse me, caller, your time is up."

Flustered I put sixteen pence in the coin box and press the button. A grinding noise announces that it was the wrong button and I have been disconnected. Frantically I press the support of the receiver up and down, "Operator, Operator! Hello, could you reconnect me?"

"Yes, what number please?"

"Andersons."

"Hello, can I help you?"

"Gloves," I croak near to despair, "Miss Bradbury, Bradley, Brady—or something."

"Hello, I'd like to order a pair of ladies' leather gloves."

"I'm afraid we only stock PVC ones or simulated fur."

"Oh no, those won't do." I think furiously for something Aunty Mary might like instead.

"Have you any fur-lined slippers."

"Slippers, hold on and I'll see. What colour was it?"

"Does du have ony unmarked lambs out on Stremness still?" Mima interrupts, sticking her head round the door of the phone box.

"One white and kind of snug, and one black with long oo."

"Eh?" squawks Miss Barclay. "One white and snug and one black with long oo?"

"No, sorry that was lambs," I shout back.

Bluey hearing the magic word shoots out of the door to look for some.

"Bluey! You fool!"

"Blue, did you say?" Do I detect a slight nervous tremor? "What size do you require?"

"Sixes," I think hard, or was it sevens?

"Hold on,"—a pause.

"I'm sorry we seem to be out of sixes at the moment."

I'm exhausted by the time I come to the end of my list, and completely confused as to what I finally ordered. A feeling that is probably shared by the shops.

The only alternative is to order from a catalogue. Then one is faced with insoluble questions such as does "green" mean emerald green or the colour of calves' sharn; will "large" be big enough, and what shades are "petrol, orchid and aubergine?" Sometimes we send for wholesale lists—the amazingly low prices fascinate us.

"Hey! One dozen men's acrylic shirts, assorted sizes, only £8.75!"

But do we know one dozen assorted men?

"How about this—fire extinguishers £4.35 for six, gift wrapped. We could give one to each house—solve everything!"

The Christmas mail is enormous, bags and bags of it, a whole tractor load and it takes Harry hours to sort out. But by and by my husband will stagger home with a heavy bag of parcels on his back.

We open them in great excitement.

"Dwine! The fire extinguishers are sold out."

"Oh dear, what on earth will we give everyone?"

"The children's cutlery sets are out of stock. What's this? They've sent four gross of clothes pegs instead!"

"Very useful."

I open another parcel and burst into giggles. "Look! It's the overall for your mother!" I hold up a shocking pink mini-skirted creation.

"Heavens!"

The house is in a shambles by now, boxes and wrapping paper are strewn all over the floor, resting-chair and sofa and even in Penny's cot where she sleeps unperturbed.

"The blue shirt for Harry!!" We gape in amazement at the shrieking concoction of turquoise and purple flowers.

"No, no." Jim shakes his head in disbelief.

"Maybe we could give it to Davie instead," I suggest.

"What were we going to give him?"

"A wallet." I delved into another box and unearthed it.

"But Harry has a good wallet already," he objects.

"Well, we could give it to Rob and give his present to Harry."

"What was Rob getting?"

"Gloves. See. Here they are. They look awfully big!"

"What size did you send for?"

"Large, I think." I can't remember of course.

Jim tries them on. They are a perfect fit for his big hands. "No, I doubt they're o'er big for Harry, or Rob either for that matter."

"Well, if we give the gloves to Ken, and Ken's present to Harry, and Davie's present to Rob, and . . ." I am sure there is a solution to it all somewhere.

"Never mind, next year we can give them all clothes pegs!" he says with a grin tipping out a mountain of five hundred and seventy-six pegs.

Although Yule has been celebrated for a long time on Foula, only recently, since the last war, have the conventional trimmings been added—Santa Claus, presents, decorations and so on. Before then the main event of the day was the menfolk going from house to house, accompanied by their Yule drams and sweets, culminating in a gathering of all the islanders in one or two houses where they danced and made merry until well into the next morning.

We enjoyed listening to my father-in-law sitting in his chair by the side of the fire telling us of those times.

"The year before the First World War when I was going to the fishing wi the Niggards men, afore Yule we drew five pounds out of wir share o' the money. This was for wir Yule stores—maybe a new suit and a pair o' shoon, for a' body dressed his best round Yule. We bought a stone o' sweeties and gave a nevfu (handful) to each of the bairns and women, but they never went in for this nonsense aboot Santi Klaas. Whisky was three shillings a bottle then for a good brand, or only half a croon for a mair ordinary ane. Some folk bought a gallon in a laim pig, du kens, an earthenware flask." He was silent for a minute and then started chuckling.

"I mind ae Yule Johnnie o'Quinister coming o'er da rigs to da Biggins wi' a pig o' whisky tucked under his airm. Laughing and leaping o'er da stanks he reached the door, when didna da pig slip oot o' his grasp and broke to smithereens on da briggy stanes. He liooch (laughed), clickit up da leggins, hooved da dregs onto Jeannie's lap and set off for Quinister again. A peerie start after, dey saw him coming again singing and jumping o'er da stanks, another pig stuck under his airm." He laughed again at the memory.

Yule Even was a busy day. Not for us the smell of turkey and plum pudding, but the mouth-watering smell of reestit mutton boiling in a muckle pot on the fire and the spicy tang of caraway seeds from the newly baked Yule Bread. We garlanded the dried piltocks and mutton hanging in the roof with paper chains and balloons. The house was given a thorough cleaning and a new piece of linoleum was laid down—for everything had to be spick and span for Yule. We also had to be sure to wash ourselves most carefully on the Eve of Yule, otherwise, we were told, "Da trows will wash you in swatts!" Swatts was a drink made by taking the ground bere meal and soaking it in water in a churn. The sediment left at the bottom was taken out and boiled into a thick sticky brown porridge called sooins, so thick was it that the women used to ask the young boys to come and help stir it. This was eaten for supper at occasions such as cairdings, when the women folk gathered at a house in the evening to card wool.

Around Yule and Nuerday (New Year's Day) a special trow, the Niuggle, got up to his pranks and mischievously hid away various household articles. These we were told would not be returned to us until the following year. Well, so far he had made off with three blinkies, the muckle tulley and one of the hens—I wondered what he was up to!

It was long past midnight before everything was arranged and we collapsed into bed. A clamour like a flock of scorries (young gulls) on a skerry woke us up just as the dawn was lightening—the bairns were up and busily investigating their presents. Two large bulging socks hung from the head of our bed too, for Santi comes to us all. Well, he is not so busy on the sixth as he is on the twenty-fifth!

As soon as the chaos was cleared enough for us to get breakfast, my husband took down his gun, filled his pockets with ammunition and various bottles, and set off south along the banks, picking up Dal on the way. At the Hametoon they were joined by more of the menfolk and they wandered along the banks passing round their bottles and shooting at rabbits, skarfs and empty bottles thrown in the sea—a traditional Yule custom here. Through the day people came along the house, glasses were filled and passed round, the bairns' toys were admired, jokes and stories were told, and before we knew it, it was time to go out for the evening.

This is the one time of the year that we all get together, come fair weather or foul—and usually it is pretty foul. This year was no exception. By evening the wind was south-west and fast increasing, hitting the back of the house with a crash and rattling the rain on the roof. Nothing daunted we pulled on oilskins over our finery and huddled in the trailer, a large tarpaulin pulled completely over the top of us. Thus swaying and bumping in the dark, the wind tearing and pulling at our cover, we were conveyed through the blackness to the Hame-toon. When the bumping stopped we cautiously peeped out from under the tarpaulin. The bright yellow light from the Niggard's window beckoned us in from the mud and rain and indoors all was warm and cosy. The room was packed with people all talking nineteen to the dozen, the bairns were playing all over the floor, swapping tales of what Santi had brought and several of the grown-up "children" were playing happily with the more intriguing toys. I squeezed myself in between Jessie and Edith on the resting-chair next to the warmly glowing stove, glad to rest after the journey through the stormy night. Snatches of conversation assailed my ears.

"Boy, did du hear wan o' yon oil pontoons sank da streen near Lerwick?"

"Faith, hits da best place for it!"

"I had the most too-tackable fancy in yon peerie lamb. I canna tell dee fu provoked I was when she wan oot o'er da dyke."

"Oh 'less. What'n a lamb was yon?"

"Boy, I mind wir faither telling me. Ae Yule dy grandfaither wanted to mak a extra special bang and put a double charge o' powder into his gun. He steadied da stock fernainst da waa o' da Ham Laamus and fired a shot. What a gluff dey got! Da recoil shoved da stane back three inches into da waa. Du can still see it."

Bottles were passed round and the talk got louder, laughter more hilarious. Eric and John Andrew were singing and playing the guitar in one corner; Harry and Jim were tuning the fiddles in another; Edith had completely succumbed to the giggles; Ken was trying to make himself heard on the phone, speaking to Andy; Francie and peerie Bobby were having an excited argument over a game of Monopoly; Rob, oblivious to the racket, was sitting in a corner reading Davie's new Christmas Annual whilst Kevin and Kenneth attacked him from behind with sticky toffee papers.

"Play us da Shaalds, Harry," shouted Aggie Jean whose feet were tapping in anticipation. Harry struck up with da Shaalds for the Foula Reel. We all grabbed partners and lined up in a set in the small space in the middle of the floor, old and young, anyone who felt like dancing, even the small bairns. Soon feet were flying as we cavorted through the reel, somewhat similar to "Strip the Willow", amid laughter and shouts of:

"No, yon way, boy!"

"Wake up lass, it's dy turn!"

"Och, I canna mind if I'm a man or a wife!"

"What! Does du no ken by noo!"

"What's du doing yon for, lass!" Someone had slyly grabbed a hold of the foot of one of the more substantially built dancers as she twirled past.

"Ooo! Guid!" She collapsed, flattening her assailants, and the dance dissolved into roars of laughter.

Eightsomes, Shetland reels, polkas and waltzes followed. Shoes were kicked off, jackets and jumpers discarded. Finally, exhausted we collapsed into the chairs again. One by one the children fell asleep and were carried ben and laid on the bed. We ate reestit mutton, yule bread, treacly loaf, cakes and biscuits till we could hold no more. Now and then someone would strike up with a song, and everyone joined in. With luck Bobby would be persuaded to sing some of his own songs. At this time of year we particularly liked to hear "Simmer Dim", a song of the long summer nights.

"Oh simmer dim, oh simmer dim,
I tank de noo, my man;
Du keeps an auld man frae his rest
Yet still du aye sheens on."

Bobby's best known song, "Fugley Isle" (Fugley was the old way of spelling Foula) has appealed to many of our summer

visitors so now you may hear it sung in Folk Clubs the length
and breadth of the country. These are my favourite verses:

"The bright pretty dancers
Will shine on thy dark shore
And the kittiwakes' sweet song
Echo blue waters o'er.
But my paths never more
Will lie o'er thy green braes
Where I played long ago
In the warm summer days.

Chorus
Fugley Isle, oh fare thee well
Childhood's home across the sea.
Never more thy peaks I'll roam
Farewell, farewell, my dear old home.

Farewell ye green valleys
Where in my youth I did roam
Wi' my ain bonny sweetheart
A love pure and fond,
With the moon slowly rising
O'er yon blue hills afar
And the ocean reflecting
The bright evening star.

We danced again, ate some more, talked and laughed till our
voices turned hoarse. By half-past six in the morning folk were
falling asleep in various quiet corners, so wearily we struggled
into our oilskins and boots, sorted out whose blinkie was whose,
wakened and dressed the bairns and were finally ready to leave.
By now Jim had got his second wind and was playing away on
the fiddle with great verve, Ken was demonstrating the back-
step to Davie, Francie had begun another game of Monopoly,
whilst Eric was strumming away merrily to himself in a corner.
But eventually we all struggled out to the tractor and huddled
under the tarpaulin, the weather being still most unpleasant.
Arriving home, my head reeling and legs shaking, I crawled
into bed and remained there in a semi-comatose state until dusk
fell.

A week later on 13th January comes Nuerday which is again an occasion for merrymaking. In Foula it is the actual New Year's Day that is important not the preceding night as in the Scottish Hogmanay. On that night however we take care to throw out all the dirty water and have in a good supply of peats and clean water. Nuerday was not held as a holiday but the folk used to work at something they hoped would go well for them during the following year, perhaps delling a patch of ground or taking up a bit of drain and if possible the men tried to go off with the boats to fish for their hansel from the sea, but of course it was rare the weather was fine enough. Mima told me how instead her father, would go down to the beach and fetch home a piece of a seaweed known as hinniwaar, of which all the children had a nibble. Early on Nuerday Harry came over to first foot us, giving us each a hansel, an apple or a bar of chocolate, for which we had to be sure not to say thank you, as that would spoil the luck. The old folk used to compete to see who could say first "My Nuer's gift, my hansel, a kishie o' dis year's gloy." The recipient of this saying was expected to give them a kishie full of gloy which was the material, usually floss (clean straw) with which thatching and kishies were made. Again in the evening we went round the houses and the merriment lasted all night and well into the early morning.

Now winter was really upon us as the wind blew unceasingly from the north-west, bitter cold. The cold penetrated through and through us till I felt like a bundle of frozen bones. Although the pressure of the seasonal work was relaxed we had plenty to occupy our time. With the colder weather the grazing dwindled as the bitter salty winds burnt the grass and we had to give our lambs extra attention if they were to survive. Every night they were rounded up and shut up in the lamb-house, and given a feed of hay. Each morning, as long as it was reasonable weather, we let them out to graze, but if it was stormy they were kept in all day and hay and water were brought to them.

Each day, as soon as Ross was safely off to school, I would hurry down to the lamb-house, dogs bounding ahead of me over the bog and a hopeful retinue of hens running behind. Opening the lamb-house door quietly, I would peep in to find lambs and foals lying from one end of the building to the other in a multi-coloured carpet. When they saw me they would get lazily to their feet, stretch and wander over to the empty hay racks to see if by chance they had left any. Plump little Morven, the foal with white feet, would rise up on her haunches and give a big yawn, then gingerly stand up taking care not to set her feet on any of the lambs. Blossom, the skewbald, was usually the last horse to wake up.

The lambs would notice that the door was open and would push and shove each other in their haste to get out. Three lambs could fit through the door at a time, and at first they would go out smoothly three by three, but then a lamb would get impatient and push out of turn and, as four lambs could not possibly squeeze through the space, they would stand struggling in the doorway until one gave way. They never learned. Every day they jammed up the door, unlike the foals who would wait quietly until the squabbling rabble got out from under their feet, then daintily step outside, one at a time in a dignified fashion.

I watched them one morning as I sheltered in the lamb-house whilst a sharp hail shower went by. The hailstones rattled noisily on the corrugated iron roof and the cold wind howled round the eaves. The lambs all disappeared into the dips and down over the grassy edge of the banks where they could graze in shelter. The foals came back to the door hoping to be let in and were most affronted when I chased them away again. When the sun blinked out again I scuttled out to the dess to fetch the hay. Under the polythene sheet that covered the dess it was warm and sunny and there was the scent of sweet hay. Shutting my eyes I could almost imagine it was summer, until a hard gust of wind flapped the polythene with a noise like gunfire.

The heavy weights on the dess made the hay extremely hard-packed, and I had to pluck it out in small wisps, until at last I had a large pile of loose hay below me. I jumped down onto it and then there commenced the daily fight to get out. The polythene sheet flapped at me like a demented octopus and, as usual, the net contrived to tangle round one of my boots and trip me up. One of these days they will get me! But this time I escaped their clutches, and gathering up a large armful of hay I staggered through the mud to the door. As usual the latch was jammed, but a sharp uppercut with my right foot dislodged it (good practice for the Can-Can, this). It took fifteen armfuls to fill the

feeding racks and half the morning was over by the time I beat
my way against the wind up to the house again.

Inside, the front of the stove was glowing red and the warm air
wrapped itself round me like a comfortable old blanket. Our
house is always warm in the winter, no matter how hard the
wind may blow, although the stove smokes terribly during gales.
When the wind shifts from north-west to west it blows down the
chimney, shooting out long tongues of flame from the front of the
stove. When the wind is south-west each gust blows the stove
damper shut, filling the house with blue peat smoke. When it
blows from north-east however half the fire blows up the
chimney, spewing sparks into the sky. But our walls are three
feet thick, the rooms are small and we have plenty of peats. In
very cold weather we light the Tilley lamp too, as it gives out a
surprising amount of heat, and its warm yellow light has a cosy
effect.

Whenever he has time to spare my husband occupies himself
with engine repairs—a pastime he thoroughly enjoys. If I am
not careful I may find myself holding nasty bits of greasy black
metal being expected to hold an intelligent conversation about
such things as cracked piston rings or worn camshaft bearings.
Sometimes, especially in winter, spare parts are difficult to
obtain and he has to make them himself from whatever happens
to be at hand.

Slowly, almost imperceptibly, the days were getting longer.
Just before dusk we would put the lambs in for the night, each
day a few minutes later. Only by this did we know the winter
was passing. The old folk used to say that the day is a cock's
stride longer by Nuerday. One day, taking Bluey with me, to
instil a little sense into his scatterbrained head, I made a sweep
of the Brae rounding up the lambs. As usual they were all
grazing down over the edge at Ham Little or nibbling seaweed
on the rocks below. I scrambled down and round the steep slopes
chivying the lambs up again, then I splashed through the bog to
check that no lambs were stuck. Every now and then my foot
would break through the soft surface filling my boot with peaty
mud. Out here, at the head of the baa, there was only me, and
the island. For the houses, crofts and all signs of human life
were out of sight. There was only the bare windswept hill, the
dark rolling waves breaking against the stark black cliffs and

the grey lowering rain-filled sky. Here in the solitude I could look at our island more objectively, temporarily freed from human ties. Many questions churned round my brain as I tried to sort out our feelings towards it, our hopes for its future, our relation to its past.

The horses were already standing at the lamb-house door waiting to go in. I opened it and drove in the lambs, counting them as they went, "61 – 62 – 63 – 64 – 65 – 66 – 67". Only 67—three were missing. I looked in the drains and found two of them skulking down by the bridge. Now, where was the other one—perhaps she had got through the fence? I made a detour down to the beach and looked up the cliff face—there she was on a small ledge above Stack na Gronna. It was only about forty feet high, but high enough for the lamb to be smashed up if it should fall, so I approached it with caution, scrambling up the ledges where the maalies nest in summer. It was the little horned lamb from Soberlie and when she saw me she stamped her feet in defiance. I could only just reach her with one hand. I pushed and "shushed" at her, but she would not budge, even when I pulled off small chips of loose rocks and threw them at her. There was nothing for it but to climb down again and go round to the top and scramble down the ledge the same way as she had gone. Gingerly I gripped the wool on her back and pulled her back with me, turned her round and gave her a gentle push. She nimbly ran off, wriggled back through the fence and darted into the lamb-house.

Inside, the lambs were all munching away at the hay racks, pushing and shoving each other, trying to reach the tastiest bits. As usual there were half a dozen of them running from rack to rack, convinced that the hay is always greener somewhere else. The peerie sean stood right under the rack where she was safe out of the crush and nibbled at the hay that dropped down. The foals reached out over the lambs' heads and pulled hay out of the top of the racks. Snowdrop, the bay, pulled out a big wisp and stood munching it thoughtfully, while several of the lambs chewed at the other end of it. Imy Face's lamb pulled the last stalk right out of Snowdrop's mouth. She gave a sigh and pulled out another mouthful. Two of the hens had already settled down to roost for the night on Blossom's back.

I got great satisfaction just standing there watching them and listening to the sound of munching—my hard work during the summer seemed well worthwhile.

My eyes lingered on the rows of hungry animals, the hard trampled dung under my feet, the driftwood stacked under the corrugated iron roof, the old window built over with rough stones, a remnant of white plaster clinging to a section of bare wall. Another picture came to my mind—the whiteness and brightness of newly whitewashed walls, a clean swept floor, faded brown pictures of unknown folk, the deep quiet tick of an old wooden clock. I remembered an old woman with a worn, wrinkled face, framed by a black hap all holes and lacy bits, her gnarled hands blotched with brown spots and blue veins, and thick black worsted stockings poking out of innumerable layers of faded black skirts and pinnies—auld Louisa o' Brae. And down through the years I still hear her querulous voice, "Na. My bonny ben end!"

11

Snowfall

Whin hammerin Winter strikks da hoose,
  My mind gyengs fae da laand;
I waak da grey hills o da sea
  An faer waaks i my haand.

Emily Milne.

Snow came with the north-west wind. Not big soft flakes gently
floating and twirling in the wind, covering the world in a
blanket of white. No, a mad world, where snow is hurtled
through the air on the fierce icy wind, barely stopping to touch
the frozen ground as it passes. On and on, the snow was flung
into the sea, where the big dark breakers rolled by from the
north. On and on, but the isle was swept bare by the storm. Only
in the shelter of the banks and burns did the snow pile up in
drifts. The garden was filled with a gigantic white drift but
round the house not even a dusting of snow had the chance to
settle on the black icy ground. The fine powder was blown
through the crannies of the old walls, filling the lamb-house
with snow and even the porch had its snow drift forced in round
the edge of the door. Heavy flans of wind battered the house
unrelentingly, until we felt quite exhausted listening to it. It
screamed past the door like an express train run amok, shaking
and shuddering the house and sucking out the air as it passed,
making our ears pop with the sudden change of pressure. My
husband battled his way to the lamb-house to feed the animals,
disappearing into the white fury and I watched anxiously at the
window for his return.

For three days the wind blew without respite, and we could
only sit inside and worry. How were our sheep faring out on the
hill? Had they had the sense to come down onto low ground, or
were they lying up in the Bruistins smoored under a snow drift.
Where were the horses? Had they taken shelter along the banks
broo and perhaps slipped over the edge? But eventually the
wind grew tired and died down to a fretful gusting, blowing the

fine powdered snow into drifts, swirling it here, sweeping it there—the isle was turned into a magic world of white. The sun came out again, casting blue shadows over the snowy landscape, and over the dark slate sea, the mainland floated brilliant white.

We rubbed the rust off our skis, emptied the spiders out of our ski-boots, and set off for the hills to see how the sheep were faring. The frosty bright air was exhilarating and we soon climbed up to the Loch of Ourafandal, which was all frozen over, not smooth and slippery however, but churned into frozen waves of ice by the wind. The hills looked unfamiliar in their beautiful white garb. Alpine, they seemed to soar sheer into the blue sky—a silent world of white. There was only the hiss of drifting, sifting snow and the deep "croup, croup" of a corbie (raven) rolling and tumbling in the sky above us. The wind had carved an overhanging cornice of snow along the edge of the ridge between the Sneug and Hamnafield and as the sun warmed it small pieces broke off forming miniature avalanches.

A lot of our sheep were gathered together in a tight bunch on the slope above the Bonxie Club scraping away the covering of snow to get at the frozen heather. We could see where they had spent the night in the shelter of a high peaty bank by the numerous round flattened marks in the snow where they had been lying and the small heaps of droppings. I counted 153 individual "beds" where they had been lying packed just like sardines. It is only during a heavy snowfall that Shetland sheep flock of their own accord into a tight group—an important adaptation that gives them a better chance of survival if they are buried in a snowdrift, their combined warmth and effort usually enabling them to break out through the snow unaided. The animals most at risk were those sheltering on their own or in small groups. It was for these we searched the deep drifts along the banks and broos, poking with a long bamboo stick to feel if any were buried. There were so many drifts. How could we ever probe them all?

"I think there's something here!" my husband shouted, poking in a particularly deep drift. The dogs seemed interested and Dandy started digging away the snow with his paws, so we took off our skis and used them as spades.

"Here's one!" My ski uncovered a woolly lump. "Still alive! I

think it's old Taggy—yes, it is." I pulled her up and set her on
her feet. She was a bit wobbly but none the worse for being
buried under six feet of snow. We uncovered another three ewes
in that drift and another two buried further up, in a gillick
(hollow) at the foot of the Gillings.

The corbie was joined by his mate—they had been cheated of
their prey this time. They looped the loop and did double
somersaults as they courted. Soon they would be nesting. We
climbed up to the top of the Sneug where the snow was deep and
soft and difficult to traverse, but the view was well worth the
trouble. The wind had sculptured the snow into an intricate
pattern of deep ripples and waves, a mosaic of white snow and
blue shadows. Jutting out below us to the west the headland of
Waster Hivda seemed far away and unfamiliar, dimpled with a
covering of drifts. The Kame swept up to the north and dropped
to the Fleck, a bowl of pure white. Further east the Stacks stood
out sharp and black against their mantles of snow. To the south
lay the Daal and the Noup, a big white hump, and the black
houses and dykes of the Hametoon, and Hamnafield, a clean-
cut, breath-taking peak of pure white, and all around lay the
very dark grey-blue sea. We sheltered by the cairn and gazed at
it all for a while.

But time soon passed. My husband suddenly remarked, "The
wind's shifted."

"So it has." I turned to the south and felt the wind blowing in
my face.

"South-east. That means a thaw. We'd better get home quick.
We have a long way to go." He jumped up and put on his skis.

"The wind feels warmer already." I sighed at the thought of
all that beautiful snow melting. The sky had clouded over and
already the snow seemed to be shrinking, losing its brilliance
and turning grey. As we made our way down tufts of heather
and crowberry started to show dark here and there above the
snow, the peat banks turned black, the icicles dripped and the
snow turned slow and sticky. By the time we got down to the low
ground the rain arrived in cold stinging lumps that soaked us
till we were shivering with damp cold. Our ski tracks turned
grey and slushy, the ground became striped with patches of dark
sodden brown and along the coastline the snow had already
vanished, giving a dirty, greyish green margin to the isle.

By next morning when I looked out, the isle was back to its normal brown and grey self with no trace left of the magic white world except for a few drifts, patterning the hills like ribs on an old carcase. My husband says they remind him of dead whales washed up on the beach and left high and dry by the tide. I never become used to these sudden thaws when snow vanishes in a matter of hours due to the change in direction of the wind, which is warmed by the sea. Sometimes the thaw affects only our island and we can see the rest of Shetland still lying white on the horizon. The bairns love the snow and always make the most of it, sledging happily over mud and grass at the slightest sign of a snowflake.

With the thaw, the south-east wind increased to storm force. All night we heard its rumble as it pounded against the rocks and by morning the coast was a white seething chaos. As usual in a south-east gale, it rained—heavy lashing drops soaking everything through and through, for there is no shelter anywhere with the wind in this direction. I struggled into oilskins and scuttled down to the lamb-house to feed the lambs, hampered by the oilskins and the fierce wind and rain, I battled backwards and forwards carrying in the hay, half of which was whipped away out of my arms before I got it into the shelter of the lamb-house. Inside it sounded as though all hell had broken loose as the heavy rain rattled and battered on the corrugated iron roof, which was shaking and shuddering until even the heavy beams were vibrating.

When I had finished feeding the animals I went down to the side of the Voe to watch the sea. Enormous waves came rolling in, heaving themselves up into a solid grey wall of water, then slowly curling over in a froth of white foam before hitting the back of the pier in a great "whumph", and hurling up a cloud of spray over the pier and the crane until even the slipway was obscured. Then slowly the white water poured back off the pier, leaving it black and washed bare. Sometimes the waves were so big they rolled over the back of the pier in a great lump of solid green water, and rushed on, unhampered, in a wall of water up to the beach at the far end of the Voe, where there was a great mass of churning red brown waar (seaweed), torn off the rocks in the storm. The wind was carrying the spume right inshore to the ruins of the old Veedal house, and to the south of me spray was being flung right up to the top of Durga Ness in an enormous white plume over 100 feet high.

"I'm gaain to look alang da cletts for driftwood," my husband said when I blew back home. "There's maybe something in the Mid Shooting Geo."

"Watch the sea doesn't take you, then," I cautioned.

I peered out through the salt-smeared window watching his progress along the rocks. I noticed Harry coming down the road and joining him. There were three "shooting" geos—holes worn deep into the rocks by the sea. The waves rushing into the caverns, compress the air within, until it suddenly bursts out in a boom of spray. The men stood for a long time watching, judging how far up the rocks the biggest wave might come, scanning the churning, seething, heaving water for a glimpse of wood.

"See yondroo, boy!" Harry pointed to where a dark red end of wood reared for a second amidst the breaking foam, before being flung pell-mell into the tunnel.

"Tak da end o' da rope and ging roond to da idder side."

Now they crouched on either side of the narrow geo, the rope stretched between them, with a slip loop attached to the middle, dangling over the spot where they hoped the log would reappear. The next wave heaved up and curled itself over, rushing into the geo in a flurry. A moment's pause and then boom and a whoosh as the spray was forced out again.

"Dere he is, boy!" shouted Harry, his words whipped away in the flying spray and wind.

A signal, the end of the rope dropped, the loop caught the end of the swirling log and the men pulled like mad. The log grounded. They had it! No—too late—the next wave rushed in, grabbed the log and flung it over and over. It jammed for a moment, then with a sudden crack it snapped in two. The wave retreated and as the men pulled up came the broken-off portion. A quick look at the next wave and my husband ran down and lifted the end up. Another wave came and the rope tightened under the strain. The wave receding down they went again both of them working at it now—heave and pull, heave and pull. Now they had it, now they had it! They carried it between them up to the old Veedal dyke and returned again to their positions at the sides of the geo to try for the other half.

By the end of the morning, they had a sizeable pile of drift-wood stacked up by the dyke, mainly small odds and ends, but including a heavy oak grating, washed off some boat, and a new bit of "two-by-four". Seen through others' eyes, it might be dismissed as firewood, hardly worth carrying to the house, but here lay our new racks, creel bars, cole pins and fencing posts. Treeless and far from the timber merchants, even finding a mast for a toy boat presents problems in Foula. All over the isle there are many such bits and pieces of old driftwood still lying where they were laid up years ago. In some cases the finder has died, or sometimes the bits just aren't of a suitable shape or size to serve any useful purpose.

Some of the wood no doubt came from boats wrecked on the isle, for there is many a dangerous skerry lying offshore, and no lighthouse to guide a ship sailing in unfamiliar waters. In the 1950s a Danish auxiliary schooner, the *North Star*, was wrecked at the Head of the Hurd in thick fog. Under sail at the time her crew were horrified to see rocks appearing on either side. They were unable to turn quickly enough and the vessel drove straight into the head of the geo (inlet). The crew launched the small lifeboat and rowed north to Ham Little where they climbed up to safety, but the boat with her cargo of wood was lost. Unfortunately shipwrecked sailors are not usually so lucky, as the wrecks seldom take place on an accessible part of the coast. In 1899 a fishing vessel called the *Teal Duck* was lost with all hands off the South Ness one dark night. The only signs of the disaster seen or heard by the islanders was the frantic barking of the ship's dog echoing out of the darkness where no island dog could be. Another time long ago one of the Biggins men, known as "Trowie Lowrie" because he was always declaring he had acquaintance with the trows (trolls), came into the house one wild night insisting he had heard the cries and shouts of "the peerie folk". He eventually persuaded the others in the house to come out and listen and they too, heard unearthly wails and screams echoing across from the back of the isle, inter-spersed with strange cracks and bangs. Impressed, the people stayed indoors that night, deeming that there was more truth in Trowie Lowrie's stories than they had thought. Only in the morning was it discovered that a full-rigged barque had been wrecked at the foot of the Kame, and the weird noises they had heard were not the shouts of the trows but the despairing cries from the doomed crew.

How many other boats may have been wrecked at the back of the isle, driven ashore at the foot of the great cliffs in the middle of winter with no chance of being noticed, let alone rescued? Even now, anyone wrecked there would have virtually no hope of rescue for the severe turbulence off the high sheer cliffs would prevent a helicopter getting close enough. As long ago as 1883 Mr Stevenson from the Northern Lighthouse Commission surveyed the island and selected a suitable site for a lighthouse, and plans went ahead for its construction. But now, almost a hundred years later, our light has still not materialized. Fully-laden oil tankers now pass "atween da lands" apparently un-aware of the dangers of the notorious shaalds of Foula. Will it take a major disaster before the island gets the light it has waited so long for?

Later that night we listened to the forecast before going to bed. "Wind going southerly but increasing to Storm Force ten and perhaps locally Force eleven (perhaps "locally" can always be translated as "around Foula").

"Hope the boats will be all right," I remarked.

"If it falls in heavy at top flood it'll clean da beach. When's da moon's change?" I looked at the calendar.

My husband made a quick calculation. "Should be top o' da flood at eleven da morn. I'll have to ging doon to check da boats."

As usual first thing next morning I struggled down to the lamb-house to attend to the lambs. It was still an hour or so before top flood (high tide) but the sea was coming in very heavy. A gale from this direction sets up a bad "run" in the Voe, the water alternately being drawn back to leave most of the seabed bare and exposed, then rushing back in a series of walls of churning water. Even while I watched, the run roared in with such force that I cringed as it hurled itself up into each little inlet, tearing at the grass along the edge, driving up over the beach to die away in a line of froth and waar just where the lowest boat lay tied.

I hurried up to the house. "The sea's taking Rob's boat."

My husband arrived down at the beach in time to see the next run catch the little white boat, smacking it round on its side. As the wave ran out again, he dashed down and fastened a rope round the aft stem.

"Look out!" shouted Lizbeth who had come down to see what was happening. "He's coming in heavy again."

He leapt up onto the deck of the old *Arthur*, out of its reach, holding tightly onto the rope as the sea tore at the white boat and swirled up waist deep where he had been standing a minute ago.

"Noo, boy. Tak her up noo, afore da next run."

He dashed down again and dragged the boat up over the grass, right up as far as it could go, next to the Ham Yard dyke.

"Boy, he's floating da flatties (dinghies)!" shouted Harry who was hurrying down to give a helping hand.

The sea picked up the two small blue boats and smacked them together.

"Man, we'll have to get dem a' oot o' yondroo."

They struggled in the lashing wind and rain, battling to save the boats, pulling them all up till they were right up at the Ham yard dyke.

"If da wind had been further up to da sooth-east he would have cleaned da beach."

"Ya, boy, dat he would. Dey'll surely be safe from da sea up here."

"Well so long as he doesna come jiust overly. I mind da folk speaking aboot da time da sea was dat bad he filled da Ham Yard. Nineteen hundred yon was."

During that storm the old *St Giles*, the large steamer which ran from the Scottish mainland to Shetland, was caught in the worst of the weather. Unable to see anything but flying spindrift and with her decks out of sight beneath breaking waves, she ran before the sea, out to the north-west, passing to the east or west of Foula, they knew not which. Half-way to Iceland the weather moderated and she headed back, fortunately arriving off the north end of Unst the most northerly island of Shetland, as she was reaching the end of her coal supplies.

From the beach the men made their way to the head of the slipway, where the mailboat was pulled up, and set about lashing it down to the cradle.

"Da worst sea I can mind was in da winter o' '36, da year afore da Nurse's hoose was biggit (built). Da wood was a' laid up dere at da side o' da road, du kens, where da stead o' auld Robbie's shed is. Well da sea took da lot, every hidmost piece o' it, and put it up upon da beach."

"Boy, dats o'er forty feet high; he'll surely no come yon bad again."

"If he's come once, he'll aye come again."

"Was dat da sam day Uncle Andrew waded in up to his waist gathering in wood by da skurtful (armful)?"

There was a lot more driftwood around then especially during the wars. On one occasion so many pitprops were floating Withoot (at the back of the Biggins dyke) that they were jammed in solid into some of the small geos. The sea was exerting such pressure on them that the men were unable to prise any out and every now and then there was a loud crack as one would spring up on end. Auld Robbie, more foolhardy than the others, was running out over the floating wood and pulling in props from the outer edge where they were more loosely packed.

Sometimes the sea brought more menacing gifts. A wandering mine would be sighted, ominously bobbing about in the breaking foam. The alert would be passed round and the men kept clear of the banks until they heard the tremendous bang as it exploded against the rocks. One large mine "ten foot long and as high as a man's shoulder" was washed up at Wirwick, where it later exploded with such force that the folk of Harrier, a mile inshore, found shattered fragments of its metal embedded in the peat.

While the men were busy trying to secure the boats, up at the house I struggled to keep on a good fire and get the dinner cooked. The wind was sucking the fire up the chimney as fast as I could stoke it up, so there was little heat coming from the top of the stove. Above the roar of the sea and the howl of the wind I could hear the distant drone of a plane circling round over the sea to the south-east of us. The sound faded away until I could no longer pick it up, then back she came again slightly further up to the north. A small fishing boat had been missing off Orkney since late last night. I peered through the window at the white heaving maelstrom. The searching plane circled round again. A cold chill crept up my back. Cold gripped my heart.

12

A Promise of Spring

Du may waander on fir ever
  An seek idder laands dee lane,
Bit some day du'll come driften
  Ta da laand o laands agen.
Shö's a laand whaar Winter's souchin
  Trowe da spöndrift an da squaal,
An da smorin moorie-caavie
  Fills da Nort winds oobin waal.

J. Peterson.

Much of our time in winter is taken up with the mere mechanics of living, especially during the severe storms that sometimes seem determined to tear our island loose. Even a trip to the peat stack to fetch an armful of peats for the fire can become quite a hazardous expedition. I always listen for a lull in the wind, then nip out and round the corner of the porch, where I stand in the lee watching the flans go roaring by, like vicious wild animals— they seem to have an entity of their own. Although only composed of wind, they are sometimes actually visible like a fast-moving heat wave, and can be heard approaching from a considerable distance away. Between the flans I run up to the face of the peat stack, where I crouch trying to find dry peats. Clutching an armful, I scuttle back to the shed, pause, then nip into the shelter of the porch. The next flan catches me out while I am still trying to get the door open, and I am bowled over into the garden fence, my long hair whipping over my face. Picking up the peats again, I flatten against the door as the next flan strikes the north end of the house. In the doorway there is a meagre six inches of lee and I can feel the wind tugging at the point of my nose. To open the door during a heavy flan would be disastrous for the wind would roar down the chimney and out of the door, causing flames to shoot out of the front of the stove, covering everything inside the room with ash, filling it with smoke, knocking pictures off the walls and even causing an untimely end to my precious pot plants by flinging them out the door. At last I get the door safely open and shut again, and stagger inside quite exhausted.

Going to the well to fetch a bucket of water is even more of a problem, and most of the water ends up inside my boots. On the other hand disposing of dirty water becomes simple and there is no need to go as far as the drain since the water is all whipped out of the basin as soon as I step outside. As our house faces the sea, we have a fine view from the window of the whirlwinds careering over the waves carrying funnels of spray a hundred feet into the air, and of the sea over the Shaalds heaving up like some gigantic crested monster, or shooting up plumes of white spray into the sky like a row of Christmas trees.

One might think that with all this rough weather I would be longing for a chance of a boat day, but quite the contrary. I listen to the forecasts with apprehension when the weather looks like moderating—not that we necessarily take what the forecasters say seriously. In fact they seem to have much in common with the man who declared, "Faith, he'll either be a fine day or a day o' gale," though there is more truth in this than one might think, a lull in the wind usually occurring as the wind changes direction to blow again with renewed strength. If the lull lasts long enough the boat may have time to nip across. The prospect of a mailday means I must turn my mind to that heap of bills and letters that I have been busily ignoring since last time the boat went. And how long ago was that. Must be three weeks ago now. Just before New Christmas wasn't it? More serious is the ever-present worry that the weather may deteriorate suddenly after the boat has left and the crew will be stuck out on the mainland for days until the next lull. And always lurking at the back of my mind is the fear that they may be caught half-way across and lost.

Outsiders picture us longing for this link with the "outside world", but I have mixed feelings when I finally receive my box and examine its contents—a few loaves of bread, packets of bacon and jars of marmalade that appear to have had a slight argument on the journey across; a wad of newspapers weeks out of date; another heap of bills which we have just newly paid; a colourful circular advertising beach wear for a continental holiday—special offer closing last week; a Great Lucky Draw coupon—first prize a Rover 2000 and luxury caravan delivered to your doorstep; two cards from a government department saying we must return form AB3 without delay, a form from the same department to be filled up explaining why we have not yet returned form AB3, and, last but not least, Form AB3. Was a mailday worth all the effort and worry it involved?

We never consider ourselves as being cut off or isolated from the outside world—we feel as much part of it as people anywhere else in this country. The very phrase the "outside world" is a misnomer for a stretch of sea, perhaps unfortunately, is not a barrier separating us from everyone else and their problems.

Winter with its long dark nights is the time for visiting friends and sooner or later the urge to have a tune comes over my husband and Eric as they get together for an evening of music, accompanied perhaps by Bobby and Davie. Mandolin, banjo, fiddle and guitar harmonize together in traditional and modern Shetland music, Country and Western, Scottish and Irish, with even an occasional Swedish or Norwegian tune thrown in, the lead is handed from one player to another, instruments are swapped round, new variations are added and improved upon, until my head is singing with a hundred melodies. Or perhaps Harry will be persuaded to take down the fiddle and entranced we will listen to the light delicate touch of the bow dancing over the strings as he plays the intricacies of a hornpipe or the heart tugging sweetness of the old, old tunes that perhaps no one but he still remembers.

Winter is also the time for chasing after dreams. How easy it is to dream; how difficult to turn a dream into reality.

We had a dream that by efficient drainage our boggy land could be made dry and fertile clothed in long, lush grass. And then, perhaps, hay turners, wufflers, buckrakes and even balers, would be possible and I, lying in the sun watching it all, would have nothing to do but smell the flowers. However, it is one thing to draw a few lines on a map and quite another to dig the actual drain. This was the second winter we had been working on it and there was nearly half a mile still to be dug. Of course part of the Brae had been drained before, as had most of the crofts, with numerous parallel ditches, or stanks, cutting up the ground into narrow rigs. The stanks at the Brae were par-

ticularly deep and the folk told us how when Jimmie o' Brae, old
Louisa's father, was takking up da stanks, all they could see of
him was the tip of the spade now and then and a peerie bit of
mud flying through the air.

On the first day of March the first skylark sang, trilling away
in the bright windy sky. The lungwees and welkies had already
returned, floating in big rafts close inshore, twinkling black and
white in the motion of the waves. We always look out for their
arrival; winter's grip never seems so relentless once the birds
are back, no matter how bad the weather might be. The days
were lengthening, now it was light until six o'clock, giving us
more time to work outside. The drain ate its way through the
heart of the bog, where it was too soft for us to stand without a
plank of wood under our feet. Balancing precariously, it was a
question of digging like mad before we sunk out of sight. The
sphagnum moss was five feet deep here. Like a vast porous
orange sponge, it soaked up water while we watched, filling up
the drain again almost as quickly as we could dig it out. It was
depressing to look behind and see the sides of the drain sogging
together again, and the heavy lumps of moss we had dug out
with so much effort drying up into mere smears of fibrous matter. In places there was hard peat full of old heather roots about
three feet down under the moss—evidence of the time when this
had been a dry headland, before indiscriminate peat cutting had
turned it into a bog.

In between the rough winter weather were occasional spells of
bright sunny breezy days, full of the smell of sun shining on the
tussocks of old grass bleached white by the wind, the smell of
mud and roots, and the waar washed up on the beach by the
storms. A brief promise of spring. The white rose put out green
buds, and purple and white crocuses cautiously poked up their
flower shoots. One mild Monday evening, standing at the door
flashing a blinkie to the mailboat, which was returning late,
having waited for the bread to come out from Lerwick, I heard
the drumming of snipe for the first time, a throbbing humming
sound that echoed through the dusk. All winter they had
skulked in the drains and bogs only uttering a single squawk
when disturbed. Now, zigzagging through the sky, drumming to
each other, they brought a memory of soft summer evenings.
But next day winter was back with us again, the wind burnt off

the rose buds and turned the crocuses into a slimy purple mess, and snow lay white on the hilltops.

Towards the end of March there came a spell of unusually calm weather, the wind was still and the sea lay pale duck-egg blue and smooth. We had not realized how accustomed we had become to the wind until now when we stepped out of the door and were met by a strange silence, almost palpable. The white rose bush put out another batch of buds and the crocuses had a second try.

The next day continued fine and Ken and Jock set off for Walls with the mailboat. It was my birthday and Jim and I had a more interesting ploy. During the past week a fair amount of wood had been floating off in Ham Little, drifting first to one side, then the other, but never coming within our reach. But this morning it had collected in a narrow inlet, known as Outer Selapiddle, so as soon as we had seen the boat off and deposited the bairns with my husband's folk we made our way over to Ham Little. The maalies were sprinkled over the cliff faces, on their old nest sites, chattering and laughing to each other. The air echoed with their cries. I shut my eyes and heard the summer.

"Watch out, love! You'll go over there da same as da quaike auld Andrew Henry carried up!"

On that occasion a young cow, or quaike, slid down the cliff at the inner end of Ham Little and Andrew went down to rescue her, climbing up again with the quaike on his shoulders.

Jim uncoiled his "banks rope" and looked around for his lesnin or stake that he had tied the rope to last time he was here. "Here he is!" He fastened the rope end securely to it.

I eyed it doubtfully and glanced down the hundred foot drop below me. "I hope it's strong enough."

He pulled it up and showed it to me then banged it into the ground again with his heel. "We dunna really need da rope but da rock's muck rotten. Go doon first and wait for me. There's a peerie green toog half way doon. Hit's safe enough. I'll steady the rope."

I slithered down, bits of wet clay and rock slipping from under my feet, and found the green ledge in round the corner from the end of the rope. A cascade of small stones announced my husband's arrival.

"It's lovely and warm here in the shelter," I said with appreciation. "Is this where Jimmie o'Brae used to sit doing his sewing?"

"No, I doubt it was doon o'er da banks at Durga Ness opposite da skerry. There's a peerie cuppie (hollow) there Dad said he went there to get clear o' his hooseful o' nagging womenfolk and watch for wood coming with the tide. He was a braa good hand at tailoring, they said. He could turn oot a well-made jacket and there's a lot o' sewing in that."

We climbed down to the bottom using the rope I had been carrying. The wood was floating at the far side, drifting into the mouth of the narrow cave, then washing gently back out again with the rise and fall of the waves.

My husband took out his creepie, as he called the three-pronged hook, and fished for the bits of wood. First came a long plank of twisted plywood.

"Dat might mak a brig for da lambs."

Then he pulled out a long pit prop with ends rounded by the action of the sea as it pounded against the rocks.

"No muckle wort. It's full of claeks (worms)." Then came a small grating. "It's braaly heavy; oak, I doubt."

Next a large fishbox with Norwegian words stamped along its sides. "Off o' a Norski. It'll mak a stock box for twa-tree crabs."

Then a lot of barrel staves—"Enough for ane or twa creel bottoms."

"Here's a piece o' candle fat of o' a Ruiski. It'll do for lighting da fire when da peats is wet."

Next he pulled out a new piece of clift (thin board), yellow and still smelling of trees, and with the owner's name scribbled on it in blue crayon. "AD Peters, I think. Wonder where he bides."

"That might be useful for something sometime," he chucked a long crooked knobbly branch onto the growing pile. After a while there was nothing left floating in the geo except an old rubber ball with a hole in it and a dead tystie (black guillemot). He tied up a bundle of wood and climbed with it up the cliff and out of sight, after first giving me careful instructions to tie on another bundle of wood to the rope when he threw it down again. "And mind and use a clove hitch or a running loop."

I considered the motley collection of wood. Knots were never my strong point. I laid the warped piece of plywood on top of the grating and tied the rope round in a combination of loops that I hoped would co-operate into becoming a clove hitch. Or wasn't it a double clove hitch they called it? I added a few more loops just in case. The plywood wriggled and would not lie still so I poked in the knobbly branch to quieten it. That should do. I gave a pull on the rope just to make sure it was secure. Whoops! The plywood twisted round and poked me in the eye, the grating fell out and nearly amputated my left foot and the knobbly branch scuttled back into the sea.

Perhaps a running loop would be better. I picked up the fishbox, put the candle fat inside it and spent several frustrating moments trying to fit the barrel staves in alongside it.

"What on earth are you taking so long about, pet?" My husband shouted down.

"O.K. I'm just fixing it!" I jammed the barrel staves in with their heads sticking out over one end of the box, wedged an empty two-gallon plastic flask in the opposite end, and tied the rope round the middle of it all.

"O.K. It's ready now!" I shouted up triumphantly.

He pulled on his end of the rope, there was a creaking noise and I was suddenly showered with barrel staves. Then the plastic flask floated down and the candle fat whizzed by my nose. I jumped back just in time to avoid being extinguished by the fish box.

"Women!" I thought I heard a disparaging mutter from up above.

Next attempt, I tied so much rope round the bundle that it looked like a cat's cradle. I hid round the corner out of reach from aerial bombardment and watched its progress nervously. It was pulled up smoothly without mishap until a corner of wood got wedged in under an outcrop of rock.

"Stand clear!" He gave the rope an almighty jerk. The outcrop parted from the cliff, paused for a moment, then crashed down in a rumble of falling rock and a stiooch of dust. I wrinkled my nose at the acrid sharp smell of broken rock, very thankful I had not been standing underneath it.

We got it all up safely eventually, first to the half-way ledge, then up to the top. We carried it over to a sheltered dip and left it there, to be fetched when we needed it.

After going up to the house for something to eat, and collect-

ing the children, my husband went to fetch in the lambs while I
started plucking hay for their feed.

A shout from my husband interrupted me, "One's gone in the
bog!"

"What!" (Child? Horse? Lamb?)

"I think it's one o' White Horny's twins."

"Is it dead?" I asked.

"Well, it thinks it is," he said, laying a soggy bundle on the
ground outside the lamb-house.

The lamb was still alive, but seemed to be nearly unconscious.

"Come on, carry it up to the house and we'll try and get it
warm," I suggested.

Of course since we had been out all day the fire was out, the
Tilley lamp was empty, the paraffin flask had disappeared,
there was no water in the water pail and we could not find the
blinkie. Eventually we sorted things out and put the lamb in a
large cardboard box in front of the fire with two hot-water
bottles. Her legs were stiff with cold, she ground her teeth and
twitched her ears, and the inside of her mouth felt frozen.

"Let's try some brandy," I suggested.

"There isn't any. What aboot whisky?" said my husband pro-
ducing the remnants of his Yule drams.

I mixed some whisky with hot water and sugar and poured it
down her throat. There did not seem to be much reaction so I
gave her a second bigger dose.

"Well, she ought to die happy anyway!"

We sat up with her till late that night and gradually she grew
warmer and became quiet, although she was still not fully
conscious and kept her eyes shut. Hoping for the best we refilled
the hot-water bottles, tucked an old bag round her, and went to
bed. Next morning when I came but, I was greeted by a "baa"
and two bright inquisitive eyes. I unwrapped the bag and helped
her to stand. Immediately she hopped out of the box, skipped
across the floor, chewed speculatively on a toy car and chased
the dogs into the porch.

It was only two days later that young Bobby came to the door
on his way to school.

"Ane o' da horses is trying to foal, just sooth o' da chapel."

We sent the bairns over to the schoolhouse with him, and
went south to see what was happening. The fine weather had

broken and a cold westerly wind was blowing. Ken was waiting beside the mare. It was Primrose, one of the small black ones. We could see that the foal was not going to be born without assistance, so we persuaded her up into the shelter of the chapel.

"Try holding her down while I examine her," I said as she flung herself down on her side.

"No sign of any feet!" I muttered worriedly.

"Well, see if you can find them inside her and pull them out."

I felt around and after a while found what felt like a hoof and with a bit of difficulty got it out.

"A chestnut! But I think it's dead. Its legs are bent up along its sides."

The other leg was more tricky, "I don't think I'll manage. I'm not strong enough to turn it and the leg's awfully stiff."

I was now shivering with cold and the wind seemed to be blowing round both sides of the chapel and meeting where we were trying to shelter. Only my arm, up past the elbow inside the mare, was warm. Ken took a turn at trying and eventually between us we managed to get it turned and out.

"I can't find any head!" I was really worried by this as I did not think we would be able to turn the head if it was also bent back along the foal's side.

I paused for a rest. "No, wait! I'm daft! It's the hind legs—see, here's the knobbly bone."

"Thank goodness," said my husband with relief. "Now he should just pull oot."

"That's what comes of flinging your heels in the air and galloping down the Kame, you silly old lump," I scolded Primrose afterwards.

The smallest foal, Flo, had become rather thin, so each day she was supposed to eat a ration of maize laced with a vitamin supplement advertised as being "very palatable" to horses. Flo of course hated it. At the slightest whiff of it she would wrinkle up her upper lip in utter disgust and snort down her nose as though to say, "You surely don't expect me to eat that!" I did not blame her either as it stank like rancid cod liver oil. She became very adept at sifting out the flakes of maize by blowing into the bucket, licking them up carefully one by one and leaving the hated supplement untouched at the bottom. The lambs always came to see what she was eating, sniffing at her mouth to find out if it was something that tasted good and licking off the crumbs of maize stuck on her nose.

Of course all the other foals loved the supplement and they had to be shut outside whilst Flo was getting hers, otherwise they pinched it all. One night Marsala, who was by far the cleverest of them all, managed to get the lid off the supplement tin and when I came down in the morning there were four very contented horses stinking of rancid oil, and only a few smears left at the bottom of the tin.

They each had their individual personalities. Marsala, being the most intelligent, tended to be the leader, but Morven was the bossiest and also the laziest, although she took good care to see she got the best of whatever was going. Snowdrop was rather reserved and was more timid than the others, rolling her eyes in great alarm at every threatening event, such as a hen flapping its wings or a dog yawning. Blossom was a gentle friendly horse who wandered around in a daydream half the time, whilst Flo was a lively frisky little thing who skipped over drains and leaped off peat banks with great abandon.

On the 29th of March the first bonxie arrived, soaring aloof above the hills surveying his domain. We were glad to see him, bully though he might be. Only a week or two and the lambing would be upon us, with its hectic chaos. Winter was almost over, gone in a flash it seemed. Had I had that nice rest I had longed for during the busy summer? Had I accomplished all those jobs I had abandoned "to be done during the winter"? No, there hadn't been time. But it was too late; we had to go on.

So during the next few weeks we made a final attack on the drain, cutting through peat with ancient tree branches buried in it. It was hard to imagine this boggy headland covered in small trees and bushes as it once must have been. Long ago much of the low ground of Foula was covered in trees—alder, birch and pine, even sycamore and oak—and bits of their branches are sometimes dug up in the peat banks. Tradition has it that the Vikings set fire to the trees when they first invaded the island, in order to get rid of the Picts, and in some places ash has been found deep in the peat, which is said to date from about that time. And they have never grown here since! Changing weather conditions may have something to do with this, as nowadays in spite of many attempts, the only trees growing in

Foula are poor stunted things which only grow as high as their shelter. In the summer the new shoots may grow up above the sheltering dykes, only to be broken and burnt by the winter storms.

But although winter was almost at an end the winter winds would continue to blow until the end of April, and it would be late in May before the grass finally turned green. The strong winds hampered us as we dug the drain, blowing us off balance and sending us scurrying for shelter from fierce showers of sleet. We skirted round a dry raised mound, presuming it to be the burial place of a cow or even a human.

There was a grave in the peat up on the Ham Moors where an Irish sailor, the son of some nobleman, was buried last century. No sooner had his boat departed again than one of the men from a nearby house dug up the body, stripped it of its fine clothes, wrapped it in old meal bags and reburied it. Quite unabashed he later went to church in the suit. The silk shirt was cut up and made into christening gowns for some of the children, two of whom grew up to be dumb, which was thought by some to be a just reward. Bodies recovered from the sea were not usually buried in the churchyard, although the Foula folk did not hold the belief which was widespread elsewhere at that time amongst fishermen, that to save a life from the sea brought terrible bad luck. There was a twelve-year-old boy from Cruglie who fell into the Voe while looking at the boats from the south side, and drowned despite the fact that a Scottish fishing boat was lying at anchor just nearby. The men were too afraid to pull him out, and the islanders never discovered what had happened to him until one of the Scots told about it when he lay dying years after.

April arrived with a snowstorm. One afternoon an ominous wall of blue-black cloud loomed up over the hills and a few minutes later the first snowflakes began to fall—big wet snowflakes whirling through the air on the north-west wind, covering everything in a heavy wet blanket. My husband ran down to the Brae to get the lambs and foals into the lamb-house before conditions became too bad to find them. The foals had gone to shelter down over the grassy edge and were very reluctant to head out into the snow-laden wind. He had to push and coax them up the slippery slope one by one. The lambs were harder to find as they had simply lain down where they were when the snowstorm struck, tail on to the wind, and they were now invisible, covered in a white blanket of snow. As he reached them white tussocks rose up, shook themselves and revealed themselves to be lambs. That night we fell asleep to the sound of the snowy wind fluttering at the window; outside the isle lay white and cold . . . how were our ewes, due to lamb next week, faring now? But during the night the wind went south-west and we woke to a familiar brown world—not a trace of a snowflake—and I was left with the feeling it had only been a dream.

We looked out for the "Borrowing Days", the last three days of March by the old style (10th, 11th and 12th April). The old folk had a saying that the weather during the three months of summer would be the same as that experienced on the three Borrowing Days. Well, this year it rained, snowed and blew!

13

Lambing

If you hear da Mirrie Dancers,
See da horsegok as he's fleein,
Dan you'll see da Voar night comin,
   quietly creepin ower da moss;
Comin trowe da licht an shadow,
   quietly creepin ower da moss.

Vagaland.

Lambing—and we were away to the hills. The lambs have to get their ears marked during the first day or two after birth otherwise they are impossible to catch. So life was very hectic at this time of year and such mundane things as housework tended to be abandoned, as only the most essential work could be fitted in after a hard day spent going to the lambs. But despite this, I loved the lambing time. The long days spent on the hills gave me a sense of freedom especially on a fine sunny day when Spring seemed well and truly here.

One such day at the end of April I set off first thing in the morning up the valley along the burn, where the bright stars of celandine spangled the old bleached grass. I stopped to admire one. Its perfectly formed petals shone like gold. And pulling up a tuft of the dried grass I saw the slender green shoots of the new growth.

As I climbed over the Harrier fence the "poors" came running to meet me and get their share of nuts, old White Seat in the lead, as sprightly as ever in spite of her seventeen years. She gave me a gummy smile as she had long since lost her teeth, a fact which did not hinder her from gobbling up more than her share of nuts.

Leaving Harrier I made my way up through Netherfandel, wandering here and there so as to have a good view of all the innumerable small sheltered dips and hollows where the sheep often lambed. In the blue sky above me the skylarks kept up a continuous chorus, the maalies were chattering up in the stony face of the Bark Hill to my left and on nearly every brow and bump a pair of bonxies surveyed me as I passed, or soared over my head with a "kak kak". They were already taking up their territories on all available land, and scraping out rough hollows for their nests. They displayed to each other, holding their wings stretched above their heads, showing off their white wing bars and uttering a loud "kee-yak kee-yak".

The ewes followed after me baaing and taking a crafty nibble at the nut bag whenever I stopped to look with my binoculars. Crumpled Horny came to show me her twins for the first time since I had marked them the previous week. They skipped and jumped around her but were quick to dart away whenever I made a suspicious move. As I walked up through the Craig a ewe lying sleeping in the sun behind an old bleached tussock rose up and looked at me then turned and sniffed at her feet. It was one I called the Ghost because of her strange pale wrinkled face. Normally very tame, she would not come down to me but kept turning round and sniffing. Obviously she had a new-born lamb beside her, although it was completely out of sight from where I was. When I climbed up to her, I saw the little lamb lying curled up in a tiny grassy hollow. It was still wet and tried to stand up on very shaky legs when I picked it up. The Ghost watched anxiously as I marked its ears, making strange snuffly grunts and licking it all over when I set it down again. It was a pretty little lamb, moorit with white freckles on its nose, four white feet and a white tail. At this age the moorit is surprisingly dark, almost black, and only becomes bleached golden in the sun as the lamb grows older, so the white markings show up very bright.

I followed the sheep track on towards the top of Codlefield. The grazing was poor here. Glancing at the hillside through the eyes of a sheep, I wondered what they found to eat—sparse bleached remnants of coarse grass, scrunchy brittle heather burnt grey by the winter winds and everywhere the ever-present faded sphagnum moss. It was a tawny golden hillside with nowhere a green shoot. Wandering towards the Bloburn burn I found a little white gimmer lamb belonging to Lizbeth and a big black wether lamb belonging to Bessie. In one of the deep hollows by the burn sheltered from the wind and smelling of sun-warmed hill, little Funny Face was standing proudly beside a

real beauty, pure white patterned evenly with big dark moorit
spots—a great big lamb with long well-boned legs and tightly
curled wool.

"You are a peerie beauty!" I exclaimed, reluctantly cutting
the spotted tips of his little ears. "You'll maybe make us a ram!"

I had to make a detour from here across to the tail of Soberlie
to check up on the lamb of a black gimmer of ours who went by
the somewhat contradictory name of White Breek's Mother's
Daughter. They were sheltering beside the old mooldie
coose—a round stone enclosure where the folk used to store
their scraped up peat dust for the kye's winter bedding, instead
of using precious straw which was all needed for fodder. There
are several of them here and there about the island, mainly on
bare stony areas where all the peat has been scraped and removed throughout the years. Earth was also removed and carried onto the rigs to improve the soil. This, mixed with many a
kishieful of sand fetched from the beach, converted the wet acid
peat into a medium on which grass, bere and even potatoes could
flourish. The bare areas are finally growing green again, but in
former times some of the landlords were very disapproving of
the practice—they however did not have to scrape a livelihood
from the reluctant ground.

The lamb was looking very unhappy creeping along with its
tummy tucked up and obviously hungry. WB's M's Daughter
watched me with a wary glint out of the corner of her amber-
coloured eyes so I tried tempting her with nuts but she darted
away suspiciously whenever I made a move. Eventually I scattered several handfuls along one side of the mooldie coose and
hid behind it out of sight. As soon as she was busy gobbling them
up I carefully wriggled round the corner, avoiding the worst of
the sharp rocks, spiky rush stalks, squooshy sheep droppings
and suchlike hazards, shot out my arm and grabbed a very
surprised ewe by the hind leg. As I had suspected she had very
little milk so the lamb would have to be given extra feeding by
bottle. I tucked the little lamb inside my jacket, and using my
much mistreated headscarf as a tether I led the ewe back down
to Harrier. Or should I say, we proceeded by a series of com-
promises—I'm not sure who was leading whom.

I was tired and hot after my struggle, but back up to the top of
Codlefield I had to go. In the little hollow just below the top I

found the original White Breeks herself standing over a lamb, her legs apart, her head down glaring at me fiercely. Oh dear, I thought, the lamb is surely dead, and right enough it was lying stretched out lifeless—a pretty black and white wether lamb. She was making a big fuss over it, nosing it and making encouraging grunts, in fact she had licked it so hard trying to revive it that she had removed all the skin off its poor little tail. She had a big full udder—I could see it gleaming pink between her hind legs—so I decided to give her her Mother's Daughter's lamb instead which would save me a lot of bother. I skinned her lamb with my marking knife and by dangling the limp bit of skin in front of her nose, persuaded her to follow me. I shut her in the old lamb-house and tied the bit of skin over the back of the little hungry lamb. She looked very droll, the skin was much bigger than her and draped around her like a shawl. She looked like an old lady tottering along on her shaky legs with her peeky face sticking out. At first White Breek's regarded her with frank disbelief, then she sniffed at the bit of skin with interested recognition, but butted the lamb over whenever she tried to suck. Finally she surely decided that she had managed to revive her lamb again after all and I left the lamb sucking happily away and wiggling its little tail. I put White Breek's young sister out again and she shot off up the hill again to the mooldie coose where she wandered around baaing forlornly for her lost lamb and making me feel quite guilty.

So up to the top of Codlefield once again. I had a long way to go yet so I hurried along as quickly as I could marking several more lambs on the way. I made a detour round the Fleck Lochs where the bonxies were bathing, rocking back and forth in the water and splashing up a shower of sparkling drops with their wings. The more enthusiastic bathers rolled over onto their backs and lay with their feet stuck up in the air, contemplating their toenails. They were too busy to stop just for me. Across the head of the Craig Burn Black Imy was lying sleeping beside her young lamb, a lovely unusual coloured animal like a young fawn. It twitched its dainty chestnut ears lined with cream and edged with black, but I passed by without disturbing them.

Next I headed south across to the Bark Hill. Here I was in the shelter and I breathed in the warm sunny air with appreciation, rich with the burnt-honey scent of sun shining on the berry heather. I love the isle in Spring as the gold and amber of the hills take on a purple tint and all the little lochs and pools shine deep sapphire blue. Up in the Bruistins there was a faint shimmer of heat haze, tomorrow was Summermill Day—the start of the summer half year. Many of our tame sheep lived up here and as soon as I appeared they came running down from all directions, some even from the top of Tounafield, bounce, bounce, bounce, like brown rubber balls as they ran straight down the very steep slope. Dad, dad, dad, went their front feet as they careered down the steep terracettes of the woodrush tussocks. I must admit it was very good for one's ego. After all, not many people would run all the way straight down a hill merely for the pleasure of a few minutes of one's company. Of course it was only cupboard love really. They jostled round me, nibbling at my jacket and pawing at the air with a front foot in anticipation.

Up in the foot of the Gillings old Rat Tail was still guarding the remains of her lamb which had died several days before. Only four little white feet and a backbone remained. A pair of fat-looking bonxies sat and watched her and every time she turned away from the lamb to snatch a few mouthfuls of grass they made a grab for the lamb's remains and took another peck at it before the ewe turned and chased them away again.

My legs carried me automatically up the steep side of the Sneug. The wind was cold up on the top and I was glad to get into the shelter on the other side and sit down for a rest on the warm scrunchy carpet of woodrush which grew so luxuriously up here. Its leaves were still tawny brown from the winter, amber-coloured when the sun shone on them, but the heart of each rosette was green with new growth. The sheep ate it only when the snow was deep but the kye loved it and would wander away up the hillside to graze it unless a close eye was kept on them. I could see Francie heading up towards the top from Wast O'er so I stretched myself out among the tussocks and relaxed in the warmth of the sun, to wait for her.

I lay on top of the world on a steep golden pinnacle floating far out in the dark blue sea. Perfect in its completeness, its alone-ness, I held my island in the palm of my hand. I held it in my heart.

"Huh! No wonder there's so many unmarked lambs around!" remarked Francie sarcastically, as she eyed my recumbent form, but she settled herself down in the sun beside me.

"Seen anything?" I asked her.

"They're popping out all over the place. I've marked eighteen lambs already. Your old black ewe has had twins."

"What kind?"

"Don't know. Couldn't catch the blighters!"

Now that I was sitting down I realized how tired my legs were.

"Either the lambs can run faster this year, or I'm getting slower," I remarked.

"Huh, too much lying in the sun, more like!" retorted Francie.

I rolled over onto my tummy and idly admired the view. Above Bloburn I could see a small figure with a bright blue jacket and red headscarf, surrounded by a huddle of little brown sheep—Lizbeth going among her tame ewes. Walking up the road which lay like a ribbon far below, were two dark figures— Mima and Ann off to look at the Strem Ness sheep. They turned off the road and disappeared over the top of Crougar.

"Hear the plane's coming in the morn."

"Oh, what with?"

"Some official bods likely."

"No peace in this place!"

"They say there's a couple o' psychology students coming in this summer to study 'the social behaviour in isolated communities'."

"I just hear dee!"

"Social behaviour!" I gave a snort.

We separated again and went off on our different routes. I made a long traverse across the steep face of the Bruistins, grumbling to myself about the sheep which wandered to the tops of the hills in the fine weather when I disturbed a ewe lying alongside a big boulder and chewing the cud with a rapt expression on her face. But as soon as she saw me, she gave an indignant snort and shot off, followed by a little spidery lamb which as far as I could see was unmarked. I set off after them, but the ewe was well in the lead, running flat out, the little lamb's spidery legs working like mad to keep pace. When she had put a reasonable distance between us she settled down into a dignified trot, casting an occasional scornful glance over her shoulders.

"Well," I thought, "I'll get you yet!" and turning my back on her and taking care to ignore her completely, I scrambled straight up the hillface and out of sight over the top of Tounafield. I worked my way along the back of the hill until I reckoned I must be opposite the ewe, then walked out to the edge of the ridge and crouched down beside a large boulder. There on the slope below me, half-way down, were the ewe and lamb now grazing peacefully. Keeping a careful watch on them I scurried down the hillside, trying to keep a slight rising fold in the slope between us. I got to within a hundred yards of them when the ewe looked up and saw me. We both took off at the same time.

I leaped, jumped and ran straight down the steep face, but the lamb, legs going for dear life, sped just tantalizing inches out of reach of the crook of my outstretched stick. I gained an inch and took a hook at the lamb with the stick, but it leapt nimbly over it and fled on down the hill. We reached the bottom of the slope still going flat out. Once we started running up the opposite slope I would soon be outrun. It was now or never. I swiped my stick, missed its neck and it hopped over without stopping. It was getting ahead of me now, first six inches then a foot, then two feet. I made a final gigantic effort and flung my stick at it. A lucky shot! It stumbled off balance and I made a grab for it, but its legs just slipped by my hand. One last effort and I flung my whole self on top of it. There was a moment of confusion but I emerged triumphant holding a wriggling, struggling little lamb.

"Got you, you peerie devil!"

The ewe had followed behind us and was watching my undignified performance with disdain—one of Francie's.

"Heaven help her when you grow up to be a ewe, spidery legs!" I remonstrated with the lamb, as I gasped for breath. It was about a week old and was already turning a more chocolatey brown.

When I had recovered I wandered down the burn looking among the sheep there, to the Loch o' Ourafandal, where the raingeese were wailing their weird cries, and then zigzagged down through the Nort Wilse. There wasn't much happening there, as the sheep there lambed slightly later than the Harrier ones, but I marked one little lamb for Aunty Mary down at the foot of the hill. It was newly born and still wet and slithery, blinking its eyes at the brightness of the world. I was heading for home now, spurred on by thoughts of a good meal and a rest.

Summermill, the 26th April by the new calendar—when the old folk reckoned the summer began. This marked what then was one of the most important events of the year, when the birds began to lay. How the islanders valued this supply of fresh eggs when there was very little else left to eat after the long winter. We always have a spell of bad weather around this time—the Summermill Ree we call it (a ree being a spell of wind and rain). Sometimes we even experience some of the worst weather of the winter at this time—in 1947 and again in 1973 the blizzards were so severe that many sheep were buried in the deep snowdrifts. It is hard to believe in these conditions that it is the beginning of summer. No wonder the nories, the first of the sea-birds to nest, lay their eggs in the warmth and shelter of a burrow.

The sky was already ominous when I set out the next day. A wall of black cloud piled up in the north, towering up into the sky as I watched, hanging there as though about to pounce on us. Up in the Craig whirlwinds were racing down out of the Fleck—little ones only a dozen feet high. One hit me with a sudden "swack", spun me half-way round, then as suddenly left me and twirled on down the hillside picking up the brown rosettes of dead woodrush and swirling them round and round, so that the hill appeared to be inhabited by lots of little brown water spouts. This was a notorious place for whirlwinds. The most spectacular that I have ever seen came sweeping down through the middle of the Fleck after a bad blizzard, spinning across Harrier—gigantic white whirlwinds five hundred feet high and about a hundred feet in diameter. They were so fierce that they were tearing up large lumps of snow off the ground and carrying them high into the air.

I got up as far as the top of the Craig Burn, where I met a solid wall of fierce buffeting wind. I headed into it, taking first one step and then another, but could make little headway and was forced to beat a hasty retreat down into the Craig again. A little later the skies let loose a driving blanket of wet snow. Visibility became almost nil, but I kept going down towards where, my sense of direction told me, Harrier lay. Sheep drifted past me in the whiteness, making for shelter round by the Bloburn burn. Already their backs had a cover of snow.

Coming over a slight rise, I fancied I heard a small bleating sound over to my right. I went over to investigate and found Auld Hoggy standing over a pair of twins newly born and still wet.

"You stupid old ewe, twins at your age!" I scolded her.

Auld Hoggy dropped her ears even more forlornly than usual. Already the lambs were chilled and too weak to stand, so I picked them up and stuffed them both into the front of my jacket. At first all went well and Auld Hoggy followed behind me baaing to her lambs, but then the stupid animal turned and ran back to where they had been born, sniffing the ground as she searched for them. I had to turn and go back to fetch her but again she would only follow me so far and then run back again. Finally I managed to drive her in front of me, running to keep up with her as she disappeared into the blinding snow. The lambs seemed to be getting heavier and heavier, the backs of my legs were soaked with wet snow, the ground was slippery and the wind kept knocking me off balance. But at last a familiar stone dyke loomed up ahead—I had reached the back of Harrier. I was not very sure where exactly I was, but followed the dyke along to my right, driving Auld Hoggy in front of me. She knew exactly where she was and ran along to the gate, where she stopped waiting to be let in. I shut her and the lambs into the old lamb-house where I rubbed them dry with hay and made sure they both had a good fill of milk before I left.

The snow eased for a few minutes as I came over the top of the Lieug and I could make out my husband standing at the house door looking for me with his binoculars. As the cloud lifted for a moment off the hill, I saw a small black figure coming down through Quiverigill—must be Francie away off her normal route. I was thankful I had retreated when I did as the wind kept rising until it became a mad thing.

"I'm going to run down and feed the hens before it gets worse," I told my husband.

"You're not going furt in this," he said flatly, as the house gave a jolt and all the air seemed to be sucked out making our ears pop as the flan swept past us.

I hesitated at the window. Another hard flan hit us and a small flotilla from a pile of fencing posts flew by and were flung like javelins into the edge of the yard. Out of the corner of my eye I saw the wind pick up the empty 45-gallon steel paraffin drum and hurl it over the barbed wire fence. Maybe it wasn't a good idea to go outside, after all!

"Did du hear Peter Manson telling o' a night o' gale when da wind was taking his corn in da yard and he was struggling to fasten it doon wi muckle flat stanes off da dyke. 'Faith,' he said, 'When the wind started to tak da stanes I thought it was time to go to da fire'."

The storm blew all night, slamming into our house time and time again. The draught blowing down the ben chimney was so strong it shifted my husband's shoes right across the room and flapped the linoleum up and down. Even the bed shook as each flan hit us. We lay listening as each crash seemed worse than the one before. Now and then we would peer out of the window to see what was blowing away next. It had moderated slightly by morning but what a scene of destruction met my eyes when I opened the door. The wind had blown down two large gaps in the garden wall, and where, oh where, were all the daffodils? Mangled, torn off at the root or burnt to tatters of brown, even the buds had been snapped off.

The wind was "carrying the Loch". Each flan tearing over the Mill Loch picked up sheets of water and swirled it up to six hundred feet high—a white spout against the dark hill. It was no weather to go outside unless one had to, so I abandoned all hope of going to the lambs.

Next morning the wind went southerly and it started to rain—heavy lashing continual rain. The hill was dark and forbidding and disappeared into nasty grey ragged cloud. The burn was swollen into a miniature river, flooding over some of the hayrigs down in the valley and turning the water in the Voe a peaty brown. Water poured out of our drains in the Brae and fell in creamy waterfalls into the sea. I plodded slowly northwards, my oilskins making walking awkward and tiring, but without them I would have been soaked by now and it was nice to start out dry. Up at Harrier, Auld Hoggy was very pleased to see me again as the water bucket was empty and all the hay eaten. Her twins were sleeping curled up together in the only dry corner of the lamb-house where the rain did not drip through the old roof. It was hard to tell which head belonged to which lamb.

I met the first of the sheep up outside the Harrier dyke. They

were wary of me and ran away when they heard the swish-swish
of my oilskins rubbing together. A little further on I came across
our Black Imy baaing worriedly in a hoarse voice. No sign of her
pretty little lamb! I imitated a lamb crying and watched her as
she ran to the nearest pair of bonxies and put them to flight with
a threatening toss of her head. She chased off several pairs in a
similar manner before she lost interest and stood baaing forlornly again. Following her example I scrutinized all the
bonxies in the area and noticed with some surprise one bird
behaving very oddly. It was waddling round and round a rabbit
hole, then stopping now and again to peer so far down it only its
tail was sticking out. I pushed my hand into the hole as far up as
I could reach and felt lamb's wool. By wriggling my arm in a bit
further I got a grip on it and pulled out the lamb, but it had been
dead for a while.

Further along I found another dead lamb—new born, it had
never survived long enough to stand up—and one poorly which I
stuffed into my jacket to keep it warm. It was very weak and
only just hanging on to life. The rain was seeping in round the
edges of my oilskins and I felt the first cold trickles running
down my back. This is the worst stage of getting soaked, when
the rest of you is still lovely and warm. You never appreciate it
or even notice it until the cold and wet start encroaching, then
you suddenly realize what you will have to surrender. Later on
when you are soaked through and through, your clothes cling to
you clammily, your wet trousers chafe and even your boots are
full of water. Then you no longer care—what's a little more
wet—and you happily wade through the burn knee deep.

Over on the tail of Soberlie I spotted two bonxies sitting
working with something down at the back of the Bloburn dyke,
so I plodded down to investigate. The birds rose up as I approached and sat down on a broo, watching me. It was my dear
little Funny Face. She lay in the middle of a small boggy hole,
all four legs had gone through the surface and her head lay
stretched out in front of her. Instead of her friendly golden eyes
were two red gaping holes from which the blood had run down
the sides of her cheeks and formed two large pools, crimson on
the green sphagnum moss. I stretched out my hand and touched
her—dead but still warm and the blood had not yet congealed.
Angrily I aimed a futile blow at the bonxies with my stick, then

sighed and pushed her under with my boot, at least they wouldn't get any more of her. Where was her lamb? I spent a while searching in holes and down along the burn, but I never did find any trace of it.

The Bruistins lay in thick cloud and the wind was now blowing fiercely in my face as I made my way slowly up the face of the Sneug. I could hear the Fleck sheep passing by in the mist above me, baaing to one another, but I never saw any signs of them. Half-way up I abandoned the attempt and turned back down through the Bruistins. I could hear a lamb wailing somewhere down among the peat hags, and by going towards the sound I eventually found it standing dejectedly sheltering under an overhanging bank all by itself. I recognized it as one of old Crumpled Horny's twins—now where had she gone? There were no sheep around so I "caddied" as loud as I could and a few faint baas echoed back from what must have been the top of Tounafield. I made my way in that direction, leaving the lamb behind as it was too fleet of foot for me to catch, and caddied again. Dark shapes appeared above me, coming down the steep slope out of the mist—old Essy Face, Young Horny, Taggy, the Clown, Graemit Face's Daughter. Suddenly the hillside seemed full of sheep but there was no sign of Crumpled Horny. I could still hear the sound of the lamb crying so I went back to it and drove it down to the Craig, where it joined up with a group of our sheep and lambs. Perhaps they would meet up with its mother again as they moved down looking for shelter.

Back into the Bruistins again, visibility was nil, but my feet automatically took me the right way. I walked over a small patch of wet peat, a dozen rows of footprints marched across it alongside me, evidence that I had come this way many times before although I had little idea as to where exactly I was. Down by Ourafandal, close into the side of the hill, there was a bit of shelter and several of our sheep were grazing there. Two of them had lambed sometime the day before, and the little lambs were creeping close alongside the ewes' tummies sheltering from the rain. One of our young gimmers had not been so sensible and was standing beside a dead lamb.

Further down the burn I found the corpse of old Rat Tail, lying half-submerged in a bog which she had foolishly tried to cross. The birds had already eaten her eyes and tongue and had pulled out long strips of intestine which were tangled up on a tuft of crowberry. So, poor auld ewe, did they get you after all? The wind was whipping up the loch into steep brown waves and carrying cream spume and sand up onto the boggy edge. Another corpse was floating off in the water. A wave lifted up her face and I recognized the twisted horns of old Crumpled Horny. Her lamb would never find her now. I peered back into the mist and rain, fancying I could hear its forlorn baaing. A gust of wind caught me off balance. I slipped and fell into a muddy pool, grazing my knuckles on a stone and tearing the knee of my oilskins. A host of bonxies rose up from the loch and circled round and round my head in the swirling grey mist, calling their harsh "kak kak".

Back home at last, and the comfort of dry clothes and the old stove glowing red with warmth. The sickly lamb was laid in a cardboard box, wrapped up in an old jumper and wedged in with hot-water bottles. A bottle of warm milk and a teaspoon of brandy had done wonders for it. I lay back on the resting-chair munching a bit of bread and cheese and writing up my list of lambs. Bad spells of weather like this are the main reason for the low percentage of lambing among the sheep here—an average of only 75 per cent most years. Lack of enclosed grazing and shortage of feedstuffs after the winter makes it impossible to bring all the sheep down off the hills to lamb in the shelter of the crofts. It is simply not possible to feed several hundred sheep off only 15 or 20 acres of croft, no matter how hard one might work.

I was just beginning to grow really warm again and my hair, hanging in wet rats' tails, was starting to steam, when there was a tap on the window and John Andrew peered in through the raindrops.

"Aggie Jean has a yowe dat canna lamb. Could du come and look at it? She's braaly poorly."

And that's the lambing. Days that you could dance with the sheer delight of living. Days you could sit down in the rain and cry.

14

Voar

Da ask is tik at da back o Vaila,
As da cowld sweet breath o da sooth wind blaas,
Whar da rigs is lyin, gold an shaila,
An da peat-reek driften by ower Waas.
Whin da green paek comes, and you hear da Kilya
Among da fleein cloods o maas.

Vagaland.

One evening in late April, as the clouds were turned pink and gold by the setting sun, my husband came into the house all smiles.

"Come furt (outside) and listen!"

He pulled me out to the door. There, wheeling and swooping in the sky above us, two swift dark birds uttered their haunting yearning triumphant cry "Eee-an, eee-an eee-an". My heart leapt inside me, seemed to soar up into the very sky and cry with them. The allens were back.

The days lengthened, suddenly the evenings lightened, taking us by surprise. The summer dim was here again with its soft translucent northern light, bringing vague yearnings for the summer nights when we were young and wandered hand in hand over the isle with only the call of the allens and the distant drumming of snipe echoing through the peace.

By the time of the lambing our old lambs from the previous year graduated to setnins (one-year-old ewes) and after the Summermill Ree was by, we put them out to fend for themselves and to give the grass a chance to grow for summer hay. I missed them for the toon seemed empty without their cheeky faces. But the gap was soon filled by several "problem children". There was Whitie with her funny pink turned-up nose and little bandy legs—her mother did not have enough milk to feed her without the extra help of a bottle—and the Menace, an unsuccessful adoption case who much preferred to stand and suck my bike. In spite of having such an unorthodox mother, he grew into a fine fat lamb and was sent out to the marts in the autumn.

Most endearing of all though was Midget—unique of all lambs—who was so tiny she could stand on my hand. When I found her she was lying in a puddle stiff and cold—I thought she was dead but carried her up to the house to show my husband as I had never seen such a small lamb before. It was only when she made a slight wheezing sound that I realized she was still alive. Poor little scrap! I laid her in front of the fire to die in warmth and peace. Imagine my surprise when I came back in again after attending to the other lambs, and she lifted up her head and gave a most decisive maa. From then on she never looked back. Her legs were so tiny—no bigger than one of my fingers—and she was not able to walk over the rough ground but spent her days lying in the shelter of a big stone. Every now and then her mother would come and feed her, half squatting down so that the Midget could reach up to her udder. Being premature, she had a big bulgy forehead and a tiny little nose, and her legs grew alarmingly bandy as they tried to hold up her body—never had we seen such an ugly little mite. It was several weeks before she grew any teeth and then she found the grass so tough that she often lost her balance trying to bite it off. She became very tame and loved to curl up on the palm of my hand and go to sleep in the warmth. Eventually she was to grow into a ewe, but remained small all her life although she had normal sized lambs.

As well as coping with the lambing we had to get on with our voar (spring) work in any spare time we could find. Hence evening would find us bent over our spades digging our tattie rig. We both used the Shetland spade, a light sharp-bladed implement with a long wooden handle and a wooden step just above the blade. We used our thigh as a pivot for the handle and worked side by side turning over a long clod of earth each time. In the old days as many as eight people would dell together, turning over a whole row with each spadeful, then taking a step back and turning over the next row. The men always took the outside edge of the rig where the ground was tougher. They liked to dig the furs (furrows) with a "full belly"—a curve which was supposed to bring fertility. Then-a-days every possible scrap of arable land was delled because they had to provide as much of their own meal as possible. Such was the scarcity of good land that one of the Ristie men took to cultivating a rig of tatties on top of the Stack o' da Gaads—a good mile's walk from his house and reached by a narrow track from the cliff edge which has since fallen away. When I look at the many small rigs patterning the slope around me, I always feel grateful that I live now and do not have to dig all of them too.

How rapidly the rigs deteriorate when they are no longer cultivated. In the drier areas Yorkshire fog and buttercups soon take over and the wet rigs grow only floss and moss. Ten years later one looks at the land and wonders how it ever grew anything. This same land the old folk once painstakingly carried in on their backs in kishies, particularly from the areas along the coast where the peat soil was mixed with boulder clay and fertilized with sea-bird's droppings. This practice produced the large scalped areas around the outside dykes particularly noticeable at the Hametoon where they stretch up to the tail of Hamnafield and far up the side of the Noup. Sand and seaweed were also carried in from the beach—for some islanders a walk of a couple of miles—in order to reduce acidity and lighten the soil. All the muck from the byre and lamb-house was also put on each spring and most houses had a special fish midden made from fish offal which made a particularly rich fertilizer.

When the rents were fixed by the Crofters Act last century my husband's great grandfather, Muckle Johnie o' the Biggins, wanted to know why his rent was fixed higher than any other, and was told it was because it was the best bere-growing toon on the island.

"Aye," he said, "I carried the toon in upon my back."

As we dug we "shapped up" the lumps with a quick chopping movement of our spades—a job I hated. We were unable to use the plough on our land as the ground was very wet and soft at the foot of the rigs; in fact there was a spring in the lower corner of the bottom rig.

I used the spade to plant the potatoes too, digging the holes with it in one hand and dropping in the tatties with the other. Consigning each to its fate, I sometimes wondered if any of them would ever come up again.

Most of the houses in Foula still have their rig of tatties, but very little grain is grown now apart from a little corn as fodder for the handful of kye. In the old days a big earthenware jar, holding perhaps 50 lbs of salted butter, was built in the middle of the seed skrew in the hairst to ensure that it would not be touched until the voar, when it would be a very welcome addition to their meagre diet, and give them the strength to carry out all the voar work. When my husband's folk kept more cows, the corn kept us all busy for many days as we wheeled countless barrows of muck from the midden to the rigs, which became patterned with small dark heaps. Then the muck had to be shapped (chopped) up fine and spread evenly over the ground with a shuill (spreader). The men would plough with the small two-wheeled tractor, the Trusty—a back-breaking job as it was awkward to work with and had to be held up all the time by the handles otherwise it dug down till it bogged in. We womenfolk would follow behind shapping up the lumps and turning over the furrows that hadn't turned right over. Sometimes the corn was ploughed in, my father-in-law going ahead scattering the seed in front of him out of a bucket, but more often we harrowed it in afterwards with small wooden harrows that we pulled ourselves with a rope yoked round our shoulders. For oats they harrowed four double drachts, for bere eight double drachts, harrowed until a rivlin didn't leave a mark, for fine-packed earth made strong stiff straw. The others loathed this job but I always enjoyed it, walking back and forth across the rig seeing the earth turn fine and smooth as I worked, smelling the good voar smell of muck and new-turned earth and watching the swallows skimming over the burn, and its golden blok flowers (marsh marigold).

Every day brought a change as the year leapt forwards into summer. The tirricks came back to their stony breeding ground out from the Hametoon dyke. Here they hovered and swooped in an excited mêlée, filling the air with their cries, lovely dainty white birds. Rob took to wearing a beret in self-defence as they started to defend their territories. Although small and fragile looking, they are quite capable of drawing blood.

The blue maalie tried to nest on top of the unused end of the last dess, but try as he would he could not get the polythene sheet arranged to his mind, and a few days later I saw him and his mate on the garden dyke. He stretched out his neck and peered over the edge down at a large clump of my best narcissi.

"Ah, hah hah hah!" he said with enthusiasm and turned to his mate to tell her of his bright idea. She appeared to be struck dumb by his brilliance and sat waving her head around, mouth agape, unable to get a word out. I jumped up, grabbed the broom and chased them away. The blue maalie got such a surprise he fell off the dyke and into the garden, where he flopped and flapped round and round the daffodils, until at last I managed to catch a hold of him and fling him out again. He flew off in a huff and went back to an unsatisfactory liaison with the dess.

When the lambing was finally over I had time to turn my attention to the neglected garden. Every house has its garden here—well, we call them gardens, though some people might not recognize these little battered wind-blown patches as such. Many a happy hour we spent browsing through the flower catalogues, gazing with wonder at the cherry trees smothered with blossom, the myriads of rose bushes with their perfectly formed blooms, dahlias the size of dinner plates and stately lilies six feet high. In a dream we saw our gardens transformed into a flowery paradise, and feverishly started writing out lists. I came down to earth with a bump when I added up the cost of my first list—well perhaps cherry trees were a bit optimistic and did I really like flowers the size of plates?

Perhaps I could allow myself just one lily—what did it say?— "Well drained soil in a sunny position". The trouble was, there never seemed to be any plants that preferred a windswept, well-salted bog. When the much pondered-over plants finally arrived with the mail I rushed to unpack them. Half of them, alas, had been transformed into a nasty slimy mess. After all what self-respecting plant could stand up to being shut up in a parcel for so long? The others were transferred at once to the garden where they were fussed over and cosseted, and their symptoms discussed with anyone who happened to be passing. What a lot of pleasure my little garden gave me, especially at this time of year when the isle was still brown and eaten bare by the sheep. Inside the shelter of the wall the bluebells were flowering, the poor battered bushes were covered with green shoots and in the most sheltered corner an occasional tulip bloomed intermittently between gales.

Down on the beach, boats had been shifted out of their winter noosts, and the men were busy scrubbing them out and painting them bright red, kingfisher blue or snowy white, perhaps with contrasting gunwales of black, yellow or brown, each man choosing his favourite colour scheme. Children and dogs could be identified by their various dabs of paint. Engines were pulled to pieces, black oily bits scattered all over the floor while the magneto baked in the oven. I kept stumbling over lobster creels in various stages of repair, as my husband occupied any odd spare minutes by weaving up a hole with bright orange courlene or fitting a new wooden bar. There was a pervasive smell of paint, engine grease, wood shavings, melted courlene and singed fingers.

Along the burn the first marsh marigolds were flowering, "blok" we call them—an ugly name for such a beautiful flower. Soon the burn and stanks would be lined with golden clumps, and the wetter rigs would be patterned with them. My husband searched the banks around Ham Little and one day came home triumphantly with a spray of his favourite flower, the little blue spring squill. I sniffed its fragrant scent appreciatively—what memories of past summers it brought back. Each day on my way to the lamb-house to feed the hens I glanced at the bare brown rigs until at last I saw the first pale green fragile shoots—the corn had breered (sprouted). Then the first sprouts of the potatoes poked their way up through the earth—dark purple with the young leaves all curled up. They were harder to spot but after a week or so each row became clearly discernible.

As expected at this time of year, we heard rumours that the County Council really intended to fix the roads during the summer. The south road had been badly cut up by the frost and the braes were rapidly turning into loose scree, while the north road had deteriorated into a string of pot-holes joined by patches of mud, and cars progressed along it in a series of skids and lurches. Still we are quite fond of our road really. It provides a green peck (early bite) for the ewes in the spring, dust baths for the peerie birds in the summer, mud for the bairns to squelch between their toes, and thrills and spills on a bike for any youngster at a loose end. But by the end of the winter when the only way to get a tractor past the worst stretch is to go off the road and drive over the moorland, we feel inclined to take the officials responsible for a run north along the road. That should at least shake up their ideas.

In the old days there were only footpaths or gaets. The main one which can still be seen running along the foot of the hill was used by the folk going to the chapel, twice every Sunday. Sunday, their only day off, provided an opportunity for visiting friends and relatives, and there was a constant coming and going along the gaet all day. The present road, which seems to prefer the steepest braes to a more level route, was a 'mealy road'—that is, it was constructed by the islanders themselves in return for wages of meal, and barrels of salt herring or beef, one shared between every four houses.

The year 1887 had been a very bad one. The crops had failed and the fishing had been poor. As a result the islanders were faced with starvation. The ministers here at the time, Jim's grandfather, and a Rev. Robertson of the Congregational Church, wrote to various businessmen for help. Mr Scott who was the landlord at the time, was approached by his friends down south and asked what he was going to do about it. His annual income from the island at this time was substantial, but he refused to help. There were plenty of limpets along the shore, he replied, only the islanders were too lazy to gather them. However the businessmen, including some in Lerwick, responded, and a supply of food was sent to the island and placed in the care of the ministers.

Since a road was badly needed on the island, it was decided that the islanders should work for their supplies and a surveyor, Mr Dryburgh, planned a route which was both level and dry. However Robertson, a somewhat overbearing individual, had other ideas, and insisted the road should go straight up over the Height of Hamnabreck, for he declared the stimulating view from the top would be an inspiration to the men coming home after being off at the fishing. No doubt it did have a profound effect on the men as they trudged up the steep unnecessary brae on a wet night with a heavy buiddy full of fish on their backs, if not quite the kind of inspiration he had hoped for!

In May, our tame wheatear came back. His territory included our house, and often when the door was left open he flew in to see if the dogs had left any crumbs of dinner for him. He was an aggressive little bird and would bob up and down on the garden wall, chattering defiance at Auld Pussy who was sleeping curled up among the bluebells. However she was too full to pay any attention, for now that the young rabbits had left the burrow she was dining well. Some years ago there was a breed of extremely

fierce cats, known locally as Ruissi cats, which lived in the hills
and cliffs and were quick to attack if disturbed. The last one was
killed by a Hametoon man who cornered it in Mucklebruik and
shot it with his muzzle loader. However, the cat sprang at him
and attacked him viciously and he smashed the stock of his gun
before he finally managed to beat it to death. That was before
my minding, but as bairns we were warned not to play near the
banks "else da Ruissi cats will get dee!"

May was the month for cutting the peats. The bairns and I
tidied up last year's roogs (heaps) and gathered up the peats
scattered by the wind, while my husband ripped the bank—that
is he marked the edge of the next strip of turf to be removed.
With a ripper, a long sharp blade set at right angles to a wooden
handle, he made a continuous cut about two feet in from the old
face of the bank. Then he flayed the bank, cutting off the turf in
fells with a spade. These fells have to be arranged along the
bottom or greff of the peat bank so that the ground where the
peat is being removed will be kept green. This is one of the
regulations of the common grazings that applies generally over
Shetland.

My husband cut our East Lieug bank first. I loved to lie in the
sun and watch him at work. The slap, slap, slap of wet peats
being flung out had a soporific effect on me. The sun was hot, the
hills reared up steep and sheer and somehow insubstantial
when seen through the shimmer of heat haze, as though they
were cut out of cardboard and set up on edge as a backdrop for
some play. The wind caressed my face and whispered through
the heather bringing scents of moor and sea while the cries of
the allens lingered in my ears. The bank was at the edge of one of
their few remaining colonies and the usual pair was again
nesting at the inner end of our peat bank. After a few prelimi-
nary swoops at the dogs they decided to accept us and perched on
top of one of the peat roogs nearby to watch our goings on. They
were very dapper little birds—I watched them out of the corner
of my eye. One was a dark phase bird, that is dark brown all
over, whereas the other was a light phase with a creamy white
belly and collar and a neat little dark cap on the crown of his
head. Every now and then one or other of them would fly off to
chivy away an invading bonxie, swooping and darting at the
much bigger bird who flew steadily on ignoring it. But the

allens' fierce cries would alert the neighbouring pairs and they all joined in, attacking the bonxie so relentlessly he was forced to retreat, leaving the allens hanging in a spiralling group, wings curved down, breasts puffed out, beaks agape, crying a chorus of triumph.

Watching my husband casting, it looked very smooth and effortless but soon his shirt was dark with sweat. Standing on the top of the bank, he cut out each peat vertically with his tuskar, a long-handled implement with a sharp cutting blade. Deftly he picked up each peat on the tuskar balancing it just exactly so, and then flung it out to lie flat and unbroken on the back of the bank. Peats from the top layer of moor are known as the outlay and these he flung up to fifteen feet away from the edge of the bank. The peat from the outside of the bank, the skiumpak, he threw down into the greff. After he had finished the outlay he would cast out a second deeper layer or moor, the peats from which he would arrange in a dyke along the top of the bank, with each peat arranged at right angles to the bank, one on top of the other like a carefully built brick wall. Between each peat he left a small gap for the wind to blow through and dry them. When wet they were about nine inches wide and two-and-a-half feet long, but they would shrink considerably as they dried. Idly I glanced at my watch as my husband cast, he was cutting fifteen peats a minute. Harry was the record holder, at a steady seventeen peats to the minute—a thousand peats an hour, or eight and a half tons weight of wet peat—surely a world record!

There is a plentiful supply of peat on the island, some of it as much as fifteen feet deep, although there is very little at the south end. The folk of the Hametoon have to fetch their peats from quite far away—some even had banks at the west end of the Daal and high up on the side of the Noup. Houses with only elderly folk or with no menfolk arrange for casters, when all the able-bodied men come for a day to cast a year's supply of peats free of charge.

So spring hurried by, everyone busy working from dawn till dusk at all the innumerable jobs. One longed-for evening, late in May, we saw the sun shining for the first time from the north side of the hills, the low clear golden light picking up the green of the valley, illuminating it. Such a green—a green to make one's heart ache with the vividness of it. Green! At last the isle was green again!

15

Foals and Fowls

White breest and blue wings
An feet at's tarry black!
Skeetchin i da warm loch
An laavin roond da stack!
Kittiwake! Kittiwake!
Du's aye welcome back!

George PS Peterson.

The first foals were not due until mid May, but Jacob had evidently thought otherwise, as by April it was obvious that Sally, the big brown mare with the white star, was going to have an early foal. She foaled a week later, early on a fine sunny morning. My husband was very pleased when he came back home from Harrier and announced, "It's a filly!"

I stuck my head out of the bedclothes for long enough to ask sleepily "What colour?"

"Black, with a big white star," he replied enthusiastically sitting down on the edge of the bed. "She's a real beauty and fine boned—du should see her legs. She's going to have a peerie head too. What'll we call her?"

"Huh! Come to bed and shut up, can't you," I grumbled, burrowing further into the blankets.

"Bed! It's a beautiful morning! Da sun is rising o'er da sea, it's aa glitter and da hills are gold, and du should just see da colour o' da moss in dis light, green just like velvet. Bed! I'm going furt to flay da Gossameadow bank."

"What?" I sat up and looked at the clock. Half past five. "You must be mad," I declared and subsided under the bedclothes again.

I spent the day up at Harrier scattering bucketfuls of nitrogen on the reseeded grass. It was so warm I discarded first my jacket and then my jumper, and soon became smothered in grey dust. The gritty granules consistently worked their way up under my finger nails and my nose was full of the acrid salty smell. The

sun seemed to shine with increased intensity, reflecting off the
brilliant white bank of cloud lying to the north of the isle. But
the fine weather did not last long. By the time I arrived home the
first big snowflakes were whirling down to melt as they touched
the still warm earth. Only a passing shower, we kept thinking,
looking to the north for signs of it clearing; but by evening it had
developed into a blizzard of unusual severity. As we watched the
drifts gathering around the house we worried about the little
new-born foal and our young setnins (one-year-old lambs) we
had blithely put up to Harrier a few weeks ago, when we believed winter was over. So we left the children with our nearest
neighbours and headed north with the tractor, ploughing
through the drifts sending up a wall of flying snow on each side.
Almost blinded by the snow, my husband could only hope for the
best as he picked a route through the drifts, for the road was by
now obliterated. Nothing could be seen in the circle of light from
the headlamps but driving snowflakes and an occasional be-
wildered bonxie rising up out of the whiteness.

We left the tractor at the Harrier gate, leaving the engine
running and the lights on, but by the time we had struggled fifty
yards we could no longer pick out the lights in the drifting snow
and could only navigate by the sound of the engine. As we waded
waist deep through banks of loose fluffy snow, I fell into a hidden
drain and broke my blinkie. Snow and fragments of glass were
packed hard round the bulb so it only gave a dull red glow. As I
struggled to my feet, my husband stumbled knocking the end off
his blinkie and pitching the batteries into the snow, and we
groped around in the dark trying to find them again for several
anxious minutes before we felt their reassuring hard smooth
shapes. A flash of the blinkie picked up the gleam of five pairs of
big green luminescent eyes sheltering up at the North Harrier
dyke—we had found the young fillies. The sheep were sheltering in the old yard and came pouring out when we disturbed
them and stood huddled in a close-packed flock in the shelter of
the corner dyke. But there was no sign of Sally and her foal, and
by this time I was resigning myself to the idea of Sally standing
beside a dead foal smothered in a deep drift somewhere.

Finally we caught a glimpse of her running round the back of
the old byre, the foal running close at her side. She ploughed
straight through the drifts most impressively. The combination

Flossie and Marcie with the author's husband.

Meeting the sheep . . .

. . . and feeding the foals.

A plane-load of ponies.

Loading a pony onto the mailboat.

A peat bank.

The islanders learn to
cut peat at an early age.

The hay harvest.

 A hay rack.

Digging out a
sheep

Snow has its
pleasures too.

Opposite: The
beach under snow.

A bonxie displaying.

Nories (puffins).

of snow, blinkies and oilskins however was too much for her and she refused to come near, but eventually we caught the foal in a deep drift. My husband carried her in his arms into the old byre and Sally followed grunting her disapproval. We kept them inside for several days until the worst of the snow had melted. Drift, as we called the baby foal, became very tame—she enjoyed having her chin scratched and would stretch out her neck and twitch her lips in appreciation. Sometimes she returned the compliment and gently snuffled in our ears or nibbled our hair. Like all our young foals she had a very engaging chubby face with big soft eyes and an extraordinary mouthful of long very soft bristles, so she looked as though she had been chewing a moulting floor brush. Although she would be black when she grew up, at the moment she was a lovely silver colour, grading from steel grey along her backbone to almost white on her legs and face.

During the first week of May we took in the rest of the mares. We were told it was easy to calculate when the mares should foal from the date they foaled the year before, but unfortunately nobody had enlightened our mares. We found it more reliable to check their udders each day instead, as they usually got their milk the night before foaling. They soon became used to this routine and would patiently munch a handful of nuts while I placed a cold clammy hand on their tummies. Of course this involved going up to Harrier every evening, but it was so lovely and peaceful up there with the sun shining from the north, low over the top of Soberlie, a soft green light and no sound but the kak of the bonxies and the plaintive cry of the allens and the quiet gurgle of the burn. No one in sight anywhere and the houses standing empty and at peace, the Wilse only an old ruin, and the sheep grazing in the old yards. The setting sun cast a golden glow over the hilltops, Hamnafield, the Sneug, the Kame where they rose up, serene and far away. I had forgotten how calm and smiling the isle could be, how kind.

When the next mare, Flossie, was due to foal I fetched her down to the house, where we could keep an eye on her. When the alarm went off very early next morning I crawled out of bed, struggled into my duffle coat and went out. The sun was already up and the isle was so bright and vividly green, every detail standing out sharp and clear in the low light. The dew still lay heavy on the grass and a flock of maas (gulls) had settled on the rigs down at the Brae which were smothered in yellow blok (marsh marigold) flowers.

At first I could not see any signs of Flossie and I walked out to the far fence before I found her lying flat out on her side. Now nothing looks so alarmingly dead as a horse sleeping on its side, and the effect was heightened by a horrible hoodie crow which was sitting on top of her bulging belly apparently sharpening its beak on her hide. It flew away when I got near, but Flossie still lay motionless. Only when I came right up to her and poked my toe in her immense tummy did she open one eye, give a large yawn and sleepily grumble as to what all the fuss was about. The crows often perched on the horses when we had them down around the house during foaling and I sometimes wondered if they had second sight and were hoping for a tasty titbit when the foal was born, but perhaps they just had cold feet and found them to be a cosy perch.

Flossie's foal was born the following night. The first we knew about it was a strange bumping noise coming from the back of the house. Going outside, I found a little dark foal bumbling around trying to find something to suck on the house wall. It had obviously decided that this big dark lump was a "super-mum", far better than its own. Flossie, as usual, was paying not the slightest attention to it and was up at the clothes line, scratching her bottom on the post. I put my arms around the foal and examined it.

"Another colt—Flossie, you are hopeless! When are you going to have a filly?" I asked her, but she was too busy looking for nuts in my pocket to answer.

"I'll call you Dunter," I said. Dunter flicked his little bushy tail in agreement, tried to stand up and fell forwards on his nose, long lanky legs in a tangle.

We had several more new foals that week and for a while life seemed to consist solely of shifting horses around as we tried to make the little bit of limited grazing stretch to cover all eventualities. This shortage of controlled grazing causes us unending problems, and sometimes life seems like a giant jigsaw puzzle in which we must fit too many pieces into too small a space. The crofts are the only bits of enclosed land as the hill grazing is unregulated scattald, i.e. it is common grazing on which all the islanders can graze any number of livestock that they might wish. This is not such a chaotic system as it sounds, as in reality the numbers will depend on the amount of winter feeding that can be made, which is severely limited by the small amount of arable ground available. As winter feeding is also limited according to the labour available it tends to mean that the younger islanders with families are increasing their flocks as their experience increases and the older ones are cutting down their flocks as they become less able, so the system balances itself very well and the total amount of livestock kept remains more or less constant from year to year.

By now we had had another six foals, all black, which was rather disappointing. We enjoyed watching them when they started to play at only a few days old. One would have thought they were attached to their mothers by a short tether as they raced round and round them, first one way then the other, but always keeping the same distance away. To begin with they were rather clumsy, but soon they learnt to arch their necks and frisk their tails so that they looked like little circus horses on a merry-go-round. Round and round and round they would canter with effortless stride. As they grew older, their "apron strings" lengthened, and they began to play with each other, chasing one another in a wild game of tag, or rearing up on their hind legs in a mock battle. They made the most amusing noises, as though their voices were in the middle of breaking, a funny high-pitched squeak interspersed with extraordinary deep gruff grunts.

Our hopes were now pinned on Carina and Clare, the last two due to foal—two chestnut fillies perhaps? Carina's tummy was growing enormous. She was a ridiculous-looking horse altogether as she had an enormous mane that completely hid her head and almost trailed on the ground. I measured it one day and found it was twenty-eight inches long, and she herself was only thirty-two inches high at the shoulder. She was a patient, kindly horse and a great favourite with the children being bright piebald. Every day Kevin would ask her solicitously, "Is your baby coming out today?", while Penny would lift up her tail just to make sure it wasn't. After we put out all the other mares to the hill, we took her and Clare down around the house where they soon made themselves at home. Any washing hanging on the clothes lines was liable to be sampled, and if the porch door was left open a banging and clumping would soon announce that Carina was at the pot plants again, or that Clare was drinking out of the water pail.

My husband had taken up his little flat-bottomed dinghy to the house to repair and upturned it at the gable of the house. One day while I was tidying up the bedroom he came into the house and asked, "Any old fibreglass material I could get?"

"I can't think of any," I replied after a moment's thought.

"Ah!—just the thing," his face lit up as he caught sight of some fancy curtain material, and he marched off with it. Very snazzy the repaired boat looked with a patch of yellow roses on its bottom. After this he tarred the bottom with archangel tar and left it overnight to dry. In the morning when I passed it on my way to the well I was astonished by its transformation—it was covered with long black and white hairs. Evidently Carina had found it a most satisfactory back scratcher.

"That darned horse!" my husband said, shaking his head in disgust.

"Never mind," I consoled him. "You've got the only hairy flowered boat in the world!"

Carina eventually foaled in the middle of June, a fine bright chestnut foal. At least she had got the colour right, even if it was another colt. He was the image of his father and was soon up on his feet and prancing around, rather wobbly in the sunshine.

Clare showed no signs of foaling. Obviously we were in for a long wait—but perhaps she was saving up for a chestnut filly this time!

One summer morning a large cruise ship anchored off the Voe. The bairns were all agog, so after a hurried breakfast we all set off down the road for the pier. We met the first batch of passengers coming *en masse* up the road past Ham, a brightly coloured army advancing on us. We summoned up smiles on our faces, kept a firm hold on the children and scuttled past, trying to quell such comments as:–

"Look, yon wife's got a bloodin' mooth!"

"Yon's no blood, boy. Yon's dat sticky stuff she's painted on," corrected the eldest scornfully.

"What does she do yon for?"

"I dunno ken."

"Look, yon wife's got purple hair!"

"Yon's no a wife, it's a man!" retorted the eldest in a carrying voice.

"Fu does du ken?"

"A wife couldna be yon ugly!"

The youngest settled the argument by announcing loudly, "I don't like all these horrid people."

Several cameras were clicking as some of the passengers took photos of us "natives"—they seemed rather nonplussed when my husband turned round, pulled out his camera and took a photo of them.

With the long fine days other visitors arrived. Our mainland VIPs took advantage of the new outcrop of small island airstrips to go island hopping and who could blame them when the isles lay invitingly golden out in the calm pale blue sea. We left off in the middle of the jobs we were struggling with to stand for half an hour at the airstrip listening to the head of this, that and the next Board, Commission and Department churning out their prepared platitudes . . .

". . . all within our power to aid the remoter regions,"

". . . amalgamation into more economic units,"

". . . growing importance of tourism,"

". . . chalets,"

". . . souvenirs."

We murmured the native grunts that were expected of us in the appropriate places, one eye on the weather tide already turning south by, the other on that wall of black cumulus building up out to the west. So with a parting ". . . can't of course guarantee anything . . . and it all depends on . . ." they went on to the next island on the list while we went back to our work.

We are no longer ourselves. As summer lengthens we must share our island with an assortment of many differing visitors, some who have come a long way, from France, Germany, Holland or America. There are photographers crouching in hides, geologists chipping off bits of rock, botanists on hands and knees peering among the grass, zoologists enthusiastically following behind the horses scooping up fresh droppings for worm counts, agriculturalists raising an eyebrow at our ramshackle fences and that inevitable gate stengled up wi da bruks o yon auld bedstead, twatree loops o rustit torny wire and a gadderie o coir.

Some of them become our friends and we pick their brains on many a subject, discuss our island with them till the small hours of the morning while they help at our crüs till they are ready to drop.

Perhaps a few summer visitors do no harm to an isolated island like this as they bring in new ideas and interests and get to know the island and its ways. Only when the numbers become too great to be absorbed and they become anonymous tourists do the islanders feel outnumbered and swamped. In a small island with a limited population the number that can be happily absorbed is small—a fact not often realized by the officials who advocate tourism for such places. There are some islands that are completely tourist orientated, and no doubt the original islanders have either adapted or left, but we feel it is important that there should still be some parts of this materialistic country which are not interested solely in making money from everyone who passes their way.

Foula being "the island of birds", many of the visitors are bird watchers who have come to see the largest colony of bonxies in the Northern Hemisphere. They are often surprised by the islanders' knowledge of birds and their ability to identify migrants, for we are unusually interested in birds and derive much enjoyment just watching them and their antics. One might be surprised therefore that sometimes the bird watchers and the islanders don't always quite see eye to eye. Suffice to say that an islander is very possessive of his island and his birds, having managed them and derived a fair part of his livelihood from them ever since man first set foot here. He does not always take kindly to the outside world imposing its own ideas of the most suitable rules and regulations of bird conservation on him. What the bird fanatics are liable to forget is that as long as the birds were used for food the islanders had to be concerned for their conservation, otherwise they would go hungry. But there was another reason, more important than the economic one— simply that they were fond of their birds and we always will be in a way that outsiders often find hard to understand.

As a further encouragement to sound conservation, some of the cliffs were divided up, the parts being assigned to the various crofts and an islander knew that if he over harvested his own area he would not be able to get more from another. His area was not necessarily the part of the cliffs nearest his croft. For example, Gutrun, at the South End, had a share of the toogs of the Nort Bank, and Mogle had a share on the North Face of Nebbifield.

The period after Summermill Day (26th April) was divided into weeks and various events were related to them. For example the bonxies began laying in earnest on the second day of the third week, whereas the lungwees didn't lay until the fifth and sixth weeks. The voar work was all done according to the various weeks. It was important to get the crops in by a certain time because of the short, rapid growing season—the old folk reckoned "a day i da voar was worth a week i da hairst". Neeps were sown in the second week, kale plants were set only in the first or sixth and seventh weeks, to avoid infestation from a fly which was believed to lay its eggs only in May. The weather followed the weeks too, the seventh and the ninth weeks often being very wintry, hence the saying "Keep a sheaf in the neuk for the seventh euk", in case it was so cold then that the kye had to be kept indoors. It was during the seventh week in 1946 that the island experienced a severe snowstorm. The islanders had just rooed their sheep and some of them died from exposure without the protection of their fleeces.

Bonxies lay three clutches, usually two eggs each time. The first and sometimes the second laying were taken for food but rarely the third, unless it was necessary to reduce their numbers. When the allen colony was so much bigger their eggs were sometimes eaten too, but again it was not considered right to take the third laying. Dunters' eggs were much prized, but generally two or three eggs were left in the nest, this being considered the number of chicks the mother bird would rear successfully. The eggs did not have to be new laid—"sitten" eggs were also eaten for when the small embryo of the chick starts growing the yolk gets a creamy consistency. The birds themselves used to be eaten by the islanders. Early in the spring the nories, welkies and lungwees were caught when they first came ashore, providing a welcome change of diet. Later the plump young norie chicks were pulled out of their burrows and roasted, split down their backs and laid out flat, crisp and oozing with fat. Although maalies' eggs were popular the birds were seldom eaten, being considered too insipid and pale fleshed—"almost as

bad as a hen". Young skarfs were stewed until they were so
tender that the meat was falling off the bones and adult skarfs
were eaten too, particularly in the winter.

There was hardly a square foot of the banks that the Foula
men were not familiar with and they thought nothing of climbing alone—sometimes they didn't even bother to take a rope. A
few years ago two attempts were made by rock climbers to climb
the Kame, to the interest of some of the islanders. The Kame,
with its vast population of nories, had been one of the most
popular fowling areas; there was what was regarded as almost a
gaet (track) down to the Little Kame, a treacherous series of
narrow ledges and tufts of grass, but as one elderly islander
remarked with complete sincerity, that wasn't real climbing of
course, the auld folk had none of this "proper" climbing gear!
Long ago, it is said, they used ropes woven from women's hair
which were greatly valued and very carefully kept. Later they
wove them from horses' hair and there was once a high penalty
enforced in Shetland for pulling hairs out of a neighbour's horse.
Sometimes they climbed together in twos or threes on the more
difficult cliffs. The climber used two ropes, the hand tow, held in
his hands, which was fastened to a lesnin (fastening) at the top,
and the body tow tied round his middle which he used to negoti-
ate awkward places, and which was paid out by his partner at
the top. He signalled up to the top by tugging on the body rope.

On one occasion Scottie o Wilse, who was a skilled banks man,
and David o Mucklegrind were climbing together on the Nort
Bank for nories. Scottie was lowermost catching the birds and
tying them to a rope round his wrist in a böli (tied up bundle) of
about thirty birds, when David suddenly saw the böli begin to
roll off the ledge. He shouted a warning down to Scottie, but the
updraught carried his words away, so he braced himself for the
shock as best he could. As it fell the böli nearly jerked them both
off balance and the rope tore the skin right off Scottie's hand so
that it was hanging from his fingertips like an inside out glove.
David managed to take the strain and eventually they struggled back up to the top and safety in spite of Scottie's injured
hand. Although it healed he never went in the high banks
again.

If something fell over the banks it was said to have "geen
afore". This applied to people, animals, rocks or anything else.

Contrary to the romantic thinking of some of our more dramatic writers of island tales not many islanders lost their lives like this. This is borne out by the relatively few accounts told of such incidents by the older islanders, though some occurred so long ago that the names have been forgotten. A man fell while climbing on the north side of the Kame, his remains being found splattered onto a small outcrop known as the Hog o Trots An and they said they took what was left of him home in a tub. Jimmie o Shodels was the last man to be killed in the banks in 1845. He fell at the back of the Noup and they found him smashed up on the cletts at the bottom, with the curn (curds) he had just eaten that morning spread out over the rocks.

Not all banks' accidents were the result of fowling. One old wife from the Hametoon used to take her cow each day to the fine green grass at the back of the Noup. She tied the cow's tether round her waist to leave her hands free to do her knitting while she walked, as was the custom, but one day when she was crossing the Murnatoogs the cow lost its footing and plunged over the edge dragging the unfortunate woman with it.

Because of the height of the banks those who fell were usually killed outright, or seriously injured. My husband's great grandfather, John Henry or "Muckle Johnie" was going after birds on Waster Hivda with his two young sons when a large boulder shifted, pinning him by the legs so that he was hanging head down. His back was injured, and although he was rescued he never fully recovered.

Even when the population was at its highest the proportion of birds and eggs that were eaten was relatively small; they were not normally preserved so that the amount caught was limited entirely by appetite. I have only heard of one household, Ristie, which sometimes salted down a barrel of young tysties and nories. An ecological system in which man is involved purely for his own food will normally remain in a stable balance from one century to the next. Usually it is only when commercialism is introduced that the system breaks down and resources are over exploited.

Which brings us to the vexed question of the bonxies. As our ornithological friends are always fond of telling us, Foula is very fortunate in having the largest breeding colony of bonxies in the northern hemisphere. Although they have now spread all over

Shetland and down to Orkney and the North of Scotland, formerly Foula and Unst were the only two places in Britain where they bred. It seems likely that they spread down to Foula from Iceland relatively recently, perhaps about the sixteenth century as the name bonxie appears to originate in Foula, unlike most of the other bird names which were derived direct from the old Norse and are common to both the Shetland dialect and Old Icelandic.

There are various references to the numbers of bonxies here during the last two centuries, contained in short accounts written about the island by passing visitors. The accounts make very interesting reading, but unfortunately there tends to be a lack of reliable information. Of course there was a tendency for visitors in the past to dramatize facts for effect, or simply to misinterpret what they observed, and perhaps Foula suffered from this more than most places due to its remoteness. If one could only sort out what might have been correct, one could write a learned history of the isle; however I shall leave that difficult task to some other time.

It would be unwise to accept the accuracy of past accounts on the size of the bonxie population and base any study of its expansion on them. Estimates of bird populations are always difficult and even a detailed scientific study of a particular group will give different results depending on the accuracy of the observers. For example casual counts of the allen population on Foula by visiting bird watchers gave an official figure of 150 pairs which remained constant for several years, but in 1975 the colony was systematically counted nest by nest in a research project involving a considerable length of time and manpower, to give a more accurate figure of nearly three hundred pairs. Unfortunately some of the more optimistic ornithologists immediately leapt to the erroneous conclusion that this represented an encouraging increase in the population, whereas in fact all it represented was an encouraging increase in the time and effort spent counting it.

The first written account of bonxies here was in 1774 when Low reported seeing six pairs on Liorafield, and he also appears to have seen quite a number elsewhere. All that we can deduce without doubt is that at this time bonxies were known to be present and breeding on Foula.

During the last half of last century, collectors from the south sometimes managed to hire a boat to land them on the island in order to obtain bonxies' eggs and skins, and the islanders were also taking the first laying for eating. For reasons of his own, Scott the landlord decided to cash in on the situation and brought the possibility of the extinction of the bonxies by collectors to the notice of ornithologists down south. It is said that he received donations of money to help towards their protection and to employ a man to keep an eye on the collectors, but that he pocketed the money for his own use. He was later awarded a medal by the Zoological Society of London for his efforts.

Great concern was now being expressed by naturalists down south about the bonxies' extinction, and in 1892 the President of the Edinburgh Naturalists Field Club considered purchasing the island for the express purpose of saving the colony. About this time the Scott family relinquished the ownership of the island to a firm of moneylenders in payment of gambling debts. The islanders profess that the colony was never in any danger and was in fact increasing alarmingly. This seems to be confirmed by the figures quoted by Edmonston, a well-known local naturalist. According to him the colony doubled from "fully fifty pairs" in 1890 to "over one hundred pairs" in 1891. The islanders' accounts suggest that this was an underestimate.

The first account of eggs being sold by an islander, in fact the only one I have heard of, was right at the beginning of this century when Andrew Henry of the North Biggins collected a kishieful of bonxies' eggs, perhaps about fifteen score, one morning from Haamar. He sold them to a baker in Scalloway who also bought gulls' eggs for baking. He received, I believe, a farthing each, which was considered a very good price. The area where he collected them was a small proportion of the total bonxie breeding area, so that the whole colony must have been at least 500 pairs and probably more. This does not tally with the only reports of numbers made round then. In 1892 Edmonston estimated about 120 pairs and in 1938 Venables and Fisher estimated about 300 pairs. But no matter which figure is correct, the bonxie has increased rapidly and estimates for the present day range from 3,000 to 6,000 pairs. Previously the islanders had made a practice of discouraging them from nesting on the lower ground by taking all three clutches of eggs from any that attempted to do so. They also collected a considerable number of eggs from the main breeding areas while going through the hills during the lambing, which helped to keep the colony in reasonable proportions. Under the Bird Protection Act of 1954 this became illegal. Very large fines were imposed on anyone caught taking a bonxie's egg, and they soon spread over most of the island even onto some of the crofts.

The bonxie here used to be mainly a fish eater, chasing other birds and forcing them to disgorge their catch. Sometimes they killed other birds, particularly young kittiwakes, and as fishing has been intensified they soon learnt to follow fishing boats for guts and other scraps thrown overboard. As the population increased, competition for food forced some of them to alter their feeding habits and naturally enough some of them took to killing birds as the main part of their diet. The kittiwakes suffered severely and the nories were soon being hunted in large numbers.

Not so long ago myriads and myriads of nories could be seen flying like clouds of midges off the Nort Bank and lining up in rows along the cliff edge and ledges but now only a few thousand are left. Of course the puffins have decreased all over Britain and one might surmise that the great skua was not entirely responsible, but looking at our immense colony of bonxies we are sometimes given to wondering if they are feeding off everyone else's puffins during the winter now they have acquired the taste for them. Up to the first part of this century kittiwakes nested here in great abundance. So many thousands packed onto the ledges of the Wast Gaad that the piltocks caught there were considered uneatable because of the taint of kittiwake droppings, but now you can count these birds in hundreds. Gone is the continued stream of kittiwakes flying all day long to the Mill Loch to fetch slie (weed) for their nests, making such a clamour that the folk in their houses had to raise their voices to be heard. Gone is the solid white flutter of kittiwakes bathing on the lochs that I loved to watch as a child. Although during the last two decades, the population has remained relatively constant, (in 1975 we counted from the sea 7750 occupied nests) I am afraid we will never again see the vast numbers of the previous century. I believe that a large part of this population drop was due to the continual harassment of the kittiwakes by bonxies if they ventured inland, thus preventing access to the essential freshwater lochs and the supply of suitable nesting material. Ecological chains are very complex and one should be very wary before interfering with their balance. The only predator of bonxies is man, and to allow them to increase without check is sure to have some detrimental repercussions. Some bonxies appear to develop very individualistic tastes. Some birds have developed great skill in catching rabbits, waiting quietly outside a burrow until a baby one comes out, then nabbing it before it even realizes its danger, or swooping after an adult too far out in the open to run for cover. And to a bird there's not much difference between a rabbit and a lamb! Contrary to ornithologists' beliefs I have never seen any evidence that a wild bird regards man's domestic animals as sacrosanct. Most of the lambs taken are puny and possibly would die anyway, but some bonxies will tackle an older healthy lamb.

The bonxie, like most predatory birds, regurgitates pellets of roughage formed from the parts of their food they cannot digest—bones, feathers, hair and so on. One year out of interest I gathered up all the pellets I saw during the end of April when the bonxies were starting to take up their territories. Despite the fact that this particular spring the lambing was going very well, I found from my results that thirteen per cent of the pellets consisted entirely of wool and sheep's bones, while several contained the complete lower jaw of a lamb. This was a surprising and alarmingly high proportion, although of course most of these animals would have been dead or dying before the bonxies interfered with them. At the moment the economic harm done by the bonxies is not of much significance: a few poorly lambs, the odd duck or chicken. But what of the future? A slump in the stocks of sand eel due to increased industrial fishing, or a big decrease in kittiwakes and nories due to oil spillage, may mean the bonxies will have to become more dependent on our lambs.

One of the birds most affected by the increase of bonxies is the allen, or Arctic skua. In the last twenty years the population of allens has decreased from an estimate of over six hundred pairs in 1955 to only three hundred pairs in 1975. Competition with the bonxies for breeding space is one important factor. The other major factor is simply that allens form a large part

of some bonxies' diets. Newly hatched chicks are at greatest
risk, a large proportion of them never surviving more than a few
days, and predation continues to a lesser extent up to the time
the fledglings start to fly when again a high proportion may be
killed. Once we had one of the largest colonies of allens in the
world, stretching over all the low-lying ground out through the
Daal and up as high as Gruitflek, up even into the Fleck. Its
decrease has been an insidious almost unnoticeable decline, a
pair less here, another missing there, bonxies moving in a few
yards last year, up to that broo this year, half-way along the
peat bank next year, until now the allen territory has been
beaten back to the areas most frequented by human beings, on
the crofts, along the roadsides, around the peat banks, by the
church and airstrip. And as the human population dropped the
bonxies encroached still further, moving in round the ruined
houses, the untrodden paths, the disused peat banks, a
reminder of things we would rather have forgotten. With the
increasing pressure from the inevitable and uncontrollable
expansion of the bonxie population, the allen population can
only decline and eventually disappear unless there is human
intervention. There is much controversy these days on the justi-
fication of culls of groups of animals that are showing big
increases. Conservationists tend to argue against them, but
what is the ultimate purpose of conservation? Is it not, after all,
the preservation of other living things for mankind's enjoyment—the pleasure an individual finds in plants and animals,
or the love of an islander for the bird that typifies his summer.

The bonxie situation is a reminder that our island is no longer
our own—we have lost control of our environment. The outside
world can impose its own conditions and regulations on our
island even to the detriment of the islander. Foula has now the
largest colony of breeding bonxies in the northern hemisphere,
but no one ever asked if that was what the people wanted.

16

June

Dee an Me, an da scent o'da meyfloors
Dee an Me, an da simmer dim,
Dee an Me, an da rosy sunset
Wi' clespit haands at life's bright rim—

Annie Deyell.

June is our best month, sometimes our only month of real summer. Now the sun wakens us up at four in the morning shining in through our bedroom window and shines brightly on all day until ten at night, making the children very reluctant to go to bed at bedtime. The ground dries up, the little pools vanish, the level of the lochs drop and they grow green scummy algae. The burns up in the hills are only a string of stagnant pools and the sphagnum moss turns pale yellow, then white. Sometimes the ground becomes so dry that big cracks appear on the bare patches of moor, and the hay growing on shallow ground is scorched and dies.

Most years we experience a drought at this time of year. The well at the back of the house dries up, and I have to fetch water from further afield. With three houses now using the lower well we all have to economize, think twice even before we do the washing. And I regret to say that as the level of the water sinks lower and lower, the heaps of unwashed garments grow ever higher—a state that sometimes is not resolved until the gales and rain of autumn. Wherever possible water has to be used twice over—the water the tatties were washed in is saved to scrub the porch floor, the water they were boiled in is tipped into the basin to supplement the washing up water. Distracted shouts of "Don't drink so much!" are not the cries of the local abstinence society but my cries as I watch the precious water ration disappearing down seemingly unquenchable throats. Flush toilets, including that of the school can only be flushed once a day. Conditions which elsewhere would be considered intolerable are a familiar problem here summer after summer.

But the hot sunny weather only lasts for a few days at a time being replaced by a thick mist that creeps in from the sea and smothers the isle in white. Visibility drops to only a hundred yards as the hills and then the houses vanish, and we are left with a cold clammy nothingness. The world turns dismal, even the green of the grass turns sour and the cries of the allens echo sad and lonely. Then as suddenly, the wind changes direction and freshens and the next few days will be bright and warm again.

We try to make the most of our little bit of warmth and find time to swim in the loch or go for a wander out to the head of the Baa to see our favourite wild flowers, the squills. They flower in carpets there, like blue mist floating over the grass, thousands and thousands of tiny blue star-like blossoms. Each minute waxy bloom is perfectly formed—some bright blue, some pale lavender, some almost white. We love our squills. We try to ensure that the lambs do not graze them too hard in the early spring, and they reward us by thriving and increasing until every dry broo is smothered with them and the air is heavy with their sweet nutty scent. Not a very profitable crop perhaps, but then none of us will ever make a fortune here—not in money. But the fragrance of a flower, the cry of an allen, the warmth of sun on one's face are worth more than a few extra pounds.

The Shetland sheep, because its wool is so fine and lacks the long hairs found amongst other types of wool, tends to lose its fleece by itself without any assistance from us. Already some of the setnins (one-year-old lambs) are running around in various degrees of nakedness, some with a piece of old fleece draped round their shoulders like a cloak, others trailing a long train of wool behind them or sporting a fluffy bustle or a white Elizabethan ruff. One sunny morning after my husband had set off to the Shaalds in his blue boat to try for bait, I took the bairns up to Harrier to roo the setnins before they lost too much of their fleeces. The dogs worked efficiently together for a change, Bluey evidently having decided that perhaps it was not quite the thing after all to hang on to Dandy's tail and pull. The bairns could hardly restrain their excitement and ran after the sheep shouting and laughing, and between us all we drove them into the crü.

I caught my first "victim"—Spooty lamb, who was most disgusted when I tied up her legs and she lay grinding her teeth in suppressed fury. Her fleece was so loose it simply lifted off, almost like a ragged blanket, although round her neck it was fixed on more firmly and required some deft tweaking to pull it off. Underneath her new wool was already an inch long, the moorit very dark and the white beautifully clean. I untied her and lifted her out over the fence. She looked very strange—a dark elegant creature instead of the rag-bag she had been before, though her elegance was somewhat marred by long fluffy tufts of wool sticking out behind her ears and on the point of her tail. The peerie sean was next. Between her old fleece and the new wool was a mass of hayseeds—evidence of her habit of standing right under the hayrack to eat. She endured her rooing with aplomb, chewing her cud thoughtfully while I pulled away. People unaccustomed to the Shetland sheep think this method of pulling off the wool must be very cruel, like tearing hair out of one's head, but actually the old fleece is no longer attached to the sheep's skin and they do not appear to mind at all.

The sun was high by now and every now and then I took a rest and sat scanning the hills. The Kame was pale green and far away, a myriad of tiny maalies wheeling out from its edge. The Sneug rose up in front of me, patterned green and gold and dappled with shadows from the clouds. I could just make out the bonxies circling in the sky above the summit and a handful of sheep meandering up the Oxnagate. To the south Hamnafield was sheer and uptilted, still amber gold from the winter, and as I watched a fragile cap of cloud drifted in from the south and settled on the top. I looked at all this and wondered, how could anyone bear to live anywhere else?

In Harrier the mares were grazing peacefully while the little foals slept stretched flat out on their sides in the sun. The reseeded grass was a lush patch of vivid green, while the grass outside, cropped close by the horses, had a faded yellow look. The mares were losing their winter coats too and were looking rather scruffy. Now and then one would amble up to the fence and give its bottom a really satisfying scratch against the wire. Jacob was prancing up and down outside the fence gazing longingly at his wives. He had already got his summer coat, a deep flaming red that contrasted with his long flaxen mane and tail.

The crü where I was working was in the midst of allen territory, and one pair had a nest only a few yards away. Every
time I stood up to catch another sheep they swooped viciously at
me crying fiercely, and when I bent down again to roo they
settled down nearby crying triumphantly that they had beaten
me into submission. After a while the cock bird grew tired of this
and stood silently watching, but his wife kept up her scolding,
sharp, cat-like cries. Perhaps it was not me she was scolding but
her mate as eventually he walked diffidently up to the nest,
drew himself up impressively, then plumped down onto the
eggs, shuffling into a comfortable position. He sat alert for a
minute, head held high and tail cocked up, then slumped down
into a more comfortable position and dozed off in the sun, leaving his wife to keep watch.

My gaze lingered on the old low grey buildings: the Wilse,
long ruined, growing back into the ground; the little house of
North Harrier built so carefully and painstakingly with cut
sandstone, I could just find a vague memory of its inhabitants in
the back of my mind; the dilapidated clutter of houses over at
South Harrier; it seemed no time at all since the folk were
there—but it was ten years already. Now they stood empty,
deserted, but there would be people living here again sometime—this I knew.

Many and many a one had lived here in the past, stretching
back how far? One had only to walk among the old grey stones to
feel how lived-in this piece of land was. No one could be lonely
here. There were old pre-Norse buildings up here—the remains
lay under this green grass, under this dark acid soil. Here were
stone cist graves containing urns of cremated ash and dried
blood, their lids carefully sealed up. Here under this grassy
mound beside the burn was a pile of burnt charred stones. Here
in the corner of this rig were crumbled fragments of soft dark red
pottery; in that rig lay the bones of some long dead man. I did not
need an archaeologist to excavate it, examine it, date it, take it
all away to some museum. It was enough for me to know it was
here, safe under my feet, lying forever where it belonged.

I half closed my eyes and tried to picture the land as it was
then, the valley clothed with small green trees, trailing
branches hanging over the burn, rustling leaves reflecting in
the water of the loch—harebells and myrtle, juniper and

bracken. Did trees once cover the ground where the road runs now, softening the contours of the low hill of Crougar, where the grey silhouette of some ancient building on the summit kept watch over the sea? Were there clusters of stone houses roofed with branches and turf, blue wood smoke rising from the fires, sheep grazing on the hillside, cattle being driven down to the burn for a drink, fish drying in the sun, bairns picking the flowers? Did a blackbird sing? Were the people happy?

But the vision eluded me. I could see only the bare gold-green hills, the white maalies bathing in the blue water of the loch, and the bonxies soaring in the sky. And instead of the song of a blackbird came the heart-stirring wail of an allen.

I worked with the setnins all day till my back ached and my fingers blistered and it was evening by the time we plodded down the dusty road for home, weary and smelling strongly of sheep. The low sun was casting long shadows down the green valley and the hill was a high dark silhouette. Out to sea, the light glinted on a fishing boat steaming north by the isle, and I could hear the faint whine of an engine as my husband's boat came round the head of the Taing, leaving a long rippled wake behind it in the pale water.

In spite of the long sunny days the weather was never fine enough for all the peats to dry out completely where they lay on the ground, and the next job was to raise them up into miniature wigwams with the damp side turned outwards. I worked at it automatically, bent over double, my hands reaching out, without stopping, for the peats and balancing them into innumerable raisings, six to eight peats in each. A dunter had made her nest on the back of the East Lieug bank, snug in between two peats. She sat close and watched me raising, following each movement with only her eyes. I left the peats undisturbed around about her and carried on further along the bank.

I enjoyed working out at the peat banks although the work was tiring and hard on one's back. The East Lieug bank had a good view of the sea and I could see Jock lying off at the Sand in his small white boat trying for a halibut, and my husband and Ken in their blue boats fishing further south. A flock of kittiwakes flew by just offshore. I could hear them echoing "kitti-

wake, kittiwake", as they drifted out of sight to the south. The
Gossameadow bank was much closer to the hill and some days it
felt almost underneath it. The hill was green now, the dark olive
green of the woodrush blending with the light yellow green of
the moss, and from here it towered up above us, very high and
steep.

All the young birds were hatching out now. Fluffy fawn
bonxie chicks were everywhere, hiding behind tussocks, tucked
away under broos, paddling through pools, scuttling away if
they thought we had not noticed them. The allen chicks were
darker and harder to find—sometimes we almost trod on them
accidentally. When I was working out at the peat bank I would
gather up both the allen chicks and lay them in safety in a little
dip next to one of the peat-roogs so they would not be trampled
on by the dogs or children. The parents did not actually dis-
approve but they always watched me carefully to see where I
was going with their offspring. They perched on top of the
neighbouring roog to keep watch, uttering occasional alert
squawks to let me know I was still being kept under
observation.

The grass was losing its vivid greenness, tinted now with a
sprinkling of daisies. Flowers were everywhere. We welcomed
back each one of our old friends—not that we had much time to
stand around admiring them for they were not the only things
that were growing. The tatties were disappearing under a
blanket of ervie (chickweed) and the corn was having a battle
with the meldie (corn spurry) which was threatening to swamp
it—time to take out the hoe. I hacked away at the ervie all day,
flinging heaps of it off onto the sides of the rig. The children
gathered it up to make nests out of it and spent hours happily
hatching out stone "eggs". I had half the rig cleaned by evening.
It was long past the children's bedtimes and I was tired, my back
ached and my hands could hardly summon up the strength to
hold on to the hoe, but I kept going, making the most of the long
light evening. I was not the only one working late—the peat
banks over on the Lieug were a bustle with activity. I could
make out the figures of Edith, and Aggie Jean bent over as they
raised peats helped by Doreen who was in for a summer holiday.
Bobby and Eric drove down to the Voe in their hill buggy and
shortly after I could hear the rumble as they pulled their boat

down the beach. Andrew was coming down the road wheeling a barrow load of peats home and soon my husband went off on the tractor to fetch a trailer load of peats for the Biggins. Harry was out on the East Lieug helping Tom with his peats, and Jock was up at the top of the Lieug starting up his motor bike. I was so engrossed watching all this activity that I accidentally chopped off three tattie plants in succession.

The sun slowly sank in the north, below the Heights, turning the sky crimson and gold. I laid down the hoe, gathered up the bairns and went indoors. It was after eleven o'clock, yet the night would remain only faintly dimmed until the sun rose again in the north an hour or two later. Sunset and sunrise merged into one single display and the skylark still sang at midnight. Now we did not need to light the lamp at all and it had a confusing effect sometimes as we found ourselves still working hard at something in the small hours of the morning, under the impression it was still evening. Some days we had to rise very early in the morning so that my husband could catch a favourable tide for fishing and we might meet someone still working from the day before—our today was his tomorrow! However, contrary to the widely believed legend that is held on the Shetland mainland, we do not normally make a habit of staying up half the night, but go to bed around eleven just the same as anyone else living in more conventional places. There is many a strange story told of the peculiar antics of the Foula folk by the mainland inhabitants which affords us much amusement. In fact when we go out there on some business, some people react to us as though we came from the wilds of the North Pole, not an island only a few miles away, and many a strange question we are asked. "Do you really live in houses the same as ours?" and "Is it true you have stoves there?"

Foula clocks are a law unto themselves anyway, which sometimes causes confusion to summer visitors who may leave one house at a certain time and arrive at another house an hour earlier. Clocks may be one hour, two hours or even such complications as forty-seven and a half minutes faster than Greenwich Mean Time, British Summer Time or any other time the owner might fancy. The clocks are our slaves—not the other way round. The times we eat, sleep or work depend entirely on when it suits us, not because of what the neighbours might think, or from some strange belief that it is a virtue to do such things at any particular time.

After the tatties had been hoed they had to be heaped, the loose earth scraped up and heaped round their stems with the hoe in a long row. Now this ought to be a simple job, but no matter how carefully I plant the tatties in neat straight rows in the spring, invariably they come up all higgledy-piggledy, and sometimes it's hard to make out any rows at all. Somehow it goes against the grain to chop off the offending tattie sprouts, but eventually I converted the chaos into some sort of order and the rig began to look quite smart with its long rows of dark heaped up earth topped with bunches of green leaves.

Next I turned my attention to the vegetables. A pair of young maalies were trying to nest in the corner of the yard and they considered the young kale plants to be most attractive nesting material. Every morning I flung them out of the nest and replanted all the pulled up plants, but during the night they would be at it again. As a result the kale was beginning to look somewhat the worse for wear. I yanked up handfuls of weeds for several hours, then:

"Does du ken dy caddies is in da Leirabeck hay?"

"Mamma, Penny's cut her toe and her guts is coming oot!"

"Could du help me caa oot yon blasted thiefy yowes o wirs?"

"Could I get a laen o da muckle spanner?"

"Where's my dinner?"

The vegetables have a poor time against such competition.

By mid June the reseeding up at Harrier was knee high, which was tall for this exposed part of the world. It rippled and waved as the wind sighed through it. The grasses were flowering, dark green spikes of timothy, orderly heads of ryegrass, coarse loose tufts of cocksfoot, and fragile sprays of meadow grass. All were unfamiliar to us and so we observed them with interest. My husband and Harry were spending any spare time they had in fixing up the mower, which as usual had gone into a decline during the winter, in spite of being kept inside. During the next few days I worked hard trying to get all the other work finished, so I would be free to work in the hay, for once I started on it I would have little time to do anything else.

For several days the fine weather held as a light westerly wind caressed the isle, blowing down off the hills, warm and smelling of flowers. A soft white cloud floated above the hills, forever reforming and drifting away, casting fragile shadows over the land. I could smell the sweet scent of drying hay long before I reached Harrier. The swathes had shrunk and shrivelled, turned crisp and dry on top. I set to with a rake, walking slowly up and down the rig, the rake going out automatically, turning over the hay so that the wet green undersurface could dry in the sun. With one eye I watched the rake, with the other I kept a watch on the bairns who were playing in the burn, making boats out of seggy leaves and with my other eyes I saw the hills basking gold green in the sun, watched our sheep grazing up on Codlefield, followed the flight of a bonxie as it hunted rabbits over at the Wilse, beating back and forth like a hawk, watched the allens soaring and swooping in the sky above, saw the pollen rise like fine white dust as I disturbed the ryegrass flowers at my feet. A handful of sheep drifted by outside the hay fence, the ewes busy snipping out the best shoots of grass, the lambs bouncing and racing up and down in an excited group. All except one that is, a big white new-born cross Cheviot lamb with a long dangly tail, who tripped demurely along at the heels of Old White Seat.

"Hey, where were you last winter!" I shouted at her, but she only gave me a toothless smirk and passed by.

I worked all day, only pausing for a few minutes to eat some soggy sandwiches, the bairns having played submarines with the bagful, and yet the sun was sinking low over Soberlie by the time I finished, turning the hills red gold, painting the old grey stones a glowing purple pink. A hard day's work and I had only turned about half an acre of hay. A mechanical hay turner would have turned it all and hardly noticed.

Home again, tired and hardly able even to chew a piece of bread. With an effort I held up the binoculars to look for the returning mailboat, picked out the stacks at the mouth of Vaila Sound, scanned the faraway edge of the sea where the distant waves formed small dark lumps—which one was the boat? I scanned to the south where the sea lay pale and silvery and then to the north where the ribbon of dark water stretched showing that the tide had turned. There she was, out on the innermost edge of the dark strip, a small, low, familiar black dot. How many times have I looked for it?

Next day was cold and grey. Up at Harrier the hills were dark, almost purple black and forbidding. They reared up and disappeared into ragged grey cloud, two thousand feet or twenty thousand—they could have been infinitely high. I looked at the grey sky and then at the expanse of hay. Up it would have to go, whether it was dry or not. I spent the day raking up the hay into rolls, carrying it in big tangled armfuls to the racks and putting it up in shaggy heaps. Slowly one by one the racks advanced down the rig. I made "heads" out of the longer clumps of hay, gathering up the stalks to make a sheaf. What would the old folk have thought of hay that long? For that matter what would they have thought of hay growing on their best corn rig, or the horses standing cropping the short grass where they used to grow bere, or the maalies nesting one at each corner of the ruin that was once their home?

The grey cloud crept lower until a white mizzle drifted down from Soberlie, wetting the hay. I plodded on regardless. The midges came out, myriads of tiny black tormentors, settling on my face, humming in my ear, biting, buzzing, driving me half mad. Only showing themselves on the rare calm days the Foula midges make up for lost time by biting with an unsurpassed appetite. Lucky men, off at the lobsters out of their reach! The young horses stood restlessly flicking their tails and tossing their heads, finally they could stand their tormentors no longer and careered off in a wild gallop, Flo in the lead. The tame cock allen had taken to perching on Blossom's back of an afternoon, he fluttered his wings frantically trying to keep his balance as she set off after the others. As she leapt over a drain she kicked up her heels and he fell off. Undaunted he returned to his favourite perch when the horses settled down again. The mizzle turned into drizzle. The day deteriorated into a battle—me versus the hay. But the hay and the midges beat me in the end, and I was forced to retreat leaving the job unfinished.

So the days passed—days of warm wind and sun when the hay was a delight to work with, scrunchy and sweet-smelling, days of cold grey when the cloud crept down from the hills trailing rags of drizzle, and the hay was damp and sticky, days when a small white cloud leapt up into the sky over Soberlie, towered blue black above us and let loose a cloudburst, and the hay became dripping wet. There were days when I hated hay, when I looked at it and wondered what on earth I was doing struggling away day after day on such a ridiculously small patch of hay. But the days did pass, and one evening I set off home down the road giving a last satisfied glance at the rows of conical hay coles, each topped with its tuffed head of grass seeds, patterning the small patch, on which the second crop of grass was already shooting up soft and lush.

17

Goodbye to the Cows

Da scent o hay, an da smell o waar,
Da swish a da sye o da busy maa'er,
Fat bees dat flit fae swaar to swaar,
Waarm, simmer haze.

Rhoda Bulter.

Johnsmas, the 24th June—Midsummer. From now on the nights would lengthen and the days shrink as summer slipped through our fingers. We expected a gale around now, the Johnsmas Ree—but the wind had a different sound from the wind of winter. Blowing down off the hills, it rolled over the top of our roof, snoring in the chimneys, lulling us to sleep, blowing away our worries and tiredness, assuring us that it would still blow whether our work was done or not. We relaxed and slept soundly, soothed by the familiar sound.

The wind blew through July. My husband, as he hauled his lobster pots, kept in the lee of the coast, dodging through the tide ranks, always with one eye on his work and the other on the weather, while I kept one eye on the clock and the other on the sea, worried in case he had been caught south-by by the changing tide, or was unable to cross the rank off Strem Ness. Around Martibillimus (or St Swithin's Day) the tide was at its strongest. The old folk believed that it was no use going off to the fishing around then, as they said the tide was so strong it rolled da hurds (boulders) o'er da bottom.

But sometimes the wind brought real gales which sent low grey cloud and fine drizzle flying through the air. Then we would wake up in the mornings and see two or three, or even half a dozen large foreign fishing boats lying anchored off the mouth of the Voe in the lee of the isle—Norwegian purse netters, spick and span and newly painted, rusty old Scottish trawlers, boats from Iceland and the Faröes. The wind and tide would carry them slowly south out of sight as they dragged their anchors, then they would steam up again and anchor anew. While my

husband and the other island men admired the fine lines of the
Norskies, it set them off again cursing the lack of a harbour here
that prevented them from keeping similar boats and competing
on an equal footing. If the weather moderated the fishermen
would come ashore and carry on incomprehensible conversations with us in Norwegian, Danish or perhaps it was Faröese.
But after a few days the wind would drop and when we looked
out in the morning the sea would be empty again, somehow bare
and lonely now they had left. Sometimes we saw them again in
the winter riding out the storms, now hidden in a seething flurry
of white spindrift, now rearing and plunging on the big black
lumps of waves, now disappearing in a sudden squall of snow. At
night they shone their searchlights on the land, afraid they
might drift ashore in the winter dark.

The isle was at its lushest in July, when the hay rigs were gold
and red with buttercups and soorocks—a testimony to the poor
acid soil. Down in the valley all the flowers were out—yellow
segs stood along the burn, sweet-smelling red clover and yellow
money-grass patterned the pasture, the brugs and barer broos
were covered with bright blue sheep's bit scabious and creamy
flowers of white clover while everywhere sparkled the little
yellow bark flowers. In the cultivated rigs blossomed the big
scented white daisies, pale yellow rungie, daa nettles, ogadoo,
all in a weedy flourishing tangle. Even the poorest of land was
flowering, the bog covered with a delicate drift of white like an
early fall of snow—the attractive white plumes of cotton grass
or Luk a Minnie's oo, and the little orange spikes of bog asphodel
or clowie floors, so called because of its scent of spicy cloves, and
here and there large patches of pink ragged robin.

Over at Ham Little was the biggest transformation of all. The
bare brown overgrazed banks of winter where I had scrambled
after the lambs every evening were now a flower garden with
clumps of purple thyme and yellow and orange bird's foot trefoil,
with banks of sweet williams (red campion) and overhanging
fronds of lacy green ferns. For so long I had looked at the bare
ground through the eyes of our hungry sheep with despair, that
now the lush greenness was almost overwhelming. Somehow it
always took us by surprise, this sudden bursting into bloom,
brief and beautiful like summer itself. When it was over and the
ground became sere and bare again, it was hard to believe it

would ever bloom again, hard to believe summer too would come again and again, yet each summer seemed like the only one and we tried to cling on to it before it slipped away and we were back in eternal winter.

One fine bright sunny day I decided it was time to give the roof its annual coat of tar. It was pleasant up on the roof, almost hot and the change of viewpoint added a novelty to my surroundings. From here the garden looked almost like a real garden, and I could see over to Lerabeck where Andrew was busy tarring his own roof. I could almost see down to the pier, if I just stood on tiptoe and—Whoops! There goes the tar bucket! A large glob of tar shot out and splashed over my husband's bike leaning against the wall. Well, never mind, perhaps he won't notice. By dinner time the roof was well tarred—so was I!

Roofs of tarred felt are of relatively recent introduction. When I was a child there were still five houses here that had the old tek (thatched) roofs and one or two of the outhouses still have them. But the tek roof takes a lot more work to keep up and has to be repaired every few years. When the house was no longer inhabited the roof fell in during the winter leaving only a ruin. Even now if a house becomes empty the croft is often absorbed into another unit, the felt roof is soon damaged by the wind and the house becomes yet another ruin. But most of the houses would be considered uninhabitable by present standards anyway as they were all condemned over twenty years ago and they haven't improved since. All except our own that is, as the man who lived here at the time was somewhat of a hermit and threw stones at any strangers who came too near, including the sanitary inspectors who came to look at the house! Added to this is the problem, now widespread over the country, of summer homes. There are five houses here at the moment inhabited only during the summer holiday, and although some of the folk are our own come back to their old homes and we are delighted to have them, it does result in there being no houses available for young folk wanting to live their lives here.

The older houses of course had no chimneys, only a hole in the middle of the roof and an open fire in the middle of the floor. Each inhabitant of the house had their own kist or wooden chest in which they kept their possessions, and sometimes there was also a tiny cupboard built into the stone wall of the house. The box beds at one end of the room afforded draught-free sleeping quarters with some degree of privacy. In this way the small house was kept relatively tidy, a fact I sometimes remember when I look round our cluttered but end. A pile of wildly assorted battered books are stacked up on the arm of the sofa balancing precariously threatening to avalanche every time one of our more high-faluting visitors sits down; a clutter of papers and magazines slide off one end of the sideboard; a heap of records pile up at the other end; dozens of boxes of slides teeter in towers on the mantelpiece; cameras cower behind the radio; used battteries marshal in every available cranny, gathering their strength for an emergency, whilst cardboard boxes breed indiscriminately in the darker corners.

It was just as well there came a spell of rain and I was forced to stay inside and put the house to rights. I covered all the clutter with sheets and spent an enjoyable day teetering on top of a pile of boxes and barrels, sloshing white paint on the ceiling which had grown a fine incrustation of black soot during the winter. This year's first batch of piltocks hanging up in the roof had stopped dripping and were smelling good and tangy. I poked the dripping brush in around about them—well, you didn't expect me to take them all down, did you? And if some of them got rather splattered, I'm sure it would make a pleasing variation to our winter dinners. I dabbed away happily with the brush rehearsing witty puns about whiting with which to dazzle my better half, occasionally pausing to spit out a mouthful of paint.

While the seasons come and go as they have done since man first set foot on Foula our lives are changing or are being changed for us more rapidly than we care to admit. I was forced to realize this when the last of the island's milking cows were sent out to the mainland to be sold. There were only four of them left and the bull had been sold two years previously so their milk was drying up. They walked sedately down to the pier with their owners, stood meekly while the ropes were fastened round their middles, then rolled their eyes in fear as the crane lifted them up and deposited them onto the deck of the boat.

Flekka and Redda, old Blacka and the Ham quaike—it was a final good-bye to dear old friends. They brought back memories of pails of warm milk frothing over on a soft summer night, of the rhythmic "swirl-clunk" of the churn, smelling of warm wood and buttermilk, of the "shush shush shush" as one worked the churn staff up and down and the soft creamy butter floated up to the surface. I thought of long cool drinks of sharp blaand, run milk smooth and wobbly and sprinkled with oatmeal and fresh baked baps spread with slices of .kirn. I seemed to hear again the echoing "k-nock, k-nock, k-nock" as the stake of a cow's tether was banged in on a summer morning and could almost see the kye waiting at the gate to be let in on a dark hairst night. Other memories came to me unbidden—rigs of corn rustling and waving in the summer wind, the scrape, scrape of scythe being sharpened on a frosty autumn afternoon, corn skrews being fastened down on a black night of gale, old Sholma being butchered on a bitter winter day and a young calf slobbering over one's fingers. From now on the island would have to depend solely on milk that came out of a tin or from a plastic sachet.

The kye stood placidly gazing at nothing as the boat steamed out of the Voe. A helicopter flew over the isle, heading out to the north-west, out to an oil rig. The sun glinted off its silver body and the harsh ominous drone of its engine drowned the purr of the boat. We silently watched it disappear out of sight. Times were indeed changing.

Two oil rigs were drilling to the west of us, the nearest a mere forty miles to the north-west—out there at the Far Haaf. And what would oil bring us? Not much of the twenty million pounds made over to the County Council by the big oil companies, of that we could be sure. They would need it all and more to cope with the enormous changes that oil would bring to the islands. We were not so naïve as to expect any to go towards providing us with the harbour we urgently needed. No. Oil would only bring us pollution and inflation.

With the binoculars we could pick out the oil rig out to the north-west from the top of Summons Head, a pale far-away Eiffel Tower. It looked harmless enough—but? Not one of us was taken in by the platitudes of the oil companies' public relations propaganda. On an operation of this scale an oil spill seems inevitable sooner or later, and in these exposed waters clean-up operations will be difficult and lengthy. Bird populations already under stress such as the nories and tysties may be irreparably damaged. How lonely will the island be then.

There was a breathtaking view from this point on the 700 foot high clifftop. To the east the sheer rock face swept down to the arch of Kittiwakes Haa and the jagged stacks lying off the north end. To the west the long wall of the Nort Bank rose abruptly to the dark forbidding face of the Kame. A wild, beautiful place, this. The grass along the cliff edge was littered with pieces of rock that had been torn out of the face by the winter storms, some as big as a brick had been flung a hundred yards inland.

For a really close-up view of the birds there is nowhere to compare with Mucklebruik. A narrow sheep track runs in through the face of the cliff just above Waster Hoevdi. Here you can reach out and run your hand over the worn surface of the striated red and cream sandstone, rub off the weathered grains of sand laid down so many eons ago. Full 330 million years the grains have stood firmly cemented in this great rock barrier and I rub them off with my finger. Further along, the track leads to a jumble of broken rocks that have fallen down out of the cliff face—the slums of the bird world. There is the almost over-powering tangy fishy smell of their droppings which are splashed over the rocks like whitewash and the air is full of their noise. Nories guffaw and laugh as they sit in rows outside their holes, lungwees and welkies kirr and whirr on ledges, scram-bling and jostling in under the biggest rocks, while under one's feet there is nothing short of pure bedlam, a squawking and flapping and wheezing and scuttling of a thousand skarfs nest-ing in every single crack and cranny several storeys deep. For farce there is not much to beat a skarf defending his nest, though why he bothers I don't know, as not even the hungriest islander ever touched skarfs' eggs. The nest is a disgusting filthy splatter of rubbish on which it sits, wings spread, beak agape to show its bright yellow lining, shaking its head so vigorously that its warning cry comes out as an extraordinary undulating wailing groan. The chicks are in hiding, scrawny ugly heads poking into the furthest cracks, big fluffy bottoms sticking out in full view. The excitement is too much for the adult who shakes the noise out of his beak so violently he loses balance and slithers backwards upside down into a hole right on top of the nearest neighbours who immediately start up an indignant croaking and flapping. The chaos spreads through the colony like a wave as one clambers from rock to rock.

At the south end of Mucklebruik is a tremendous straight narrow cleft in the cliff known as the Sneck o da Smaalie, up through which one can climb. After the brilliant sunshine outside, inside the Smaalie all is gloomy and dank, water drips incessantly down the moss-encrusted walls, the laughter of the nories sounds more like the gloatings of trows echoing up from the bowels of the earth, and under one's unsuspecting feet lurk the gruesome remains of sheep that have plunged to their death. But as we wriggle up through the chimney-like hole at the upper end of the Smaalie a wren bursts into vivid song and we are out into the bright sunny world again.

Off the coast here a square-rigged ship was wrecked one September night in 1883. The sailors had no idea as to their whereabouts and a rumour went round that the island was inhabited by cannibals. Rather than be eaten by savages, the crew decided to go down with the ship and helped themselves to the ship's rum to deaden their senses. But one of them, Tom Black, decided to take his chances ashore and persuaded his chum to keep sober and come with him. As the ship was driven onto the rocks the two men leapt for their lives. Tom scrambled ashore safely but a large wave came in and tore his chum away. It was a night of poor visibility, but the only way out of his predicament was up. Up the cliff that loomed above him. So up he climbed in the darkness, up and up, not knowing where the summit was. But he reached the top safely.

As dawn was lightening John Henry was going out to the west end of the Daal to fetch home a kishie of peats, when he saw this bedraggled tattered figure stumbling towards him. Being a deeply religious man he wondered if he was seeing a vision and asked fearfully,

"Are you earthly or unearthly?"

"Flesh and blood, flesh and blood," was the reassuring answer.

John took the stranger back to the Hametoon with him and he stayed there until the spring. The men went back that day to look for survivors but all they found was the ship's mate lying half-way up through the cliff face on a small ledge. He had been killed outright by a stone falling on his head. For the first three or four days Tom Black still feared for his life and lay awake on the resting-chair all night just in case. They said he would stare up at the blackened roof and mutter "Pitch and tar, pitch and tar", not realizing it was soot. Years later one of the men away at the sailing met up with him again down south and he was delighted to hear news of his island friends.

We were expecting Clare, the last remaining mare, to foal during July. The night she was due to foal we were in the middle of a summer gale, the wind gusting fiercely from the south-west, sweeping clouds of drizzle over the isle. I hunted round the house, up by the old dyke and down below the yard and finally I found her sheltering out in the old Groups peat bank, tail on to the wind and wet. The wind whipped her bedraggled mane across her face and her sides were grey with drops of water, but she seemed contented enough so I went back to the warmth of my bed.

Early next morning I went out to check up on her again. The wind howled forlornly down from the hills, a wet white mist shrouded the isle and the air smelt of wet sour peat, damp heather and the raw salt tang of the sea. As I walked out into the whiteness, dark shapes loomed up in front of me and turned into peat banks, stone dykes, old broos. I wandered up and down checking the sheltered spots but found no signs of Clare. There was nothing but the howl of the wind and the 'kak kak kak' of the bonxies. Once I thought I heard a wild high whinny echoing through the whiteness but the toon was empty.

I ran back home and woke up my husband. "I can't find her!"

"Well, she must be gone oot. Did du mind and check da gates was tied shut last night? Da wind's maybe blown ane open."

"Yes, I did." Or did I? I could not remember anything clearly except the wind and the mist and Clare standing with her wet mane blowing across her face. I went out to look at the gates and found the one at the far fence in the outer half of the Groups was hanging open, swinging shut again between the gusts of wind. I shut it and looked around for the piece of rope to tie it so the wind would not burst it open again. Then I remembered. I had used it for a tether and the gate had never been tied up again since, I could have kicked myself for forgetting. Well Clare probably on her way north to look for the other horses. Later on during the day I looked north, keeping my eyes open for hoof marks and fresh droppings. It was strange walking through the mist with only a section of the road in sight. Whiteness lay on each side and I seemed suspended in time, walking up and down on the spot. Above, the allens cried and wailed with sadness. I found the horses sheltering along the Harrier dyke, bedraggled and dark with wetness. They were hard to recognize and little yellow-nosed Clare was not with them.

Back home again I made my way south along the banks. Squelching through the mire at the back of the dyke. The plumes of the bog cotton hung sodden in the rain, runnels of peaty water ran down the faces of the black wet peat banks and the wind shrieked dismally as it blew through the telegraph poles and swirled the white mist into eerie shapes. Dark forms swooped out of the mist and circled round my head with a harsh 'kak kak kak'. The mist distorted everything deceptively, so that the bonxies seemed huge and menacing and I had to brace myself against ducking involuntarily. Ahead of me a black shape rose up out of the whiteness and looked at me, I ran forwards—a horse! No. It was only a ewe.

Then I found a fresh heap of droppings and a few hoof marks. So, this was where she had gone. I followed the marks. Here she had stopped to roll—I could see black hairs tangled in the wet berry heather. Here she had stopped to eat a few mouthfuls of green grass near the cliff edge. I followed the hoofmarks along the edge. Here she had been running—the prints were cut deep into the short turf—across this little dip, up over this bump, down the other side and straight towards the very edge. Two deep skid marks were cut into the black earth—and nothing more.

I stood for a long time staring at the marks, staring down through the mist to the white boiling foaming waves breaking on the black rocks far below. Staring till the rain seeped round the edges of my oilskins and trickled down my back. And I hated the wind, hated the mist, hated the bonxies, hated the horse, even hated myself.

I rolled my hatred into a black ball and flung it down after the horse.

18

High Summer

An in ida lee
Anunder da hill,
Da beach at da nowst
Is shaltered an still.
Da smaa shingly stanes
Lies swittlin togedder—
Hoosh! Hears du dem harkin
Fornent ane anidder.

George PS Peterson.

The June sunshine and the July gales between them had dried the peats until they had shrunk and curled up. The berry heather was putting out long green shoots in the shelter of the raisings and big shiny black beetles and brown centipedes had taken up residence underneath. It was time to stack them up in heaps or roogs where they would remain dry till we fetched them home. At last even the bare moorland was flushed green with summer as the large mats of berry heather turned emerald and their first berries were ripening against the warm sphagnum moss. The bairns spent their days "at da berries" gathering handfuls of the small black fruit. The peerie ones swallowed them in mouthfuls while the older ones munched them up and spat out the pips and skins, until they came home at the end of the day with their mouths stained dark purple.

Many of the birds feed on the berries too—not just the starlings and blackbirds but even the allens and bonxies—and their purple seed-filled droppings are scattered everywhere, even over my clean washing hanging out to dry. Perhaps they have been partly responsible for the spread of the crowberry since last century. Unfortunately the sheep do not eat it, not even in the hardest winter when they are compelled to eat the coarsest sedges and rushes and even the moss and lichen. So the green covering of the isle in summer is deceptive as regards grazing since large areas produce very little nourishment at all.

"Untouched by the hand of time" is a phrase often applied to islands but wherever man is found there is change, even in the very vegetation which at first glance appears stable. In my own lifetime, I have seen the bare stony scalped areas grow green and rushes and crowberry invade neglected crofts. My husband's father spoke of the days when bracken, extinct for thirty years, grew out on the West Lieug where the berry heather is now dominant—bracken tall enough for the bairns to hide in. Tom told how his uncle could remember when small stunted bushes of juniper, grew up in the Fleck. It is not such a big jump after all to the days when much of the low land was wooded. And there are more obvious changes—the painful change in the island's economy from fishing to crofting, the shift in emphasis from kye to sheep, the end of the era of the banks and the dependence on birds, the loosening of the hold religion had on the island life, the drastic decline in the population from 267 in 1781 to around 40 at the present time. Even when I look back at the valley over a mere ten years, what unforeseen changes I see—a uniform covering of grass instead of rigs of waving corn, fences along the road, horses standing at the gate instead of kye, folk gone, bairns born. So the world rolls on and we go with it, not looking back, but going forwards, perhaps blindly, but always with hope.

Out at the Gossameadow banks the allen chicks had already grown their feathers. Of the nine pairs that had been nesting when we were casting the peats here, only three were left with five chicks between them. Our favourite pair were quiet, placid individuals, one dark and slim with a hint of light round its head and the other plump and short-set, very white, the white on its head meeting broad at the back of its nape and its dark cap faded to a pale fawny grey. Their chicks took after them. One was a bonny speckled chestnut, with a bright chestnut nape, plump and well fed. The other was smaller, drab, dark brown and not much more than a bundle of bones. They were full of the wander-lust and sprinted off on their long blue grey legs heading for bonxie land, but when they reached the edge of their territory the parent birds would swoop at them, chivying them back with sharp cries. The parents kept watch from the top of an old roog, standing side by side, occasionally conversing with other allens passing overhead, or if provoked enough one would dart up and chase away the invaders.

I flung the nearest peats onto a dry hummock on the back of the bank. They were only a fraction of their wet weight now and smelt good. There's no smell like that of sun shining on dry peat, a fine warm smell that tickles your nose. The peats from further away I carried in armfuls until it seemed that my arm had been stretched to at least twice its normal length, so I set to work with the barrow instead. Now, as every self-respecting Shetlander knows, filling up a barrow with peats is not just a job—it's a work of art, the aim being to fit in at least one more peat than is the very positive maximum, whilst avoiding ending up with a load which will tip out when you run into that hidden stank in full view of your watching neighbour. Having arranged a suitably precarious load to my satisfaction, I picked up the handles of the barrow and staggered off. For an alarming minute the barrow threatened to run amok but, gathering up my reserves of strength and my legs which kept wandering off to one side, I gained control over it, and we galloped off. After a while the pile was big enough and I began to build it into a roog, flinging the scattered peats up on top and arranging the outside layer so the rain would run off.

The peats I fetched to build the second roog were on the edge of the next pair of allens' territory. One of the birds was quite normal, i.e. not averse to giving you a few cracks across the head just to prove who was boss, but not holding any permanent grudge. The other, a sleek dark grey-brown bird, reminded me of an allen Peter Manson used to tell about that would sit on his head tearing his cap to shreds whenever he went to the peats. Our grey allen was equally persistent and every time I passed with the barrow she let out a squawk and unerringly hit me a wallop just behind my ear. At first I tried to ignore her, but I soon found myself developing a permanent cringe, so next time I hear her squawking I dropped the barrow, grabbed a big hard peat and flung it straight at her as she zoomed in for a direct hit. Being the world's worst aimer, the peat missed and she caught me a glancing smack across the forehead which was followed a second later by a stunning blow from the returning peat. This seemed somewhat unfair. Finally I developed the technique of balancing the barrow on one knee whenever I heard the rush of wind through her wings as she dived, and protecting my head with my free arm—progress was slow and erratic.

A big, light-coloured bonxie, was standing on a bump just in front of the roog I was building. As I watched he sauntered quietly up to the little dark allen chick who had been investigating a tuft of sheep's wool tangled in the heather. Perhaps mistaking the bonxie for a parent bringing food, the chick ran fearlessly right towards him and squatted at his feet. The marauder made a sudden downwards stab with his beak at the middle of the chick's breast just as I let out a shout and dropped the barrow. Thwarted the bonxie flew up and was immediately noticed by the allens who chased him off the colony screaming and hitting him. I carried the chick to the far side of the territory, unharmed except for a few lost feathers. The bonxie returned to his bump where he stood watching, and it wasn't more than a couple of barrow loads later when he was back in again stalking towards the little dark chick. Though I chased him away again, I knew it was hopeless. When I returned to the bank the next day the bonxie and his mate were squabbling over the remains of the chick on their look-out bump. When I picked up the corpse they flew up a few feet in the air and landed again only two yards away, where they stood side by side watching me.

The chestnut chick continued to thrive and soon was fluttering on his first flight a couple of feet above the ground. The dogs spent most of their time crouched flat to the ground keeping watch on him. When he set off for a run, Dandy would immediately head him off. The chick sometimes retaliated and pecked him on the nose, but usually sat down again looking rather baffled. Sometimes Bluey got excited and nudged the chick upside down and he would lie on his back waggling his blue grey legs, looking ridiculous. But a few days later on my way north to Harrier, I noticed that the parent birds were not sitting on their usual look-out post on top of the old roog and when I went over to investigate no bird swooped down on me. I tried to pick them out among the allens that were circling in the sky above me, but could not positively identify them. I knew then that something had happened to the chick. I looked angrily at the bonxies that squatted singly or in pairs every thirty yards or so all over the moorland to the west of me. If looks could kill!

By the end of August all the allen chicks in this small colony
had been killed except one. One! One young bird to fly away to
take its chances in the outside world. What were the odds
against it ever returning?

One day the world will wake up and find that many other
things have dwindled away unnoticed. For so things go, not
dramatically with a sudden wiping out of a population, but just
a gradual chipping away until what is left is too few for anything but decline. But nobody cares—worse, nobody even
notices.

But I watched the young bird flying seawards accompanied by
a handful of adults, watched them, now chasing each other
through the sky screaming and swooping, now hanging motionless wailing in unison. I cared. Yes we care. But it's only a bird!
Only an island!

The year had turned a full circle again, summer was at its
zenith. The sound of the mower echoed through the evenings
and hay rigs that had been tinted gold, red and blue with flowers
and waving clumps of rür lay a few days later shorn, pale
green and bare. Again the crüs occupied much of our time—the
running through the hills, the barking, shouting, baaing confusion, the smell of sheep, the laughter, the tiredness. We came
home at night through the dew-soaked grass with the rustling of
the rür and the far-away croon of a leerie lingering in our
ears—and the high dark hill not brooding, not menacing but
simply passive, accepting.

One summer evening as I watched Jim's boat steaming into
the Voe I heard him shout, "Coming aff to try for twa tree lür
(pollack) north by?"

Abandoning the hay (for once it would have to take care of
itself), I herded the bairns down the Orknaman's gete where the
boat was lying alongside the rocks and bundled them in. It was
one of those soft summer evenings when the sea lies smooth and
pale pearly gray, almost oily in its consistency. The boat left a
long ever-widening wake of ripples that caught the gentle evening light as though carved out of translucent glass, and the
mainland seemed far away, a dark blue line floating above the
silver horizon. I sat curled up in the bow listening to the
"lap-lap" of the ripples against the boards still warm from the
day's sun—the boards that separated me from the deep expanse

below. Out to sea I noticed several white birds diving straight down into the water.

"See the gannets out there."

"Yon'll be mackerel dere after. We'll try for some wirsells." He laid the helm over to the side and the boat turned in a sweep. As we drew away from the shore the landscape altered as the island took shape. At first just the high straight peak of Hamnafield loomed up dark behind where the land parted at the Voe, then the low rocky cliffs to the north and south drew out, and the Sneug, and then the Kame, marshalled alongside Hamnafield. Finally the rounded hump of the Noup and the curved sweep of Soberlie arranged themselves at each end of the isle. And still we sailed away, far out into the glassy sea, until the isle lay stretched out on the horizon, floating poised, as though about to fly away.

As I looked at its high peaks so stark, so bare, sweeping eternally to the north, I felt for the first time a loneliness. So beautiful it lay, yet so aloof, so uncompromising—no sign of human warmth.

My husband slowed down the engine and we drifted north with the tide. Hardly had we paid out our lines than we were pulling them in again, a mackerel tugging on every hook, and in no time we had a fishbox overflowing with beautiful iridescent fish. Round us floated rafts of birds—black and white lungwees twinkled and winked in the low sun, nories paddled frantically as the boat approached and dived under at the very last minute, black skarfs watched us indifferently.

We steamed back towards the north end of the isle, through the rank off Strem Ness where the tide curled the pearly glass surface of the sea into beautiful dark whirls and flutes, past the long low boulder beach of Hiorwick, skirting round the pointed stacks of the Broch and Sheepie until we lay off the back of the Gaada Stack. A good place this for lür (pollack), a fish that we especially prized salted and dried for the winter. We paid out our lines, taking care not to snag them on the rough bottom and sat waiting, jiggling the line gently with one hand to make the brightly coloured plastic lures dart around as if they were sandeel. The Gaada Stack is the most spectacular of the island rocks, standing up out of the sea like a three-legged giant, 125 feet high. From where we lay the light shone through the double holes. A few ledges halfway up were packed with lungwees from whom came a continual gentle "kirr, kirr, kirr" as they bobbed and bowed to their neighbours. A flock of kittiwakes were sitting on the sloping rock opposite the Broch, some resting with their heads tucked under their wings, others preening and fussing their feathers. Suddenly they rose together like a cloud of snowflakes, wheeled overhead and drifted away to the large breeding area at Kittiwakes Haa, their cries of "kittiwake, kittiwake" echoing through the still evening. A bonxie chivied one of the stragglers, forcing it down to the surface of the sea where they fluttered a few moments in uneven battle.

A tremendous tug on my line interrupted my reverie. I could feel the fish yanking frenziedly this way and that as I pulled it up until nearer the surface it hung limply, a heavy weight. Then I had it on board, gasping and flopping its chunky tail, a big heavy thick-set fish with orange marbling over its normal fishy colours—a bonny thing of a lür! After a couple of hours we had over threescore of them ranging from three to ten pounds in weight. My husband carefully kept the big creamy pink livers and their emptied stomachs when he gutted them. Tomorrow I would stuff the stomachs with liver and pepper and we would dine off liver muggies, the tasty oily oniony mealy mess of crudi mudi, gree (melted livers) simmered gently on top of the stove and poured over steaks of juicy fish, and newly dug black potatoes bursting out of their skins. In the old days feasts such as this kept the folk well fed all summer for even if all the fish had to be cured and sold to mitigate their ever-increasing debts, the heads could be stuffed with livers and boiled.

We went home the long way, round the back of the isle, sailing close in under the great cliffs, in under the towering height of Soberlie that swept up so steeply from the Kittiwakes Haa where the kittiwakes set up a continual cacophony of cries. The sun sank lower towards the north horizon lighting up every smooth overhanging facet of the iron-stained rock until they flashed a crimson red.

I strained my eyes searching that great overhanging rampart; near the top there used to be a hole known as Peggy Henry's Hoose. The luckless Peggy Henry was suffering from what was known as leprosy, a common enough disease in the old times though whether it was really leprosy is doubtful. At any rate it was believed to be contagious and fatal and the unhappy sufferers were made to live apart, usually in little felly houses made from turf. But Peggy Henry chose to live in a hole in the cliff, with a sheer drop of 500 feet below her and the wide empty horizon before her and the wild sea-birds her only company. One of the men from the Nort Toons had been her sweetheart and every night he carried food and drink up the hill and laid it on a stone near the cliff edge. One night when he got there he found the food from the day before still untouched. He shouted and cried for Peggy but there was never an answer. Whether she slipped accidentally or whether she found her fate too hard to bear and flung herself out to join the sea-birds was never certain.

From Soberlie to the Kame the Nort Bank stretched unbroken, a tremendous wall of rock carved away by the mighty ocean rolling in from the North. Maalies whirled round and round out from the cliff face, gliding downwards, soaring upwards in apparently aimless flight. This was the cliff that was famed afar for its countless nories. The men of those days knew every ledge and fingerhold.

We steamed past the foot of the Kame 1,220 feet high, and gazed up in awe at that pointed sliver of a peak, a witch's tower soaring into the sky. And our stomachs turned over at the thought that we had stood on top of that insubstantial summit. The cliff dipped slightly to Nebbifield, a massive smooth bare face of rock a thousand feet high showing the red brown and cream-coloured striations of the layers of sandstone inclined up to the north. Seals lay sleeping on the rocks like giant swollen slugs, occasionally scratching sleepily with a flipper or shuffling into a more comfortable position. As we approached one of them, a big dark grey bull, opened one bleary eye and stared at us. He lifted up his head and his tail and poised in a crescent shape on top of the rock, then flopped back as though exhausted by even this small effort. It was too much for one of the boys who let out an excited shout. Immediately the entire group was awake and humphing for the water at top speed. They dived in and we watched them swimming under the water, pale green shapes, then they surfaced and lifted their heads out of the water watching us with wide open limpid eyes.

A purely local wind blew down off the high cliffs. It was a warm balmy breeze with a subtle mixture of scents, of sheep basking in the sun along the bank's broo, of the berry heather from the wind blown moorland, of blue peat reek drifting from the chimneys in the soft evening air, of seaweed-covered rocks lapped by the summer sea, of wild flowers patterning the hay rigs, of sea birds crowding the cliff ledges—scents of home and happiness.

From Nebbifield to Waster Hoevdi the cliff swept in an unbroken curve as though carved out by a giant's knife. My husband stilled the boat an arm's length from the cliff face and I gazed up at the tremendous overhanging face that loomed above us, 650 feet high. I felt vertigo churning up my stomach and dragged my eyes away, focusing them instead where the foot of the cliff dropped straight into the sea. I peered down into the dark deep water but saw no bottom. The largest colony of guillemots nested on Waster Hoevdi and I scanned the ledges trying to estimate the numbers—ten thousand, possibly more? They have been increasing these last few years despite the hazards of pollution and the predation from the bonxies and gulls. The chicks leave their ledges when they are only three weeks old. From the ledges came a great confusion of loud kirring and chirring and peep-peeing of the chicks. It was not possible to make out whether the adults pushed the chicks off the ledges or persuaded them to go, or whether they left of their own accord. Hurtling down through the air a chick would tumble and somersault, frantically flapping its half grown wings to land on the water with such force it almost seemed to bounce. One or both the parents would follow the chick down and would stay with it until it reached full adult size. A flock of maas (gulls) and bonxies circled, as excited as birds following a fishing boat gutting a big catch, and many a chick was caught in mid air.

The sun sank slowly down towards the north horizon turning orange, then red, painting the sea with gold and purple swirls and ripples. As we watched, it slipped below the horizon, a glowing red semicircle, a diminishing quarter, a brief shining crimson glimpse—then it was gone. A distant trawler was silhouetted dark against the golden sky with black specks of birds following behind her.

Off the nose of Waster Hoevdi a group of neesiks or porpoises gambolled, rolling their round black backs above water only a

few boat lengths away. Just to the north of us two killer whales
passed by going somewhere, their straight pointed fins cutting
through the water, occasionally lifting themselves out of the
water giving us a glimpse of their black and white sides and the
spout of steam from their blow hole as they submerged. Both the
neesiks and the killer whales are common enough around the
island. More occasional visitors are the great big whales we
sometimes meet off in the tide ranks at the ends of the island.
Once one reared its huge head out of the water only a hundred
feet away and smacked it down violently on the surface of the
sea, so near that we could see its tiny, piggy eye and smell its
stale fishy breath.

Once, and only once, we were privileged to see a sight that no
one here had ever heard tell of before. It was the last Sunday in
June 1966—one of those beautiful calm, pale blue days. We
were sitting at the table having a late lunch when my husband
glanced out of the window. His eyes widened in surprise. What
could it be—a tidal wave, a strange cloud, a mirage? About eight
miles offshore an unusual phenomenon stretched from opposite
Sumburgh Head at the south of the mainland right to the north
where it disappeared out of sight behind the back of the Taing, a
long line of breaking white waves with what looked like a
narrow band of rain showers above it. Looking at it with the
binoculars we saw it was a school of thousands and thousands of
whales. They swam at a speed of about nine knots, a fast speed
for a whale and were keeping to the deeper water. It took over an
hour for the tail end of the procession to disappear to the north
and we watched it in utter amazement, unable to comprehend
what the vast number might have been. All the whales in the
world seemed to be there.

I often used to scan the horizon for them in following summers, longing to see them again. But with the coming of oil and
the resulting sea traffic I now know I never will.

19

What of the Future

Dey tackit Est, dey tackit Wast
But aye da norie kept his nest.

Gideon Manson.

In the past the average population on Foula appears to have been around 150. In 1790 it was 143, and although it is said to have suffered severe decreases due to the muckle fever (small-pox) on several occasions, it soon recovered to its normal level. During the last century the population increased substantially as it did over the whole of Shetland, reaching its peak in 1881 when there were 267 inhabitants in Foula with 33 children at the school. The islanders tended to marry later too, until at the end of this era they were marrying towards the end of their child-bearing years and families were relatively small. Some in fact never quite got around to marrying and courted all their lives. This would suggest that the island was overpopulated and in fact housing was a real problem for a man wanting to marry, his own small home being crowded enough already. By this time it was no longer permissible for a man simply to break out a new croft from the hill.

After this the population steadily declined as with the decline of the fishing industry families emigrated to the mainland and even further afield. Obviously there are many reasons for the decline of any population whether of people or of birds, all form-ing a complex tangle. Students of these phenomena may put forward one particular reason or another as being the most important, depending on their own individual experience and knowledge. Take the puffin for example, which suffered a big decline all over Britain in the 1960s, the ordinary bird watcher blames pollution from the industrial nations, a specialist suggests collapse of the burrows from overuse while the islander blames the bonxies and the maalies. I don't suppose any single factor was the sole cause—it's the total effect that counts. Too many adverse factors work together and the balance is tipped whereby the population decreases. Who could point to any one cause as the last straw? Perhaps only the norie himself.

Two of the main reasons I would pick out in our own case are the collapse of the indigenous fishing due to lack of a harbour and the modern educational system. The fishing has already been discussed and obviously the loss of use of the island's only major resource must have a drastic effect on the population. The educational drawbacks are more insidious. At twelve years old all the children must leave the island and continue their education in Lerwick, the only town in Shetland, whether they are academically inclined or not.

Naturally the children must be able to have the best education available, none of us would wish them to be educationally deprived just because they live here, but the complete removal of an age group must give an unbalanced aspect to the population, and when it is that of the next up-and-coming generation it can only be harmful to the island's future. The teenagers aren't here to give their views and outline their hopes for the future. Decisions in the island's policy are made without regard to them, yet without them how can the island continue to survive? They *are* the island's future, some day it will be theirs.

Twelve to eighteen is an important formative phase in a child's life. If a child is removed from his own home environment and plonked down somewhere entirely different, he may be very homesick at first but in time he becomes familiar with the new way of life and develops interests and skills that relate to it. When the time comes to leave school he finds that he hasn't learnt the skills necessary to enable him to cope with life on his island. He can't cast peats, he has no knowledge of meads and tides, he can't handle a sheep, let alone a sheep dog, and even the sheer physical aspect of living off the land and sea after years of town life is daunting. In the meantime the parents' economy has not expanded in relation to the growth of their absent child and they may now find themselves unable to support him financially if he should return.

All around him is a society in which the size of the wage packet seems to be the most important thing in life, in which people are always discussing the poverty line, rampant inflation, declaring they are facing abject poverty on incomes twice that of his parents. No wonder he doesn't return to the island. He is genuinely scared that he won't manage. He doesn't realize that if we can do it, so can he, and he doesn't have the courage even to attempt it. So the only course he sees open to him is to get a job on the mainland. Next follow early marriage, a caravan, a council house, insurance policies, hire purchase, electricity bills and rent demands. Almost unknown to him he becomes trapped in an urban existence.

During the past thirty years three children have remained at the island school until the age of sixteen all three are still living on the island. But during the same period, of the island children educated away from the island only one has returned to settle permanently. It is interesting to note how the emphasis has shifted. At one time, the question for the young folk was whether or not to leave the island—now it is whether or not to return. And it's far far easier simply not to leave, than it is to come back.

Many people consider this inevitable, maintaining that children will always choose the urban life, it being in their eyes far more rewarding. But sometimes I wonder how they would feel if their own children were removed from their home towns and educated here. I wonder if their cities would then be viable. Families are very close here and many cannot face this break. When the oldest child has to leave the island the whole family often go with him.

There are many other subsidiary factors. The increased dependence on crofting due to the loss of the fishing must of necessity limit the population. One croft cannot support a family so several are amalgamated. It's very tempting to gather a large number of crofts together and run sheep on them instead of on the hill, and at first sight it makes sense economically since the sheep are in an enclosed area of good grazing under proper control. But it is a short-sighted practice for the grazing soon deteriorates as the sheep eat out the finer grasses allowing coarse grasses and rushes to take over, so the crofter needs more crofts—and more. Over much of the mainland the hill grazing is being divided up and fenced in, enabling better control of the livestock, but so little of our island could be fenced in effectively. It would be fine for the crofter who gets a portion of low ground at the back of his dyke but what of the poor man who gets the back of the hill? Not that agriculture is much of a proposition

208 FOULA.

here anyway. Oh yes, we try to kid ourselves that we cope, but
take away the subsidies and grants and where would we be? Not
that the subsidies and grants aren't justified in the present
agricultural situation. During the past decade the increase in
the price of Shetland wool and lamb paid to the producer has
been small and has not kept pace with inflation. It is interesting
however to note that if the prices received for wool and lambs
today were of the equivalent value of ten years ago, our income
for our produce would be an amount equal to that we receive as
subsidy, in other words we would be agriculturally viable and
need no subsidy. But what other solution is there? The housewife demands cheap food as a right, and payment of subsidy
directly on the produce inevitably results in the buyer dropping
his price.

Let's have no illusions. What do we contribute to the rest of
the world? Very little. A few sheep, a little wool, the odd sheep-
skin and Fair Isle jersey, one or two lobsters, none of it amount-
ing to very much. Our children, yes, they leave to serve as
teachers, nurses, builders, fishermen, mechanics, precious to us
but only a handful of workers to anyone else.

On the other hand, we are fully aware of the high cost per
head of the provision of facilities such as the teacher, nurse,
roads, the telephone and so on. Distance from the mainland and
the small size of the population will always make this
inevitable. Realization of this high burden on the government
makes folk here reluctant to agitate for improvements that
people elsewhere consider as their rights.

We are also aware that some people think it would save a
great deal of inconvenience and expense if we would all go and
live somewhere else. Officialdom is never so outspoken as to say
so direct, no doubt it would create a bad public image, but we are
often given to wonder if there is a policy to rid such islands of
their inhabitants, not by force or persuasion, but simply by
long-term neglect, delay and obstructionism. If this is the case
they will have a mighty long wait. Tenacity and perseverance
(some might call it obstinacy and downright pig-headedness)
are the main characteristics of the Foula folk.

If the official attitude would only change to a more positive
one, islands like this could have a new lease of life. If, instead of
sending in their so-called experts for half an hour of polite chat

once every five years they were to talk to the ones that matter, the youngsters leaving school, the young couples setting up home in Lerwick, the ones that are out there instead of here, and ask them why they do not return to their isle, I think the answers would surprise them. It's not the things the experts consider important that stop them returning—its seldom even the so-called isolation. I have never yet heard any of the younger generation complain about that. No, it's just the simple fact that there is no available employment or housing. To give them their due, some officials and others are genuinely concerned about the problem, but they tend to put forward their own solution, usually a blanket one that they expect to apply to all islands. One can just imagine them sitting before a map drawing a sweeping red line and declaring that all to the west of it should be developed, say for tourism, while all to the east of it should turn to arts and crafts. But, although they have many problems in common all islands are different. The fact that the indigenous island population would be no better off and would eventually leave or die out is neither here nor there—except to the islander.

The cure for an island must come from within—it is futile for so-called experts to try to push it in whatever direction they consider most suitable. The island must be allowed to move under its own power, no matter if to an outsider it sometimes appears to be going backwards or even round in circles. Admittedly it is difficult for an islander to say what his particular island wants for its future for as the population drops it becomes very much just a handful of people each with his own individual and often differing hopes and interests. But surely the best solution in a case like this is to ask the younger generation what they want and then try to see it is provided?

It is only when the young islanders no longer have any interest in returning that an island truly dies.

An island needs its own islanders. Changing over most of a population to in-comers does not seem to result in a stable viable community, but rather an artificial one consisting of a series of people who come for a while, find life too disillusioning and leave again. Perhaps it is because they come for the wrong reason, to "get away from it all", "to escape from the rat race"—negative reasons only. They don't like their own environment and try to get away from it, whereas an islander lives on an island for a positive reason—it's his home and he has a strong attachment to it, strong enough to make leaving very painful. The few in-comers who do come to be considered real islanders are the ones who came and stayed because they had a real affection for the place. Unfortunately they are not common.

Of course not all the young islanders wish to return. Some are obviously attracted to urban life with all its artificial excitement, some are interested in a career which of necessity must take them further afield, some just want to see more of the world than this little corner. The attraction of urban life is the standard reason given for the decline of similar communities in the Highlands and Islands. But in our own case I think the proportion thus affected is smaller than one would expect considering all the modern influence in this direction. Perhaps our isle has more positive attractions than others—certainly there is no other like it, elsewhere seeming very dull and tame in comparison. We are frequently surprised to hear of other islands with far greater problems of depopulation yet they appear to be more favoured with low fertile land and natural harbours—who could ask for more? Yet these advantages obviously weren't enough, which leads us to suspect that the most important reason for an island's decline is not a tangible one at all. The most important reason is purely psychological—an island, or any community, is viable because it itself believes it is. As long as it has belief in itself a community will struggle on through disasters and setbacks far worse than any we have experienced. This is perhaps why an island needs its own islanders, because they have an inherited belief in their island. They know they can manage because their forefathers did—back as far as they can count kin. As long as they have this belief they will keep adapting to change—if one method of livelihood is not successful they will try another, change from fishing to crofting, from kye to sheep, from sheep to something we haven't thought of yet. Only if they become discouraged and believe the island finished, then it will die, whether it is economically viable or not. Therefore our island will live as long as *we* believe it will, or our children or our grandchildren. What the rest of the world believes doesn't matter, it may either hamper us or help us, but in the end it's we ourselves that control our own viability. When you are young you don't realize this, evacuation seems a very real threat, the future of the island appears to depend on a vague "they" who will perhaps force you to leave. Only slowly do you realize that the future is yours. It's up to you.

The attitude of others to our island has changed considerably over the last hundred years. Once it was considered just a piece of land the same as anywhere else and treated as such. People lived there in the same conditions as they lived in the rest of Shetland and indeed in most of rural Britain. They had their own particular traditions and ways of doing things but basically life was much the same. However improved communications brought Foula more to the eye of the public and it profited popular writers and the mass media to romanticize and dramatize the island. It became Britain's remotest island, the Edge of the World, the furthest outpost, cut off for months on end while the brave and noble natives starved—all calculated to appeal to the public's imagination and provide them with a few minutes of sensationalism. But the isle hadn't changed. It was still the same little piece of earth with folk going about their business as ever. Only now it could be officially declared "Out of this World". A very handy phrase for officials not wanting to provide it with the required amenities or even keep up the few it had. "Out of this world—you can't expect us to treat it like the rest of the country."

Although there is never any question of mass evacuation such as occurred in the case of St Kilda, it is unfortunately an inescapable fact that in the past its population, too, dwindled slowly away. We will live out our lives here, and our children too in their time, but what of their own children, what of the future? Will the island be empty after they are gone?

And we wonder if it will matter. But it does matter, it matters to us intensely. Why? Obviously there are personal reasons, we want to live out our lives here because we are happiest here and we hope our children will find the same contentment. As well as individual feelings, another important motive is survival of the tribe, a primitive instinct that has never been shaken off no matter how civilized man claims to be. There will always be "us" and "them"—Foula and the rest of the world. We may squabble over petty incidents, disagree over major issues, even dislike each other, but there is still a bond between us.

But does it matter to anyone else? Visitors sometimes ask what value this small isolated community can have to the rest of the world. It contributes so little to the country's economy and the people seem to have such a struggle to maintain their low standard of living. Would it not be better if they all left? Yet if they did there would be an immediate outcry. Why was this allowed to happen, they would ask, and learned books would be written to explain the reasons for the island's death.

I could warble on about the "way of life" and the importance of preserving it, the standard answer given by students of such things. Not that we don't have our way of life, but it isn't their concept of it. Our way of life isn't their happy illusion of a Utopian island of dreams where one has all the time in the world to stand and watch the hay grow. Nor is it the way of life imposed upon us by poverty and adverse conditions because we cannot do any better. The only folk wishing to preserve the spade instead of the plough are those who don't have to do any digging. Our way of life is more subtle—a harmony with our island, an understanding of it, an acceptance of the hard aspects as well as the good. With the increasing spread of urbanization this relationship with the land is disappearing, the city dweller no longer has the stimulus of man's natural environment, he has to invent his own artificial "island" to provide him with kicks, hence the appalling increase in materialism. Obviously this cannot be solved by everyone going "back to the land" for the population has become too large for this to ever be practical. But let those who have a real island to return to be encouraged to do so. It is possible to make a reasonable livelihood here, despite the fact that the cost of living here must be the highest in Britain due to the island's remoteness. One visiting departmental official, deploring the ever-rising inflation, declared that we islanders were lucky, it didn't effect us, we could "live off the hill"—a misconception shared by all who haven't tried it. But it is true we can, if necessary, tolerate a low standard of living. Our food is there to keep us alive, our clothes to keep us warm and dry. We don't need the elaborate cults of fancy food fads or the latest way-out fashions that others seem to consider so important for the titillation of their jaded senses. We may sometimes be frustrated, irritated, infuriated, driven to despair by our isle but we are never bored.

Modern industrial society, if it is to be efficient economically, requires its people to conform to a uniform standard. Its bureaucracy has no use for the small group whose needs are different, who cannot be tidily lumped in with the others. An insidious pressure is brought to bear on the local sub-cultures through the mass media, advertising and education to homogenize. The result—a drab uniformity spreads slowly over the world. Places like this where life appears "different" become important because they provide variety, they become designated as areas of interest to cater for the recreation of the masses, and it is advocated that the locals be carefully preserved to provide colour. Even if Mr Man-in-the-Street doesn't actually travel to one of these "different" places at least his life can be brightened by dreams of "getting away from it all" and his imagination stimulated by dramatic stories of the Edge of the World.

It could be argued that it is of military importance that the island be inhabited, occupying as it does quite a strategic position off the west coast of Shetland. It is feasible that if the island was uninhabited a foreign power could establish a base here for sabotage of the oil industry without any fear of discovery. Obviously it would be cheaper for this country to maintain the present population rather than build and man a precautionary military base. It might also be argued that the habitation of small outlying islands such as Foula, should play an important part in extending the hoped for EEC Fishing Limits to the maximum distance.

It *is* important to maintain the communities in the remoter parts of the country. If you allow Foula to be depopulated, are you to allow the same thing to happen to Shetland, or to the whole of the Highlands and Islands, eventually to the whole of rural Britain? Are we to end up with the country's entire population living only in the major cities? If not where are we to draw the line. Is not Foula as important to Shetland as Shetland is to the rest of Britain?

The above arguments might convince those already inclined in our favour. They won't convince the others. I know there must be an answer far more important than these, one that would be irrefutable, one which if presented to the world would bring help to our problems. I thought that if I wrote a book I would find it.

But I didn't. I only found love and that is not enough.

But sometimes in the heart hole of winter as I platch knee deep through the mud on my way to the banks to hoove another dead ewe into the sea, it comes to me that maybe there is no reason, that it is of no importance, the world will not miss us. And I look out over the windswept sodden landscape to another time when we and our descendants will have passed away, when the isle perhaps will lie empty or populated by a people far different than our own. But then I look to the hills, black defiant against the winter sky, or out to sea where the big grey breakers roll by from the north and I know it does not matter. Long, long after we are gone from this world, the isle will still be our island. The wind will still roar through the hills, the seas still pound against its cliffs. The isle does not need us, it can stand alone.

This is our sorrow and our comfort.

Glossary
of dialect words not explained in text

Aa (a') – all
abön (abune) – above
ae – one
aest – east
afore – before
ageen – again
ahint – behind
allen – Arctic skua
an – and
ane – one
anunder – below
ask – haze
at – that
athin – within
atween – between
auld – old

Baa – underwater rock
bairn – child
banks – cliffs
bell – throw
ben – bedroom of a cottage
bere – barley
biddy – a thick oatcake
bigg – build
blaa – blow
blaand – sour whey
blinkie – pocket torch
blok – marsh marigold
bloodin – bleedin
böl see *bül*
bonny – pretty
bonxie – great skua
braa – grand
braaly – very
brag – boast
breest – breast
bricht – bright
brig – bridge

briggy stanes – flagstone path in front of a house
broo – small bank
brugs – steep terraced bank
bruks – remains
bruinni – thick oatcake
buiddy – fisherman's basket
burra – heath rush
burrope – buoy rope
bül – sheltered resting place for sheep
but – living room of a cottage

Caa – drive
caddy – motherless lamb (also to call upon a lamb)
caird (caerd) – card (wool)
cairnie – a heap of stones
cast – dig peats
clett – flat sloping rock
clood – cloud
clowie flooer – bog asphodel
coo – cow
cole – small haystack on the fields
coortin – curtain
coose – heap
corbie – raven
cowld – cold
craigs – crags (also fishing from the rocks)
crü – enclosure where sheep are penned
crub see *planti crub*
crudi mudi – chopped up onions and fish livers boiled with oatmeal
curn – curds

Da – the
daa nettle – hemp nettle
dadd – thump
dan – then
daylicht – daylight
dee – you (thee)
dee – die
dell – delve
dem – them
der – their
dere – there
dere – they are
dess – a large haystack
dey – they
dim – twilight (especially in simmer dim)
dis – this
dönna – do not
doon – down
doot – doubt
dracht – the drawing of a narrow; double dracht twice over a rig with a harrow
dunter – eider duck
Dwine! – Devil take it!
dy – your (thy)
dyke – wall

Ee – eye
ee – one (occasionally)
eela – inshore fishing for piltocks
een – eyes
eenoo – just now

Fae – from
faer – fear
fell – slab of turf
felly – made of turf
ferdi maet – food for a journey
fernenst – against
fir – for
flan – a gust of wind
flay – to prepare a peat bank for casting
fleckit – spotted
flee – fly

flooer – flower
floss – a rush
foy – a party
frae – from
fu – how
fur(r) – furrow
furt – outside

Gadderie – a collection
gaet – a path
gaird – guard
geen – gone
geo – a steep sided inlet of the sea
ging – go
glisk – a glimpse
glöd – glow
gloy – straw
gruity – oily and rancid
g(y)aain – going
gyeng – go

Haaf – distant fishing grounds
haand – hand
hadd – hold
hail – haul
hairst – harvest or autumn
hansel – a good luck present
heather berry – crowberry
hert – heart
hich – high
hindmost – last
hird – carry home oats or hay
hocken – greedy
hoose – house
hoove – throw
horsegok – snipe
hurds – boulders

Ida – in the
idder – other

Ken – know
kilya – the clamour of seagulls
kishie – a carrying basket
kye – cattle

Laamer – amber
laamus – lambhouse
laand – land
laek – like
lane – alone
laavin – hovering
leerie – Manx shearwater
leet – heed
leggins – bottom of a jar
lesnin – stake to which a
climbing rope is fastened
less! – alas!
lightsome – cheerful
linn – piece of wood over which a
boat is hauled
lubba – coarse hill grass
lug – ear
lum – chimney
lungwee – guillemot
lür – a pollack

Maa – a seagull
maa'er – a mower
maalie – a fulmar
mair – more
makkin – knitting
makkin wires – knitting needles
Melashun (da) – the Devil
mesel – myself
mintie – tiny
mirrie – merry
Mirrie Dancers – Northern
Lights
mony – many
moold – (peat) mould
moorie caavie – blizzard
moorin – drifting (snow)
moorit – brown
morn (da) – tomorrow
muckle – big

Nae – no
naethin – nothing
neep – turnip
neist – next
neuk – corner

noost (nowst) – shelter on land for
a small boat
nort – north

O – of
o'er – too (over)
ogadoo – sow thistle
oo – wool
oob – moan
oot – out

Paek – pick (green paek – the
first growth of grass in Spring)
paet – peat
peerie – small
peeriewise – gently
piltock – a young saithe
planti-crub – an enclosure where
cabbage seedlings are grown
platch – squelch
ploo – plough
plukker – sea scorpion
poo – pull
prunk – alert

Qua? – who?
quaar? – where?

Raingoose – red-throated diver
rank – tidestream
ree – a spell of bad weather
expected at a certain time of year
reest – to cure meat by salting
rig – a small field
rikker – a fishing device that
depends on bare hooks
ripe – to harvest potatoes
rivlins – shoes made of hide
roo – to remove a sheep's fleece by
gently pulling it off
roond – round
roost – rust
rür – a type of reed

Sae – so
santed – spirited away

scarf see *skarf*
scordet – scored or cracked
scorie – young seagull
screw see *skroo*
sean – a lamb born late in the season
segs – leaves of the yellow flag
seggy – made from segs
seich – sigh
setnin – a one-year old ewe
shaalds – shallows
shaila – grey (wool)
shalder – oyster-catcher
shapp – to chop
shaw – show
sheen – shine
sho – shoe
shoon – shoes
shörmil – edge of the sea
shourd – to prop up
simmer – summer
skarf – shag
skeat – spit (of rain)
skeetch – splash
skrew (skroo) – corn stack
skurtful – armful
smaa – small or narrow
smo(o)r – smother
snaa – snow
sneedled – white faced
soorock – sorrel
sooth – south
spöndrift – spindrift
spootie drum – wild angelica
stane – stone
stank – ditch
stead – foundation
stenkled up – botched up
stiooch – a cloud (of dust)
stjagi – flanking fence of a crü
stock box – a floating box or cage for storing lobster
stook – corn stack
strae – straw
streen (da) – last night
strikk – strike

Summermill – start of the summer half year on 26th April
sunse (the) – the Devil
sye – scythe
swaar – swathe
swittle – splash

Ta – to
tak – take; takking up – undertaking
tank – thank
tapmist – uppermost
tattie – potato
tek – thatch (also a variety of coarse grass)
tik – thick
til – to
tink – think
tirrick – tern
tömald – tumult
toog – projecting bit of land on a cliff
too-tackable – exceptional
torny – thorny
trow – a troll
trowe – through
trucked – trampled
tuilly – knife
tushkar – peat spade
twatree – two or three
tystie – black guillemot

Unken – unfamiliar

Voar – Springtime
voe – a long sea inlet

Waa – wall
waal – wail
waand – fishing rod
waander – wander
waar – seaweed
wan – one
wast – west
welkie – razorbill

werna – were not
whaar – where
whup – coil
wi – with
windlin – small bundle of straw

wir – our

Yon – that
yondroo – over there
Yule (Yöle) – Christmas

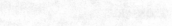

Index

Advance, 49
Airstrip, 25, 57
Allen (Arctic skua), 149, 156, 173, 178, 196

Ben Hope, 60
Black, Tom, 192
Bonxie (great skua), 61, 169–74
Borrowing Days, 135
Bronze Age, 14

Church, 55
Cod, 43, 44, 46
Cody, Jimmy, 50
Craigs, 45
Crowberry, 195
Crü, 32–41, 77–8
Cru Kaitrine, 56

Driftwood, 118–20, 123, 128–30

Fair Isle, 60
Far Haaf, 42–5
Fishing, 42–6, 50
Fugley Isle, 109

Garriocks, 47
Gear, Robert, 16, 48, 50

Haddock, 43
Hame Sea, 46
Hay, 26, 29–30, 67–75
Henry, Andrew, 128, 171
Henry, Peggy, 201
Herring boats, 49
Hirta, 27

Island Lass, 51

Jamieson, Peti, 70
Jeromson, Johnnie, 16, 48

Kale, 25
Kame, 12, 27, 62, 168, 202
Kittiwake, 172
Kye, 189

Lambing, 136–48
Leerie (Manx shearwater), 23
Lighthouse, 121
Ling, 43, 44
Lobsters, 21, 24
Loganair, 57, 97
Luirs (pollack), 200
Lungwee (common guillemot), 23, 203

Manson, Johnnie, 44
Manson, Magnie, 48, 49
Mailboat, 13, 48–54
Mooldie Coose, 138

Neolithic man, 14
Norn, 14
Norsemen, 14
North Star, 120
Nuerday (New Year's Day), 110

o'Biggins, Muckle Johnnie, 17, 151, 169
o'Brae, Louisa, 114
o'Brae, Jimmie, 129
Oil, 190

o'Quinister, Johnnie, 105
o'Shoadels, 18
o'Wise, Scottie, 168
Oxnagate, 34

Patrick, Earl, 15
Peats, 156, 179, 197–9
Pier, 50
Piltocks, 21, 25, 82, 189
Planti crubs, 26
Population, 13, 42, 46, 205
Potatoes, 88
Prestwick Pioneer, 83

Reestit mutton, 82
Rikker, 43
Road, 154
Ruissi cats, 156
Rür, 30

Saithe, 44
Scotts of Melby, 15, 171
Sheep, 32–41, 76–82, 94–5,
    99–100, 111–13, 116, 131,
    136–50, 176–7
Shetland ponies, 36, 55–61,
    85–93, 97–9, 113, 131–3,
    159–64, 193–4

Sinna, 27
Skarf (shag), 191
Sleekie, 22, 43
Sneug, 60
Spreader, 43
Stane biter, 45
Summermill, 143, 167

Tammy norie (puffin), 12, 20, 62,
    143
Teal Duck, 120
Tek, 27
Telephone, 92
Thieves' Hole, 23
Trail, 48
Trowie Lowrie, 120

Umphray, Laurie, 15

Voe, 12, 66

Westering Homewards, 54, 89
Whales, 204
Wool, 32, 40, 176

Yule (Christmas), 102–9